Reclaiming
the Source

Reclaiming the Source

Connecting what we see,

what we think,

and what we believe

Charles Owen Fọlárìn Schleicher

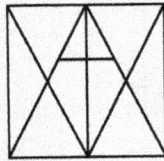

WHERE IT'S AT PRESS
Madison, Wisconsin

10 9 8 7 6 5 4 3 2 1

Printed by Where It's At Press
Includes bibliographical references and index
ISBN-13: 978-0692544754 (Custom)
ISBN-10: 0692544755

This book was printed in Garamond
with Bernhard Fashion BT, Cambria Math, and AvantGarde Bk BT on the title pages

Table of Contents

Acknowledgments

I would like to thank my wife for suggesting, indeed insisting, that I write my thoughts on Genesis down and make a book out of it. You cannot blame her for the outcome, but that there is an outcome of any sort is entirely at her instigation. I would also like to thank my two children, my son in particular, for their support and enthusiasm for my undertaking this project.

Thanks to the various sources of illustrations for giving me permission for using their material. The atomic structure diagram in Figure 2 was taken from the Quantum Universe website (http://www.the-universe.ie/quantum-Universe.html) and used with permission from Juli Rimonde. The IBO summary in Figure 4 is taken from the Independent Birth of Organisms website (http://www.mattox.com/genome/) and used with permission from Jeff Mattox. The map of the Persian Gulf in Figure 7 is taken from the article "Has the Garden of Eden Been Located at Last?" located on Lambert Dolphin's Library (ldolphin.org) and is used with permission from Lambert Dolphin. The illustrations of the hydroplate theory in Figures 10 and 11 are taken from the Center for Scientific Creation website (http://www.creationscience.com/onlinebook/) and is used with permission from the Center for Scientific Creation. The image of an Egyptian wall painting shown in Figure 12 was taken from the Reader's Digest Bible, (The Reader's Digest Association, Inc., 1971) pp.10-11; but their Rights and Permissions Department informs me they do not own the copyright for the image. Nennius' genealogy of Germanic peoples shown in Figure 15 is taken from the book *After the Flood* by Bill Cooper and is used with permission. All sources are included in the bibliography at the end of this book.

In the age of the internet, it is sometimes difficult to reach the creator of every graphic available on the worldwide web, but I have done my best to acquire permission for the use of each and every illustration used in this book. At the time of writing, illustrations seen in Figures 1, 3, 5, 6, and 14 could not be located on the internet, nor copyright holders reached.

Greatest thanks of course belongs to God for giving me the pleasure of learning and a devotion to His word.

For my wife,
my children,
and for my brothers and sisters

Introduction

A book on the history of the world and a biblical worldview demands a rigorous examination of something called epistemology, that is, our way of knowing, how we decide what it is we know. But first it demands that I lay my own cards on the table.

I take the Bible at face value. I did not grow up that way and was set in my mind to be a paleontologist at the age of six, when I read the TIME/LIFE book *Evolution* cover to cover. I devoured everything I could get my hands on about evolution, especially about dinosaurs, usually at an adult non-specialist level. At the age of seven I suddenly became aware of the idea that evolution and the Bible story of creation were at variance with one another. I felt as though I was at a crossroads between choosing the Bible and rejecting evolution on the one hand, or choosing evolution and rejecting the Bible on the other hand. I was about to reject the Bible when one day on the playground at school I reasoned out the possibility of theistic evolution and was fine with it after that. I didn't know that other people had already thought about this, much less that there was a name for it ("day-age theory"), but I reasoned that if God had been around for eternity and would be around for eternity, twelve billion years would probably seem like a week.

My later shift to creationism was sudden and actually unexpected. It was a direct result of my conversion at age 17, which involved no one but God and me. No one witnessed to me, but God converted me very directly. Evolution/creation had not been an issue for me since I was seven years old, but from the moment of my salvation, a literal understanding of the first and subsequent chapters of Genesis was totally natural for me.

About two years later I backslid. I did not lose my faith in God, but I did go back into sin. Accompanying this was a gradual return to theistic evolution. To make a very long story short, I eventually returned to the faith of my adolescence, so to speak, and gradually pulled away from "evolution-ism" toward creationism.

I mentioned above that I take the Bible at face value. I will not describe myself as a fundamentalist— not because there is any ambivalence on my part in taking the Bible at face value, but because there is not. Apart from the fact that *fundament-*

1

alist is increasingly accepted as meaning "violent fanatic," and I'm not one, there is the fact that many people who qualify as fundamentalist according to both popular and religious circles pick and choose what parts of the Bible they will take at face value. I am more accurately described as a radical Christian. This is not a book about theology, but radical Christianity can be briefly introduced by three essential elements: taking the Bible at face value from cover to cover with no regard for the culture that one is living in; that is, we claim Bible culture as our own and to the extent that the culture surrounding us conflicts with Bible culture, the surrounding culture is wrong; *sin* means willfully transgressing God's commandments and *salvation* means being forgiven our sins and being given the ability to literally stop sinning; conversion is completed by having original sin or the sin nature removed whereby a person is made holy by God.

While I discuss scientific ideas in this book, it is more about ideas than about science. This is no more a professional treatment of science than it is a professional treatment of theology—I have academic credentials in neither field. The motivation for writing this book is that I have seen how Christians who want to take the Bible at face value nevertheless do not make it the starting point of their knowledge about the world. This is largely because few churches have realized the role of worldview in any person's belief and therefore don't teach a worldview, leaving the non-theistic worldview of western society unchallenged in the minds of Christians. The situation is exacerbated by the fact that some Christians first come to experience the Gospel as adults, whereas evolution is introduced to children at about the second grade in school and at a much earlier age outside of school in the form of children's books and movies about dinosaurs and cave people. Consequently, Western Christians read the Bible with one mindset and look at the world, and especially facts of history and prehistory, with a different, non-Christian mindset.

This issue has been addressed in relatively recent years by the Answers in Genesis organization. Ken Ham and his associates have tried not only to show the foundational role that the Book of Genesis plays in Christian spirituality, but also the way that beliefs about origins is the basis for one's spiritual, religious, ethical, and social beliefs and ultimately, policies. Answers in Genesis, however, has been closely connected with the Institute for Creation Research, which has had problems in its approach to the role of Genesis and science in a Christian worldview. This in turn has resulted in problems that are addressed later in this introduction and in subsequent chapters.

The testimony of a theistic evolutionist I once read on the internet alludes to the song "The Solid Rock". The allusion involved the question of whether one's faith was based on (creationist) science or on Jesus Christ. I think that image bears on the problem with creationists whose faith is shattered by scientific evidence for evolution. It seems to me that the testimonies of such people reflect not just a paradigm shift from young earth to old earth or creationist to evolutionist, but a conflict over what is the ultimate root and judge of knowledge.

People are taught that the Bible is infallible, but learn through the culture that science is the true solid rock, the true standard by which all knowledge is ultimately judged. Later they take science classes which present them with interpretations of data contrary to their understanding of the Bible. Once this happens their faith is instantly shaken, or even obliterated. Because all along, their solid rock was science, not the Bible.

This, as I understand it, is the motivation behind the most thoroughly thought out ideas of theistic evolution. Theistic evolutionists want to believe that the Bible is infallibly correct. But they already have the unshakable faith that science is the ultimate source of knowledge and therefore the Bible can only be supported as correct insofar as it rests on the solid Rock of science (i.e. our current understanding of scientific data).

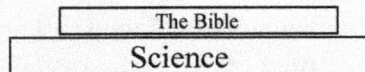

The Bible
Science

If it doesn't, one can either 1) fudge the evidence to maintain the delusion that the Bible **does** rest on science (as some creationists have done), 2) fudge the Bible to maintain the same delusion (as theistic evolutionists have done), or 3) conclude that the Bible is part of the "other ground" which is "sinking sand".

This is not so much of a problem for non-Western Christians. Outside the West, the modern scientific method is useful and respected, but is not the solid rock. An American scientist told me of the time he spent on an island country in the Caribbean. He said, "They thought I was really stupid because I believed that the earth is more than 6000 years old." (And then, in a gem of postmodern relativist expression, he added, "and maybe I am, I don't know.") If he had spelled out for them all the scientific evidence to the contrary, it would have made no difference because science is not their solid rock. I have seen this demonstrated in many parts of the developing world.

It does no good to advocate a division of powers: "the Bible reveals moral truth, science reveals physical truth." Everybody's ethics are directly derived from their worldview, which in turn is "hopelessly" bound up with our understanding of the physical universe and its origin.

Theistic evolutionists at least implicitly recognize this. Choosing theistic evolution would be pointless without recognizing that the Bible's morality and ethics are in question if its science is wrong. This is alluded to in a couple of ways on the web site of theistic evolutionist Glenn Morton: many of the people testifying of how they lost their faith because of the creation/evolution issue said that this wasn't the main issue. The main issue was that the God of the Bible and the morality of the Bible did not seem morally valid. This usually goes hand in hand with rejecting the Bible's scientific validity.

This idea of science being the solid rock on which all knowledge is ultimately judged was most dramatically demonstrated in this statement:

> When one bases their faith upon the rise or fall of a scientific theory, they are on real "sinking sand." When I left for college, I believed these sorts of either/or statements - many people do. If I had learned the facts of geology or biology or physics or astronomy or anthropology or geochronology or ... under the teaching of someone other than a godly professor, the crisis to my faith would have been much more severe. I feel it is very unlikely that I would be a Christian today. I would probably be a bitter agnostic and not because of science but because my Christianity set me up to fail.[1]

It couldn't have been science. Science is never at fault for making someone lose faith. It's got to be Christianity's fault. Which means, since we don't want to really reject Christianity, that it's "this *version* of Christianity" which is at fault, but there's some other Christianity out there that is okay. And if *that* Christianity turns out not to work someday, then *that* Christianity will have failed and we go searching for another Christianity which will serve us. In other words, science is the Solid Rock. Science never sets anyone up to fail. We don't talk about your science or my science. Somebody's Christianity can be wrong and still be called

---

[1]Steve Smith, in *Steve Smith's Testimony* (http://home.entouch.net/dmd/ssmith.htm)

Christianity, but if anyone's science is wrong it's not his or her science because if it's wrong, it's not science; science doesn't lie! Contrast this with Paul's reference to "another gospel, which is not another." (Gal 1:6,7) In other words, Paul had the same view of the Gospel that Westerners today have about science. For Paul and the early Christians, there could be many sciences (or philosophies), but only one Gospel. If anyone's Gospel was wrong then it wasn't his or her Gospel, because if it was wrong, it's not a Gospel; the Gospel doesn't lie! We need to have—we *can* have—the same perspective today.

Another example:

> There is no leeway for any other interpretation of the Biblical text since Henry Morris studied it and figured out what it really means. Now that he has found out exactly what God meant, all observations must fit within his (Morris') explanation of Genesis because God would not lie. It is not at all illogical to throw out interpretations/explanations of observed natural phenomena (biological, geological, astronomical, or what have you) even though there is no sufficient or reasonable alternative offered from their group. Petrified sand dunes in Utah CANNOT be subaerial, even though they show a complete set of characteristics that match present day subaerial dunes and the evaporite deposits in the lows between them demand a subaerial environment of formation, because they HAD to have been deposited in the flood and God doesn't lie. Varves CANNOT be annual features because they HAD to have been deposited in one year and God doesn't lie. Your example of the meander through carbonate rock CANNOT have been produced by eroding solid carbonate because it HAD to happen subaqueously and within minutes, hours or a day at most since the Bible clearly says that all geological formations except the basement rock and a thin upper veneer were laid down during the year of the flood. God doesn't lie! In ICR's logic, to ignore or deny problematic natural observations is not to be deceitful. (A perfect example of this is John Morris' statement that he has never seen a geological fact that did not fit equally as well or better in the flood model than any other model.)[2]

---

[2] Steve Robertson, 2/14/98 email to Glenn Morton, published in "Steve Robertson's Story: a Case History of What Happens to a Young-earth Advocate who works in Geology" (http://home.entouch.net/dmd/robertso.htm)

This is an excellent statement. The claim here is that, in effect, the Bible is not really the solid Rock at ICR, rather creationist scientific ideas are. For example, "Petrified sand dunes in Utah CANNOT be subaerial, because they HAD to have been deposited in the flood and God doesn't lie," suggests that only two possibilities exist: petrified sand dunes are subaerial and evolution is true, or the Bible is true in which case the sand dunes were deposited in the flood. I am not a geologist, but isn't this a bogus dichotomy? My point is that it seems from Steve Robertson's witness that Morris has equated his interpretation of scientific data with the Bible itself ("the Bible clearly says that all geological formations except the basement rock and a thin upper veneer were laid down during the year of the flood"). Note that I didn't say "Morris' interpretation of the Bible" as Mr. Robertson would. Where petrified sand dunes in Utah came from has precious little to do with the interpretation of the Bible and a lot to do with interpretation of scientific data (albeit *motivated* by Biblical interpretation). The irony here is that creationists, like evolutionists, are treating science as the Solid Rock; they prove the Bible is true by trying to show that it doesn't contradict science.

The water canopy hypothesis is another example. It can't work; therefore creationism is dead, right? Not at all, as Walt Brown's hydroplate theory demonstrates. There are multiple scientific possibilities within the same biblical worldview.

What we find in the Bible at face value, what we believe, is non-negotiable. What we experience directly through our senses is, as a rule, trustworthy and non-negotiable also, but we must be very careful to distinguish what we actually observe, and what we think about what we observe. The latter is always at least potentially debatable. What we think about physical observations (scientific ideas), secondary ideas that we derive from the Bible (theological ideas) and how we interpret our inner experience, all fall under the category of what we think; and that is negotiable. As a foundation, it is sinking sand.

But someone still may object, saying, "Where would we be if we used the Bible as our textbook for science? We would never progress!" We don't use the Bible as our science textbook. The point is that no science textbook is the center of our worldview. That leads to my belief in the true division: between generalities and particulars. The Bible is the final authority in everything that it discusses, including science and history, insofar as it touches on those subjects; but modern disciplines fill in the particulars. As it has been said before, "The Bible is not written in the language of the modern scientist.... However the Bible does contain scientific truth and Scripture and true science are in agreement."[3] Putting it yet another way, we use the scientific method to explore the physical world, but as with logic, we recognize both its explanatory power and its explanatory limitations. Science works, it's okay, and we use it. It's just not the Solid Rock.

Perhaps if those who changed from creationism to evolutionism had been given this perspective from the start, they would never have lost the faith, or even resorted to theistic evolutionism. As it was, they were raised to believe that "science **is** king, but that's okay because as our tailored hyperprotective selection of data shows, the Bible conforms to science anyway."

It is partly because of this false approach that I have stayed away from virtually all creationist literature and have gathered most of my information on origins-related science from non-Christian scientists, including non-creationist, non-evolutionist theories (hence my self description as a creationist "for want of a better word").

Something which I have found very educational is the 1961 book, *Physicist and Christian; a dialogue between the communities* by William G. Pollard.

In his remarkable book, Pollard expounds on five points by which westerners commonly contrast science and religion:
- demonstration vs. blind acceptance
- public vs. private knowledge
- fact vs. faith
- impersonal vs. personal knowledge
- orthodoxy vs. heresy

The first of each of these pairs is seen as characteristic of science, the second as characteristic of religion. Pollard argues persuasively that not only are both members of each pair to be found in both science and religion, but both members of each pair are found *to the same degree* in each.

> It is true that when I give a popular lecture as a physicist, I can count on having an audience which is spontaneously and even subconsciously convinced in advance of the validity, importance, and undeniable truth of the enterprise of physics as a whole. Moreover, the idea that I might speak of a private physics of my own would not even occur to them. I have never yet been called upon by a modern audience to defend myself or explain what possessed me to embrace physics. It is equally true that whenever I give a popular lecture on a theological topic, I can count on

---

[3] A Series of Bible Studies, Vol.1, p.1. The Apostolic Faith Church, Portland, OR.

having an audience equally convinced in advance that religion, although possibly proper, respectable, and even admirable, is nevertheless a private peculiarity of individual people and therefore essentially unreal. Here the idea of a Catholic faith which is the common public witness of the whole body of the faithful through the ages is alien to contemporary ways of thinking about Christianity. I can almost always count on being called upon by puzzled people to explain what possessed me to embrace such a faith with the degree of seriousness implied by my taking Holy Orders.

In this sense it is true that in the twentieth century science is public knowledge and religion is private. But it has often struck me that had God given it to me to live in the sixth century or even the twelfth instead of the twentieth, the situation would have been exactly reversed. Had I spoken on Christianity in that period, my audience would have been spontaneously convinced in advance of the complete validity and universal truth of what I represented, and it would have seemed completely natural that I should want to be a priest of the Church. On the other hand, if I had then subsequently become interested in the works of Democritus and Archimedes and fascinated by Greek physics, it would have seemed an anomalous thing for a well-established cleric to do. I would certainly then have been called upon to explain over and over to puzzled people what could cause a priest to divert himself wholeheartedly and zestfully into an enterprise as private and subjective as physics. Conversely, in any talk on physics then, I could have counted on an audience prepared in advance to hear only a private testimonial to an inner experience, interesting perhaps, but basically unreal and unimportant. In the sixth century Christianity would have represented public knowledge and science would have been called private knowledge.

The point of Pollard's work is that science and Christianity are both about knowledge, both about faith, and most important of all, both defined and sustained by community. In other words, both are completely parallel. I would take the conclusion one step further: that both science and Christianity can have the same function. Each can be the foundation of a worldview and each can supply optional particulars. One must choose, on faith, which will play which role. Pollard's quote above shows that both science and Christianity have played both roles for society at large at different times in history.

But, again, the basic point that William G. Pollard makes here is that scientific knowledge comes to us through the scientific community. A scientific idea is "valid" not because it is necessarily more principled or best fits the data, but because it is accepted by the scientific community. But how does the scientific community come about?

I know how the Christian community comes about: faith in God through Jesus Christ and obedience to His word saves us from sin. Then as we consecrate our lives to God, He sanctifies us. That makes us all of one accord. Without that divinely bestowed unity, there is no Christian community. So a true Christian community is bound up with humble submission to the absolute truth of God. Such is not the origin of the scientific community. So what is it's origin?

In the real world, a scientific community emerges from a consensus which is based on the prevailing philosophical ideas of the time, and that consensus is built in the usual worldly way: a combination of merit and politics. Merit is dominant in proportion to the godliness of the association of scientists, politics is dominant in inverse proportion to the same.

Everyone's view of the world is founded on faith. The question is, faith in what? Everyone's view of the world requires a perception of facts. But how do we know what the facts are? Everyone's view of the world is supported both by demonstration of facts and by blind acceptance. How do we tease apart what the world knows by demonstration and what is blindly accepted? Can we take facts that anyone, regardless of belief, can observe and connect with a view of the world that genuinely has the Bible as the solid rock of our knowledge? In the chapters that follow, we will present a view of the world that attempts to connect what we see, what we believe, and what we think about what we see and believe. Along the way we will try to make clear the distinction between these three parts of our worldview: what we see, what we think, and what we believe.

1
The Solid Rock

"Genesis is foundational to Christianity. Christ quoted from it; the rest of the Bible refers to it or quotes from it more than any other book. If you do not have a believing knowledge of the Book of Genesis, you cannot hope to attain a full comprehension of what Christianity is all about."

– Ken Ham and Paul Taylor,
The Genesis Solution

Creation is a fascinating topic; there's a lot of merit to studying it, for a variety of reasons. One of them is that all moral truth has a physical grounding. One of the greatest fallacies of liberal theology in the late nineteenth century was in stating explicitly that science reveals physical truth and not moral truth, while religion reveals moral truth and not physical truth. It's an extreme version of an idea which *is* true: that the Bible is not a science textbook. The purpose of the Bible is not to elaborate on the structure of the physical universe, or to describe orbits of planets and so forth. But anything the Bible says that touches on factual claims about the universe is accurate.

And the fact of the matter is, everybody's moral compass, everybody's standard or belief about morality and ethics, is founded on a physical basis. This is true even for people like Stephen J. Gould who used to insist that science cannot reveal moral truth. In fact, his own sense of morality and his own sense of moral philosophy stemmed directly from his beliefs about factual or about scientific claims. So the whole series of social, cultural, and moral movements that we have today stems from beliefs about the physical universe. Now, if people are attracted to Hinduism or Hindu spirituality, it's in part because they believe that the universe is billions and billions of years old and Hinduism talks about billions of years (even though Hinduism's account of creation does not in any way jibe with the evolutionary creation myth).[1] So many people today believe that animals have

---

[1] Hindu creationism believes the earth is billions of years old—and so is mankind, which "devolved" from pure spirit beings. Billions of years ago all life appeared as it exists today. Works that constitute examples of what could be called "scientific Hindu creationism" include *Forbidden Archeology* and *Human Devolution*, both by Michael Cremo of the Bhaktivedanta Institute.

all the same rights as human beings— again because of belief in evolution. People who feel it's more immoral to kill a chicken than to kill an unborn human baby are deriving their morals, ethics, and philosophy from evolution. People's beliefs about the physical origins of themselves in particular and of the universe in general, do have a direct bearing on their morality and their sense of what is right and what is wrong.

So to understand, appreciate, and agree with what is right and what is wrong in God's sight, it is essential that we get God's perspective on our origins. That's why creation is so important to study.

To start with, we will look at just the first chapter of Genesis. It's a tremendously powerful chapter. The unique importance of Genesis derives from its function and relationship with the Bible as a whole. The Old Testament is the foundation of the New Testament and each has the same organizational structure. Each testament can be divided into four sections: the covenant books, the historical books, the wisdom books, and the prophetic books.

Books of the Bible

OLD TESTAMENT

COVENANT

Genesis
Exodus
Leviticus
Numbers
Deuteronomy

HISTORY

Joshua
Judges
Ruth
1 Samuel
2 Samuel
1 Kings
2 Kings
1 Chronicles
 2 Chronicles
Ezra
Nehemiah
Esther

WISDOM

Job
Psalms
Proverbs
Ecclesiastes
Song of Solomon

PROPHECY

Isaiah
Jeremiah
Lamentations   } major
Ezekiel   prophets
Daniel
Hosea
Joel
Amos
Obadiah
Jonah
Micah   } minor
Nahum   prophets
Habakkuk
Zephaniah
Haggai
Zechariah
Malachi

NEW TESTAMENT

COVENANT

Matthew
Mark
Luke
John

HISTORY

Acts

WISDOM

Romans
1 Corinthians
2 Corinthians
Galatians
Ephesians
Philippians
Colossians
1 Thessalonians
2 Thessalonians
1 Timothy
2 Timothy
Titus
Philemon
Hebrews

} Pauline epistles

James
1 Peter
2 Peter
1 John
2 John
3 John
Jude

} Universal epistles

PROPHECY

Revelation

Within each testament, the covenant books are always the foundation. So the covenant books form the foundation for the New Testament. And the New Testament as a whole takes the Old Testament as a whole as its foundation. The New Testament literally does not make sense at all without the Old Testament. And, again, the Old Testament has as its foundation the covenant books (the Torah). And finally, unique to the covenant books of the Old Testament, the first covenant book serves as a foundation for the rest of the covenant books (this is not true for the covenant books of the New Testament). So Genesis is the foundation of the Law, which is the foundation of the Old Testament, which is the foundation for the whole New Testament. Genesis is the foundation for the whole Bible.

Because of its essential position in the Scriptures as well as its information for the ultimate origin of everything, it is legitimate to ask for the ultimate origin of Genesis itself. Traditionally the answer to this question was: Moses wrote it. Apart from there not being clear evidence that Moses wrote the book in the first place, there remains the question of how he or anyone else could have access to the information, since it necessarily starts before there were any people (or any universe, for that matter). It was attempting to answer this question that opened the way to the document hypothesis, an ultimately misguided theory of the origin of Genesis that we will discuss in more detail in the next chapter.

But archeological discoveries of the late nineteenth and early twentieth centuries led to a new and more historically based perception of the composition of Genesis than the document hypothesis: the tablet theory of P.J. Wiseman.

Wiseman, an air commodore for the U.S. Army in the early twentieth century, became an informal but avid student of archeology during his tour of duty in Mesopotamia. There he recognized a feature common to clay tablets: the use of colophons to title documents and the use of catch phrases to link and order different tablets together into a larger whole. Wiseman was to the first to compare the style of Genesis with the style of other ancient documents and found clear use of the colophon in several places in Genesis. Wiseman thus analyzed Genesis as a series of tablets, each followed by a colophon as shown in the table below.

Tablet	Verse	Wording
I	2:4	"These are the generations of the heavens and the earth".
II	5:1	"This is the book of the generations of Adam".
III	6:9	"These are the generations of Noah".
IV	10:1	"These are the generations of the sons of Noah"
V	11:10	"These are the generations of Shem"
VI	11:27	"These are the generations of Terah"
VII	25:12	"These are the generations of Ishmael"
VIII	25:19	"These are the generations of Isaac"
IX	36:1	"These are the generations of Esau"
X	36:9	"These are the generations of Esau"
XI	37:2	"These are the generations of Jacob"

It had long been understood that these phrases introduced genealogies. But in reality, they do not in many cases. Wiseman solved this dilemma by drawing a parallel between the phrase "these are the generations of x" (called *toledoth* phrases after the Hebrew word translated "generations") and the colophon phrases used on ancient clay tablets. This would mean that Genesis originated from as many as eleven or twelve tablets that were assembled together in the same order in which we have them today (as opposed to the patchwork arrangement hypothesized in the document hypothesis).

Moreover these tablets used catch lines just as did the clay tablets in Nuzi and Mari.

GENESIS	CATCH LINE
1:1	"God created the heavens and the earth"
2:4	"Lord God made the heavens and the earth"
2:4	"When they were created"
5:2	"When they were created"
6:10	"Shem, Ham and Japheth"
10:1	"Shem, Ham and Japheth"

10:32	"After the Flood"
11:10	"After the Flood"
11:26	"Abram, Nahor and Haran"
11:27	"Abram, Nahor and Haran"
25:12	"Abraham's son"
25:19	"Abraham's son"
36:1	"Who is Edom"
36:8	"Who is Edom"
36:9	"Father of the Edomites"
36:43	"Father of the Edomites"

To interpret the toledoth phrases this way, Wiseman understood the word *toledoth* not to mean 'genealogy' (as implied by the translation 'generations'), but to mean 'history', 'origin'. This analysis not only maintains the reliability of the Genesis accounts, but is more informed by documents from the time that Genesis was produced. Nevertheless there appear on the surface to be some problems with this proposal:

- Tablet 4 is at least as much about the flood as it is about Shem, Ham and Japheth's origins. But it is followed immediately by a list of their descendants.

- Tablet 5 is about the descendants of Japheth, and Ham, as well as about the descendants of Shem; why then is it called the origin of Shem?

- Tablet 7 has no information about Ishmael, but is immediately followed by a list of his sons and their distribution.

- Tablet 8 has no information on Isaac and *only* info on Ishmael, but is immediately followed by the story of Isaac's family.

- Tablets 9 *and* 10 are both supposed to be about Esau; what's up with that?

- Also, Tablet 9 is not about Esau at all, but about Jacob, who was neither Esau's "origin," nor his descendant.

The second "Esau tablet" would by Wiseman's rendering not be the story of

Esau's origin, either, but a list of his descendants! This contradicts Wiseman's own theoretical pattern for the tablets.

Clearly here what we really have is the story of Esau's descendants which is framed at the beginning and end by the phrase, "These are the generations of Esau" in the thirty-sixth chapter of Genesis. This demonstrates clearly that the phrase, "These are the generations of x"can refer to the descendants of x.

Taylor (1984) solves some of this difficulty by suggesting that Ishmael's tablet and Esau's tablet are appendices within larger texts.

Tablet	Verse	Wording
I	1:1 to 2:4a	"These are the generations of the heavens and the earth"
II	2:4b to 5:2	"This is the book of the generations of Adam"
III	5:3 to 6:9a	"These are the generations of Noah"
IV	6:9b to 10:1	"These are the generations of the sons of Noah"
V	10:2 to 11:10a	"These are the generations of Shem"
VI	11:10b to 11:27a	"These are the generations of Terah"
VII	11:27b to 25:19	"These are the generations of Isaac"
VIII	25:19 to 37:2a	"These are the generations of Jacob"
IX	37:2b to 50:26	[no colophon]
Appendix	25:12 to 25:18	"These are the generations of Ishmael"
Appendix	36:1 to 36:8	"These are the generations of Esau"
Appendix	36:9 to 36:43	"These are the generations of Esau"

The lack of a colophon on the last "tablet" is explained by the reasonable supposition that it wasn't a tablet at all: being the history of Joseph it had to have been written after the Israelites settled in Egypt and was most likely written on papyrus and therefore not in the tradition of clay tablet documentation.

The appendices or "sub-tablets" as they are called by Sewell (2001) fit at or near the end of the larger texts. This clears up some difficulties, but note that each of these appendices *begins* with the toledoth phrase, which then is immediately followed by an account of descendants. If this style was current in Ishmael's and Esau's time, it is quite probable that it also applies to the tablets of their

contemporaries, i.e. Isaac and Jacob. This suggests a reanalysis of Genesis'
underlying structure to look something like this:

Tablet	Verse	Wording
I	1:1 to 2:4a	"These are the generations of the heavens and the earth"
II	2:4b to 5:2	"This is the book of the generations of Adam"
III	5:3 to 6:9a	"These are the generations of Noah"
IV	6:9b to 10:1	"These are the generations of the sons of Noah"
V	10:2 to 11:10a	"These are the generations of Shem"
VI	11:10b to 11:27a	"These are the generations of Terah"
VII	11:27b to 25:11	[no colophon]
VIII	25:19 to 35:29	"These are the generations of Isaac"
IX	37:2 to 50:26	"These are the generations of Jacob"
Appendix	25:12 to 25:18	"These are the generations of Ishmael"
Appendix	36:1 to 36:8	"These are the generations of Esau"
Appendix	36:9 to 36:43	"These are the generations of Esau"

This leaves tablet VII (the story of Abraham) without a colophon. It also
means that the appendices aren't really appendices at all, since it's now clear that
they are not couched within one of the other sections. But what if we continue the
reanalysis back to Noah? What if the title of each section after the flood begins
that section?

Section	Verses	Wording
I	1:1 to 2:4a	"These are the generations of the heavens and the earth"
II	2:4b to 5:2	"This is the book of the generations of Adam"
III	5:3 to 6:9a	"These are the generations of Noah"
IV	6:9b to 10:1a	"These are the generations of the sons of Noah"
V	10:1 to 11:9	"These are the generations of the sons of Noah"
VI	11:10 to 11:26	"These are the generations of Shem"
VII	11:27 to 25:11	"These are the generations of Terah"
VIII	25:12 to 25:18	"These are the generations of Ishmael"
IX	25:19 to 35:29	"These are the generations of Isaac"
X	36:1 to 36:8	"These are the generations of Esau"
XI	36:9 to 36:43	"These are the generations of Esau"
XII	37:2 to 50:26	"These are the generations of Jacob"

By this analysis, Tablets I-IV follow the pattern given by Wiseman and Taylor, but since Tablets II and III are followed by genealogies, the phrase "the generations of x" is reinterpreted as introducing either genealogies or at least family history. So the colophon that ends Tablet IV begins Tablet V which is a self-contained document, framed as it is by nearly parallel statements:

> Now these are the generations of the sons of Noah, Shem, Ham, and Japheth: and unto them were sons born after the flood. (10:1)

> These are the families of the sons of Noah, after their generations, in their nations: and by these were the nations divided in the earth after the flood. (10:32)

The story of Babel may be an appendix to this Tablet or just an original part of it. This makes "the generations of Shem" very short and "the generations of

Terah" very long.[2] It also means that certainly after Tablet V, all subsequent tablets would have to have been written by someone other than the "x" of "These are the generations of x". None of this is impossible, or even improbable, though it might seem unattractive for Abraham's story to be in a document that begins with his father's name and not his own. But Genesis 13 and 14 is about Lot and his family as much as it is about Abraham. And Genesis 19 is exclusively about Lot and his family (Abraham does make a cameo). So "Tablet" VII can legitimately be said to be about "the generations of Terah," not just about Abraham. Such a title also reflects the early date of the document, when the fame of Abraham had not eclipsed that of the rest of his family and Abraham, Sarah, Lot, and Co. would still have been seen as all members of Terah's family.

I have started putting "Tablet" in quotes because another fact that corroborates a change in style from Tablet V to the subsequent "Tablets" is the length. Using chapters as a measuring stick (and chapters aren't of a set length, but in Genesis all 50 chapters are of comparable length) we see that Tablet I is one chapter long; II is three chapters; III is one chapter; IV is three chapters (slightly under four); V is one chapter; VI is less than a chapter; and VII is a whopping 14 chapters! Like VII, VIII is about twelve chapters long and IX is over thirteen chapters long. As Sewell points out, this suddenly greater length strongly suggests that something other than clay tablets were used. In any case, it certainly marks a stylistic change in the writings of the patriarchs—a change that almost exactly corresponds with the change in the use of the toledoth phrase.

If as Sewell suggests, the greater length indicates that the later documents, VII-XII, were written on papyrus or parchment, then that would mean that using the toledoth phrase could continue even after clay tablets were no longer used. So there would be no problem with the toledoth phrase being used to introduce the story of Joseph and his brothers.[3]

---

[2] It also removes the problem of the Table of Nations being titled the "generations of Shem"— the Table of Nations is largely not about Shem at all and in any case it certainly is not about his origins. Taylor has tried to deal with this by intereperting *toledoth* as meaning 'history' and the name of the individual as the author. Thus "These are the generations of Shem" is understood to mean, "these are the histories written by Shem". But then how are we to understand the completely parallel construction of Genesis 2:24: "These are the generations of the heaven and the earth?"

[3] The phrase "The book of the generations of Jesus Christ" that opens the New Testament is an example of the toledoth phrase used as late as the first century AD, and definitely not on clay tablets. There the phrase is indeed about Christ's ancestry, not His descendants. Furthermore, the toledoth is put at the beginning, not the end, and what it's put at the beginning of is a genealogy. This clearly shows that, at least by the first century, the toledoth was understood as introducing a genealogy or at least a family

Conclusion: the Book of Genesis was assembled from twelve documents written at dates unknown except that documents I-III were of antediluvian origin and IV-XII were roughly contemporary with the events they describe. The "colophon last" analysis of the texts works only for Tablets I-IV at the most, but not after that. Tablet V marks the transition from the end colophon to the introductory phrase by blending the devices of the colophon and the catch phrase. After the time of Noah the following changes appear in Genesis documents:

- the toledoth phrase introduces the document rather than closes it
- *toledoth* is understood not to mean 'ancestry,' or 'origin story,' but 'story of descendants'
- the documents are written on some material other than clay tablets (papyrus, parchment, leather).[4]

This suggests that the practice of putting the colophon at the end of the document was an antediluvian style that was suited for clay tablets (or whatever material was used before the flood), but not considered appropriate for other media of documentation in the postdiluvian world.[5]

We see then strong evidence that Genesis preserves unique and very ancient written documents. The literary style of these documents shows that they were (more or less) contemporary with the events they describe, and the first six sections in particular were written in a style that reflects a structure and medium which was appropriate to the second and third millennium BC, long before Moses' lifetime. That does not, per se, prove that Genesis is divinely inspired; but it does disprove most of the assumptions undergirding the document hypothesis. This means the scholarly arguments foundational to disregarding the possibility of divine revelation are invalid.

Genesis is therefore a crucial book, packed with meaning and packed with importance, full of critical, central information for helping us to understand the truth of the universe, the existence of God, our relationship with God, every fundamental issue that humans concern themselves with. Starting then with the Bible as our way of knowing and the book of Genesis as the first principles of our way of knowing, we will in this book combine some things we can learn from

---

history.

[4]The tablets of Ishmael and Esau are short enough to really be clay tablets, but they still follow the style of the papyrus sections and so could have been papyrus or parchment as well.

[5]Obviously the practice of using clay tablets for writing was carried on in Mesopotamia for centuries after the flood and where they were used colophons continued to be placed at the end of documents.

reading Genesis with what we know about science. Now, what we know about science is shifting sand, that is, it can always change, it can always improve. Insofar as I write about science as it intersects with the truth about the Bible, that part of it may change. But the truth of the Bible, leading up to and including the sacrifice and resurrection of Jesus Christ, itself is timeless. It is the solid rock of our knowledge.

2

Goodbye, proud world(view)!

"[Evolution is] a system which is so repugnant at once to history, to the tradition of all peoples, to exact science, to observed facts, and even to Reason herself, [that it] would seem to need no refutation, did not alienation from God and the leaning toward materialism, due to depravity, eagerly seek a support in all this tissue of fables."

– Pope Pius IX, quoted by Andrew Dickson White in *A History of the Warfare of Science with Theology in Christendom*

Having looked at the place that Genesis has in the overall structure of the Bible, we have seen that its function is unique: it is the foundation for the worldview that supplies the context for everything else that is written in all other books of the Bible. When we recognize that, we equally recognize that that is not the function that Genesis has in Western societies today. Whether one is a creationist, evolutionist, or some other persuasion, science, not the Bible, is the final criterion for judging the validity of ideas. Did Genesis ever actually function as the foundation of a people's worldview in the real world? Did it ever in Western (European) society? If not, why not? If so, how did Genesis cease to be the foundation of our worldview and evolution take its place?

Of course Genesis was indeed the foundation of the worldview in Judah and Judea. When asked about the institution of divorce, Jesus refuted the validity of that institution, based solely on the book of Genesis and its description of the original foundation of marriage. Even in Europe Genesis once served as the foundation of a worldview. In the late classical age, Augustine of Hippo, refuting the cosmology of his time where it conflicted with a literal reading of the Bible wrote, "Greater is the authority of Scripture than all the powers of the human mind."[1]

---

[1] "Major est quippe Scripturae hujus auctoritas, quam omnis humani ingenii capacitas." *De Genesi ad Litteram (The Literal Meaning Of Genesis)* 2.5.9. In the thirteenth century, Vincent de Bauvais, in his *Speculum Naturale 4.98*, quoted Augustine as writing, "Non est aliquid temere diffiniendum sed quantum Scriptura dicit accipiendum, cujus major est auctoritas quam omnis humani ingenii capacitas." This was translated by White (1896:325) as "Nothing is to be accepted save on the authority of Scripture, since greater is that authority than all the powers of the human mind." While de Bauvais did not

As recently as the late eighteenth century we have this from the French naturalist Georges-Louis Leclerc de Buffon:

> If it were admitted that the ass is of the family of the horse, and different from the horse only because it has varied from the original form, one could equally well say that the ape is of the family of man, that he is a degenerate man, that man and ape have a common origin; that, in fact, all the families among plants as well as animals have come from a single stock, and that all animals are descended from a single animal, from which have sprung in the course of time, as a result of process or of degeneration, all the other races of animals. For if it were once shown that we are justified in establishing these families; if it were granted among animals and plants there has been (I do not say several species) but even a single one, which has been produced in the course of direct descent from another species... then there would no longer be any limit to the power of nature, and we should not be wrong in supposing that, with sufficient time, she has been able from a single being to derive all the other organized beings....But this is by no means a proper representation of nature. We are assured by the authority of revelation that all animals have participated equally in the grace of direct Creation and that the first pair of every species issued fully formed from the hands of the Creator.[2]

Note first of all that Buffon's hypothesis of common descent is actually based on *degeneration* rather than progress. If apes and man have a common ancestor, it is man, not ape. By extension the common ancestor of fish and amphibians would be amphibians, not fish. Working in this way, this would mean that if all animals were descended from a single animal, it would logically be *man*. That is as strange to the evolutionist as it is to the creationist. But this assumption that diversification of life should come by degeneration is itself based on Genesis, which states that in a fallen world things left to chance or nature degenerate rather than improve, descend rather than ascend.

But what is perhaps more noteworthy in this quote is that nearly a century before the *Origin of Species*, Buffon recognized that an argument for common

---

accurately recall Augustine's words, his citation does reflect the spirit behind the phrase actually written by Augustine.

[2] Georges LouisLeclerc, comte de Buffon, *Histoire Naturelle*, 1749-89:IV.31

organismal descent for all organisms could be made on the basis of homology of organisms; yet this conclusion could be overruled "by the authority of revelation". Genesis was the foundation of the worldview; all ways of looking at the world had to be reconcilable to it or be understood as false.

So we have seen that Genesis was the foundation of a theistic (and generally Christian) worldview for much of Europe's history from the classical age to the eighteenth century. What happened? The popular belief, that evolution overthrew the theistic worldview, turns out to be incorrect.

The correct answer is twofold: one cause was the general collapse of faith in Christianity as a way of being and therefore as a worldview; the second cause was a gradual trend on the part of theologians toward analyzing the Bible as a strictly human document, with the result that they began to believe it *was* a strictly human document.

It began shortly after the Protestant Reformation in which the medieval Catholic worldview was challenged and in some countries overthrown. Worldviews do not let themselves be overthrown easily, especially one that is the basis of a despotic social and political system. Fox's *Book of Martyrs* is full of the massacres unleashed on whole populations for questioning the received world order. Eventually the political leaders in these towns fought back, first in a spirit of self-defense, then for their own agenda: what started as bloodshed over worldviews became wars over political power: the papacy versus the nation states versus the so-called Holy Roman Empire. Kenneth Clark in his book *Civilisation: A Personal View* wrote that the collapse in faith in Christianity started as a result of these wars,

> the horrors that were to descend on Western Europe, both sides proclaiming themselves as the instruments of God's wrath. Fire rains down from heaven on kings, popes, monks and poor families; and those who escape the fire fall victim to the avenging sword. It's a terrible thought that so-called wars of religion, religion of course being used as a pretext for political ambitions, but still providing a sort of emotional dynamo, went on for one hundred and twenty years, and were accompanied by such revolting episodes as the massacre of St Bartholomew. No wonder that the art of the time...should have abandoned all that belief in the decency and high destiny of man that had been achieved in the Renaissance.[3]

---

[3] Kenneth Clark, *Civilisation* (New York:Harper and Row, 1969) 161.

Clark uses art as an insight to the culture as a whole and the loss of faith seen in art was a reflection of loss of faith in the hearts and minds of western Europe.

> For almost a thousand years the chief creative force in western civilisation was Christianity. Then, in about 1725, it suddenly declined and in intellectual society practically disappeared. Of course it left a vacuum. People couldn't get on without a belief in something outside themselves, and during the next hundred years they concocted a new belief which, however irrational it may seem to us, has added a good deal to our civilisation: a belief in the divinity of nature....those parts of the visible world which were not created by man and can be perceived through the senses. The first stage in this new direction of the human mind was very largely achieved in England – and perhaps it was no accident that England was the first country in which the Christian faith had collapsed. In about 1730 the French philosopher Montesquieu noted: 'There is no religion in England. If anyone mentions religion people begin to laugh.'[4]

Perhaps it was also no accident that England was also the country of Charles Lyell, Charles Darwin, and Thomas Huxley.

But it was not the country of Buffon; France was. And in mid-eighteenth century France, as we have seen above, a theistic worldview had not yet collapsed. But it was the place where began the second cause of the collapse of Genesis as the foundation of a worldview.

Jean Astruc was an 18th century medical professor on the faculty of Paris who wrote an anonymous work entitled *Conjectures sure les memories originauz dont il paroit que Moyse s'est servi pour composer le livre de la Génèse. Avec des remarques qui appuient ou qui éclairscissent ses conjectures* ("Conjectures on the original documents that Moses appears to have used in composing the Book of Genesis. With remarks that support or throw light upon these conjectures"). This work proposed that Moses compiled the Book of Genesis from at least two complete, independent sources. He reached this conclusion by noting that some biblical passages use the name *Elohim* for God, while others use *Jehovah Elohim*. He reasoned that this meant those passages came from two different sources, which he labeled "A" and "B". He still believed Moses was the author of the book and attempted to tease out the two

---

[4]Clark, 269.

original documents from Genesis as we have it.[5]

German theologian Johann G. Eichhorn was influenced by Astruc's work and in 1787 built on it, adding various linguistic or literary patterns as criteria to differentiate the two posited original documents, in addition to the original criterion of the different names for God. Eichhorn's work in turn influenced other German theologians to pursue this hypothesis that Genesis was compiled from other original documents, an idea that came to be known as the "document hypothesis". Eichhorn also maintained the Mosaic authorship of Genesis for most of his life, but other theologians such as H. Ewald and F. Tuch further deconstructed Genesis into three traditions, the Yahwist, Elohist, and Priestly and argued that other books of the Pentateuch were also assembled from these three traditions or documents. W.M.L de Wette attributed the book of Deuteronomy to a fourth tradition, the Deuteronomist, and in 1805 dated the composition of the book to the time of King Josiah, circa 621 BC. Having influenced theological thought in Germany, Eichhorn was in turn influenced by it himself: by 1823 he no longer believed in the Mosaic authorship of Genesis.

All of this happened long before the publication of Darwin's *Origin of Species* (1859) or, for that matter, Charles Lyell's *Principles of Geology* (1830). But the change in Eichhorn's belief clearly pointed out the direction that the document hypothesis, and higher criticism in general, were leading. In Astruc's original work, "A" and "B" were equally reliable and true sources which Moses had compiled in writing the inspired Book of Genesis. By the mid-nineteenth century, these traditions were seen as completely human in origin and motivated as much by political motivations of the authors as by a desire to accurately record history. Divine inspiration played less and less of a role in the books of the Law, and of the

---

[5]It is worth noting that authors who did argue against Mosaic authorship in the seventeenth century included Thomas Hobbes and Isaac de Peyrere. Hobbes is known for his book *Leviathan* (it was in *Leviathan* that he refuted the Mosaic authorship) and Peyrere also proposed pre-Adamite creations of human beings, that there were multiple races with separate origins, and only the Jews were descended from Adam and Eve. That these men were attracted to rejecting Mosaic authorship seems to suggest an association between that idea and a spurious, even dangerous spirituality. In Peyrere in particular we see a single author espousing two ideas that are both commonly seen by evangelicals as derived from evolution: biblical higher criticism, and racism. We see here that both predated evolution, but received a major boost in prestige from evolution. In the seventeenth century, however, both ideas were condemned as heretical because they contradicted biblical and Catholic worldviews.

Richard Simon had also challenged Mosaic authorship in the strictest sense, but still believed that Genesis was accurate, was written by Israelite chroniclers who recorded all Israelite history in written form, as it happened, and that Moses had instituted this system of chronicling.

Bible generally, and human motives, including less than pure motives, were increasingly seen as the driving force in biblical composition. Therefore the Bible, especially the Book of Genesis, could not be taken at face value or trusted as a historical document.

So, contrary to popular fundamentalist opinion, it was not evolution that led to higher criticism and the rejection of the Bible as the perfect word of God; rather, the rejection by churchmen of the Bible as the perfect word of God led to evolution becoming a worldview. If the Bible could not be trusted as factual, then it could not serve as the foundation for the Western worldview. Already Christianity had ceased to be the worldview in Europe due to the "wars of religion", but an old worldview can be seriously modified or even replaced without giving up the original cornerstone of that worldview. The Catholic and Protestant worldviews were fast fading in the intelligentsia of western Europe, but it had still clung to Genesis as a truth tester. Now churchmen themselves were on the vanguard of declaring that Genesis could not be trusted. This left a great yawning gap in the hearts and minds of people in western society as a whole, and as Clark wrote, "People couldn't get on without a belief in something outside themselves." What could be called upon to fill in the gap?

It has already been noted that by the late eighteenth century the middle and upper classes in Great Britain looked to nature rather than to religion for inspiration, and for a worldview. And even before that, Western Europe as a whole had come to prefer the scientific method to church doctrine as the surest way of knowing something. With scholarship of theologians themselves presenting the Bible as a purely human document, people in the English speaking world, and Europe generally, looked to the story of nature to replace the stories of Genesis to serve as the foundation of their worldview. And the place that one could find a real *story* of nature was in Darwin's theory of evolution.

Evolution started out as a theory of the diversification of life. Darwin was explicit about insisting that his theory did not speak at all to the problem of the origin of life.

> I believe that animals have descended from at most only four or
> five progenitors, and plants from an equal or lesser number....I
> should infer from analogy that probably all the organic beings
> which have ever lived on this earth have descended from some

one primordial form, into which life was first breathed by the Creator.[6]

This statement of Darwin's from the end of his *Origin of Species*, reveals that his theory dealt exclusively with the diversification of life forms, not the origin of life itself. Much less did Darwin deal with the origin of the earth, or of the sun and moon and all stars, of the very universe. It was Thomas Huxley, an agnostic, (he actually coined the word *agnostic*) who proposed the origin of life from non-living matter by means of evolution.

By this time evolution and the document hypothesis of the Pentateuch reinforced each other. Julius Wellhausen championed the idea that the Pentateuch was the product of four oral traditions (the Yahwist or Jahvist (J) the Elohist (E) the Priestly (P), and the Deuteronomist (D)) in a nomadic religion that was transmitted through the prophets and eventually was codified in the law (the reverse chronology of the Bible, where the law was given first before the advent of prophets). These traditions varied in sometimes contradictory ways and were all collected and finally written down during or after the Babylonian exile in the sixth century BC. Eventually editors and redactors tried to harmonize the sometimes conflicting versions of these folktales. Part of the support scholars offered for the hypothesis was the understanding, believed as fact at the time, that writing had not been invented before 1000 BC. This was based on negative evidence: writing earlier than that date had not yet been discovered.

Negative evidence is not very strong evidence and of course it was soon contradicted by very concrete evidence when discoveries from Sumer showed writing well before 1000 BC, as far back as 3000 BC. But even after these discoveries, the document hypothesis held on because it was based less on evidence than on the belief that the evolutionary myth was true and therefore the Bible was not, at least in a historical sense. In the modern world Genesis, in its original function as a foundation for a worldview, was unneeded and unwelcome. Meanwhile, Darwin's own theory of evolution was running into trouble on purely scientific grounds at this same time.

For one thing, Darwin himself submitted a theory of inheritance called *pangenesis*. According to pangenesis, every organ of the body produced minute hereditary particles, called gemmules, which would make copies of the respective organs; so for instance, the eye produced eye gemmules, kidneys produced kidney

---

[6]Charles Darwin, *On the Origin of Species*, 2nd ed., (London:John Murray, 1860) 484. The words "by the Creator" were added to the second edition.

gemmules, and so on. The bloodstream carried gemmules from every organ to the reproductive systems of male and female to form gametes.

The advent of Mendel's work in genetics proved pangenesis incorrect, and moreover threatened to discredit Darwin's emphasis on natural selection as the mechanism for evolutionary change. By the 1920's the Darwinian theory of evolution was seen as obsolete and its days numbered. Strictly speaking, *Darwin's* theory of evolution has actually passed from the scientific scene.

About the same time that Darwinism was waning in scientific favor, the document hypothesis and historic scepticism about the Bible's authenticity began to be challenged as well. We have seen that one of the contributing factors to Genesis losing it's place as a foundation of western civilization's worldview was the development of higher criticism. The origin of higher criticism was in Astruc's theory of Genesis. But Astruc did not contrive his theory with the intention of overthrowing Genesis. The theory came not from skepticism, but from ignorance: ignorance of the writing styles of the very ancient world. That ignorance continued through the nineteenth century and allowed the document hypothesis to develop until faith in Genesis was shaken to the point of requiring a theory like evolution to replace it as the cornerstone of the West's worldview.

But even as materialism/nature worship replaced Christianity as a worldview and evolution replaced Genesis as the foundation of the West's worldview, the relatively new field of archeology was literally uncovering new information which challenged the skepticism of biblical higher criticism. Two of the many existing examples can illustrate this.

The use of camels by Abraham and his people was seen as anachronistic and therefore further proof that Genesis is historically inaccurate, since camels were only known to have been domesticated by 1500 BC. But Andre Parrot in 1961 discovered camel bones dating back to 2500 BC in the center of the ancient city of Mari, indicating much earlier domestication than was previously known. He and others also found artworks from well before 1500 BC depicting camels, confirming this result. It is now recognized that the use of camels by Abraham and his family is completely realistic.

In 1918 William Albright wrote an article rejecting the historicity of the war described in Genesis 14 and claiming it had been written in 500 BC. Forty-three years later, after archeological evidence supported the authenticity of this chapter, Albright wrote another article stating that his own more recent studies "established the absolute antiquity of the contents of the chapter".[7] Two years after this Albright wrote,

> During these fifteen years (between World Wars) my initially skeptical attitude toward the accuracy of Israelite historical tradition had suffered repeated jolts as discovery after discovery confirmed the historicity of details which might reasonably have been considered legendary.[8]

The point here is that there has been a consistent pattern of the students of the document hypothesis rejecting the historicity of various events or passages in the Bible based on a lack of archeological evidence, only to have their views discredited again and again when said archeological evidence did turn up. Among the most remarkable of archeological finds of this sort are the discoveries of ancient extrabiblical literature—secular literature aside from the Bible written in the days of the biblical patriarchs. Whole libraries of such literature have been discovered: more than 17,000 tablets at Ebla, over 20,000 at Nuzi, over 25,000 at Mari, some dating back to the mid-third millennium BC. Tablets at Ebla mention biblical place names like Haran, Ur, Lachish, and Jerusalem which is still referred to simply as Salim. Sodom and Gomorrah are mentioned as well as the fact that they are part of five "cities of the plain." Biblical names— Serug (*Sharugi*), Terah (*Turakhi*), Abram (*Abarama*), Jacob (*Ya'qub-il*), Laban, etc.—while not necessarily identifying the same individuals as in the Bible, are nevertheless found as authentic names of the patriarchal period.

> Abraham's adoption of Eliezer of Damascus (Gen. 15:2) can be illustrated from the Nuzi texts, which show that it was the custom for childless couples to adopt a man as their heir. If later a son were born he would have to yield to the real son (Gen

---

[7]W.F. Albright, "Historical and Mythical Elements in the Story of Joseph." *Journal of Biblical Literature*, 37.3 (1918): 112-43.

W.F. Albright, "Abram the Hebew: A New Archaeological Interpretation," *Bulletin of the American Schools of Oriental Research*, no. 163 (1961): 49 :

"The name of Amraphel king of Shinar has been found in Akkadian inscriptions in Sumer (biblical Shinar); the name of Arioch king of Elassar is rare and is not attested after the middle of the second millennium BC, in the name of *Arriwuk* a contemporary of Hammurabi; the name of Chedorlaomer, king of Elam, is now known to be an authentic name in Elamite; and the name of Tidal king of nations/Goyyim is thought to be the same as the Hittite name *Tidkhaliya*."

[8]W.F. Albright, *History, Archaeology and Christian Humanism*, (New York: McGraw-Hill, 1964) 309.

15:4). The incident in Gen. 16:1-2 which tells of Sarah presenting her handmaid Hagar to Abraham to beget a child is illustrated by a tablet of adoption which stipulates that a barren wife must provide a slave girl to her husband to beget a son. This particular tablet and the Hammurabi Law Code require that the slave's child be kept—a rule which was preempted by the divine command to send Hagar and Ishmael away. Esau's sale of his birthright to Jacob is paralleled in Nuzi by a man's transfer of his inheritance regarding a grove to his brother for three sheep.[9]

The increased knowledge of archeological data and the increased respect for the historicity of the Bible did not displace evolution, or its corrolary in biblical studies, higher criticism. But it did lead to a new and more historically based perception of the composition of Genesis than the document hypothesis: the tablet theory of P.J. Wiseman discussed in Chapter 1.

But the idea of evolution itself, the concept of a strictly materialistic origin of life, had caught the imagination of European thinkers. Genetics replaced gemmules and, for a time, even natural selection as the mechanism of speciation, but the great story had permanently replaced Genesis as the cornerstone of the western worldview. Exactly seventy years *after* the *Origin of Species* D.M.S. Watson wrote,

> Evolution itself is accepted by zoologists not because it has been observed. to occur or is supported by logically coherent arguments, but because it does fit all the facts of taxonomy, of palæontology, and geographical distribution, and because no alternative explanation is credible....not because it be can proved by logically coherent evidence to be true but because the only alternative, special creation, is clearly incredible.[10]

As early as 1896, Andrew Djckson White had written,

> The theory of an evolution process in the formation of the universe and of animated nature is established, and the old theory of direct creation is gone forever. In place of it science has given us conceptions far more noble, and opened the way to an

---

[9]Edwin Yamauchi, *The Stones and the Scriptures* (Grand Rapids, MI: Baker Book House, 1972) 38-9.

[10]D.M.S. Watson, "Adaptation", *Nature* 124.3119 (1929): 231-234.

argument from design infinitely more beautiful than any ever developed by theology.[11]

Notice from this quote that evolution was here to stay not because it is more reasonable, or more observable, but because it is "more noble," "infinitely more beautiful" than Genesis. This is, if nothing else, an honest statement. Societies, and individuals, don't change their worldview because of logical reasoning, but because of emotional and cultural factors that make the incoming worldview a more attractive way to make sense of the world. Science is just the way of making one's analytical intelligence comfortable with that worldview. "All worldviews yield poetry to those who believe them by the mere fact of being believed," wrote C.S. Lewis.

The West had lost faith in Christianity. Theologians had lost faith in the Bible. The West needed something to believe in and looked to nature for inspiration. Darwin wrote about origins in nature. The West took it from there. This in turn introduced the idea that evolution could be defined as a strictly materialistic process of diversification and complexification that applies not only to biological organisms, but across the board to all natural phenomena on all scales from the microscopic, to the stars, the galaxies, and to the universe itself. Evolution in this new definition could produce an entirely materialistic atheistic account of creation. Even after particulars in Darwinism were proved incorrect, the myth was needed and it was already bigger than Darwin, anyway.

> Consider for a few moments the enormous aesthetic claim of [Christian theology's] chief contemporary rival - what we may loosely call the Scientific Outlook...Supposing this to be a myth, is it not one of the finest myths which human imagination has yet produced? The play is preceded by the most austere of all preludes: the infinite void, and matter restlessly moving to bring forth it knows not what. Then, by the millionth millionth chance - what tragic irony - the conditions at one point of space and time bubble up into that tiny fermentation which is the beginning of life. Everything seems to be against the infant hero of our drama - just as everything seems against the youngest son or ill-used stepdaugther at the opening of a fairy-tale. But life somehow wins through. With infinite suffering, against all but insuperable obstacles, it spreads, it breeds, it complicates itself: from the amoeba up to the plant, up to the reptile, up to the mammal. We

---

[11] Andrew Dickson White, *A History of the Warfare of Science with Theology in Christendom*, vol. 1 (London: Macmillan, 1896; reprint ed, New York: Dover, 1960) 86.

glance briefly at the age of monsters. Dragons prowl the earth, devour one another and die. Then comes the theme of the younger son and the ugly duckling once more. As the weak, tiny spark of life began amidst the huge hostilities of the inanimate, so now again, amidst the beasts that are far larger and stronger than he, there comes forth a little naked, shivering, cowering creature, shuffling, not yet erect, promising nothing: the product of another millionth millionth chance. Yet somehow he thrives. He becomes the Cave Man with his club and his flints, muttering and growling over his enemies' bones, dragging his screaming mate by her hair (I could never quite make out why), tearing his children to pieces in fierce jealousy till one of them is old enough to tear him, cowering before the terrible gods whom he has created in his own image. But these are only growing pains. Wait till the next Act. There he is becoming true Man. He learns to master nature. Science comes and dissipates the superstitions of his infancy. More and more he becomes the controller of his own fate. Passing hastily over the present (for it is a mere nothing by the time-scale we are using), you follow him on into the future. See him in the last Act, though not the last scene, of this great mystery. A race of demigods now rule the planet - and perhaps more than the planet - for eugenics have made certain that only demigods will be born, and psycho-analysis that none of them shall lose or smirch his divinity, and communism that all which divinity requires shall be ready to their hands. Man has ascended his throne. Hence forward he has nothing to do but to practice virtue, to grow in wisdom, to be happy. And now, mark the final stroke of genius. If the myth stopped at that point, it might be a little pathetic. It would lack the highest grandeur of which human imagination is capable. The last scene reverses all. We have the Twilight of the Gods. All this time, silently, unceasingly, out of all reach of human power, Nature, the old enemy, has been steadily gnawing away. The sun will cool - all suns will cool - the whole universe will run down. Life (every form of life) will be banished, without hope of return, from every inch of infinite space. All ends in nothingness, and "universal darkness covers all." The pattern of myth thus becomes one of the noblest we can conceive. It is the pattern of many Elizabethan tragedies, where the protagonist's career can be represented by a slowly ascending and then rapidly falling curve, with its highest point in Act IV.

You see him climbing up and up, then blazing in his bright meridian, then finally overwhelmed in ruin.[12]

As evolution took on the role of Christianity, the role of an all-encompassing worldview, the scientific method was set as not just a method for testing hypotheses, but as *the* way of knowing. And the scientific community became charged with the same function as the Church: to define, preserve, and propagate the Truth, the Sound Doctrine.

> Is evolution a theory, a system, or a hypothesis? It is much more: it is a general postulate to which all theories, all hypotheses, all systems must henceforward bow and which they must satisfy in order to be thinkable and true. Evolution is a light which illuminates all facts, a trajectory which all lines of thought must follow. This is what evolution is.[13]

We have come full circle: we nearly started with a quote from an eighteenth century French naturalist stating the supremacy of divine revelation; we have ended with a quote from a twentieth century French cleric stating the supremacy of evolution. We will say no more about the development of evolution, and this work will not debate the interpretations of scientific data. What we think about what we see—that is, our interpretations of observed scientific data—is motivated by what we believe, be it the Bible, the story of evolution, or some other worldview. We should now see that more than scientific data is involved; and why those who believe in evolution really *believe* in it—devotedly, regarding it worthy of such energy.

> There is a beauty in this myth which well deserves better poetic handling than it has yet received: I hope some great genius will yet crystallise it before the incessant stream of philosophic change carries it all away. I am speaking, of course, of the beauty it has whether you believe it or not. There I can speak from experience:

---

[12]C.S. Lewis, "Is Theology Poetry?" in *They Asked for a Paper* (London:G. Bles, 1962) 154-6. Originally published in *Socratic Digest* no.3, 1945.

[13]Pierre Teilard de Chardin, quoted by Theodosius Dobzhansky in his aptly titled essay, "Nothing in Biology Makes Sense Except in the Light of Evolution"in *American Biology* 35.3 (1973):129. Dobzhansky was clearly wrong when he wrote that, "there is no doubt at all that Teilhard was a truly and deeply religious man and that Christianity was the cornerstone of his worldview." Deeply religious, yes, but there can be no doubt from the quote above that Christianity was *not* the cornerstone of his worldview. Evolution was. Christianity merely supplied some of the particulars.

for I, who believe less than half of what it tells me about the past, and less than nothing of what it tells me about the future, am deeply moved when I contemplate it. The only other story— unless, indeed, it is an embodiment of the same story— which similarly moves me is the Nibelung's Ring. Enden sah ich die Welt.[14]

Let us return to a story different than either of these; a story my faith holds still to be the noblest, most beautiful, and truest of all.

---

[14]Lewis, 156.

3
In the beginning

> The heavens declare the glory of God; and the firmament sheweth his handywork.
> Day unto day uttereth speech, and night unto night sheweth knowledge.
> There is no speech nor language, where their voice is not heard.
> – Psalm 19:1-3

We have seen how the Bible in general, and Genesis in particular, fell out of favor as the foundation for the worldview of western civilization. It has remained the foundation of the worldview of Christians, radical Christians especially, and this has led to a greater cultural separation between them and society at large. At this point we begin our odyssey through the book of Genesis itself, reading what we know and believe, and connecting it to what we see and to what we think about what we see. We will move through the first eleven chapters, starting with the first verse of the first chapter.

The very first verse of the first chapter of Genesis says, "In the beginning God created the heaven and the earth." I take that not simply to be a summary of the rest of the chapter, but in fact the first activity of God in creation.

The created universe is made up of trinities. God's fingerprints are all over the universe insofar as the triune nature of God is seen all over His creation. The created universe is made up of three basic things: space, time, and matter/energy. Space and matter are explicitly mentioned here in the first verse:

In the beginning God created the **heaven**

which is all of outer space, all the universe – and nothing in it, no stars or galaxies or anything like that, just empty space. Space is something even if there's nothing in it. And if space is nothing else it is the possibility for the existence of some thing, some matter. There's a place for it to be and that's what God created—the heaven. First and foremost it's simply space.

and the **earth.**
Well, matter *was* the earth.

Now, there are some current theories in physics saying that space itself may be made up of particles.[1] Without going into that in detail, suffice it to say at this point that the heaven was empty space and all the matter that God created in the universe was in the earth. That was it: the heaven and the earth, space and matter. We'll go into a little more detail about that later.

As we have just seen, the created universe is a trinity: space, time, and matter, and each of those is in turn made up of trinities. Space is also made up of three dimensions: height, depth, and breadth. People can hypothesize about four, five, twelve dimensions, whatever, but in our universe as we experience it, as everything in the universe experiences it, there are just three dimensions. Time is made up of three parts: past, present, and future. And matter is made up of three things. But it gets a little more complicated when we talk about matter. All matter is made up of molecules and all molecules are made up of atoms. And each type of atom is called

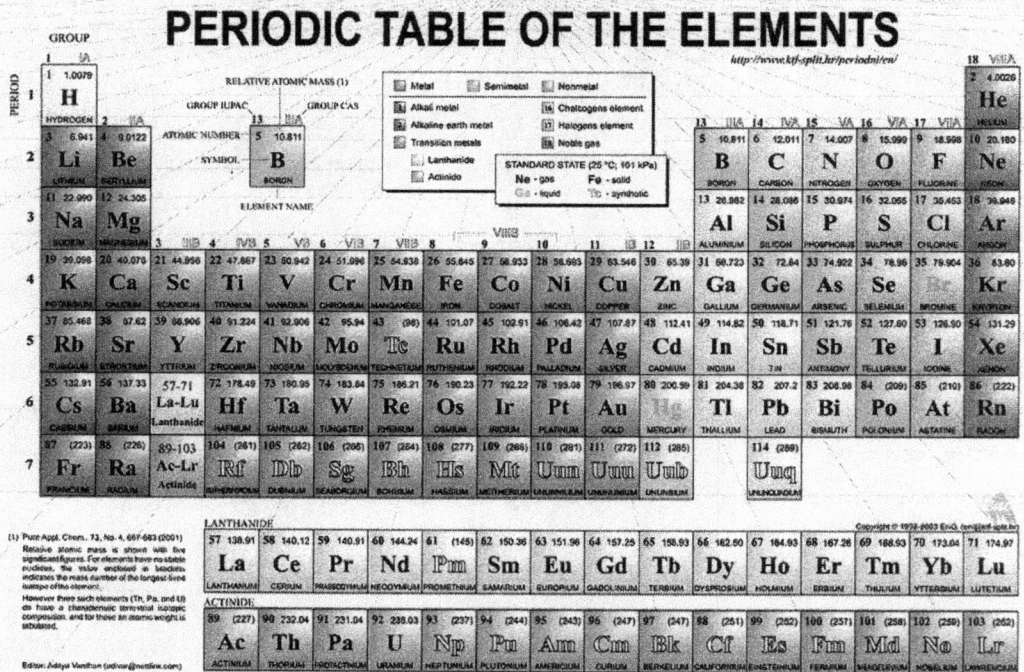

Figure 1. The Periodic Table of the Elements of Matter

---

[1] See "The Bountiful Fullness of Empty Space" by Lambert Dolphin: www.ldolphin.org/emptyspace.html . Also see "Matter is made of waves" by Gabriel LaFreniere: http://www.glafreniere.com/matter.htm

an element.

There are roughly a hundred stable elements in the universe that naturally occur without being produced in a laboratory. And the only place that has them all naturally occurring is the earth. I don't know of any other planet that has all 100+ elements. But the earth has every element there is. It appears that God basically created every kind of atom there was, packed it all together in a ball (or shapeless mass) and there was the earth. So the earth does represent the creation of all matter, or at least every *kind* of matter. And the elements are all just the logical formation of every kind of atom: one proton, one neutron, one electron, two protons, two neutrons, two electrons, and so on and every variation thereof all the way up to those 100+ elements all together in one mass, at that time a shapeless mass, because verse two says,

> And the earth was without form, and void; and darkness was upon the face of the deep. And the Spirit of God moved upon the face of the waters.

"Without form, [that is, shapeless] and void [empty]." Shapeless and barren. "And the Spirit of God moved upon the face of the waters." Here we see the action of the Spirit of God in creation.

> And God said, Let there be light: and there was light.

Before we get to light, let's talk about atoms a little bit more. Each atom is made up of a nucleus and electron(s), and each nucleus is made up of protons and neutrons. Protons and neutrons, in turn, are made up of quarks so we see a pattern here of not only a trinity, but a pattern of a trinity made up of a singularity plus a duality. Each atom is made up of a nucleus and electrons; it seems to be two things.

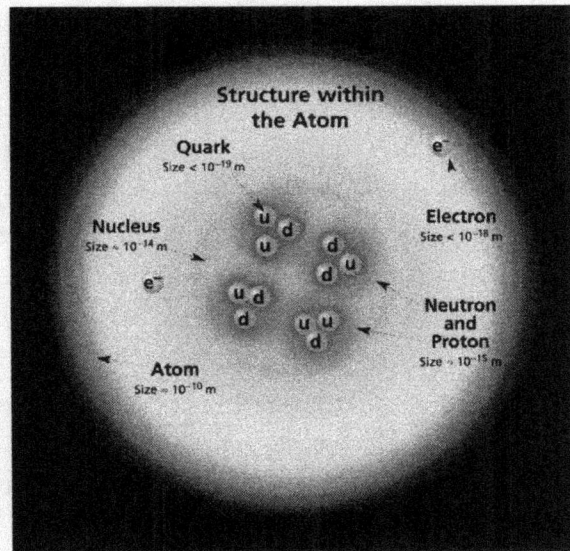

Figure2. Structure of an atom according to the standard model

But the nucleus itself is made up of protons and neutrons so there are three basic parts to an atom: protons, neutrons, electrons. The protons and neutrons go together to form the nucleus; that's the duality. The electron is left by itself; that's the singularity. And the protons and neutrons turn out to be trinities also because each proton and each neutron is made of three quarks. Because electrons are such a different kind of particle from quarks they belong to a type that has its own name: leptons. It turns out that there are three kinds of quarks and three kinds of leptons; these three types are called the three "generations" of matter. The first generation is the only one that is stable, while the other two generations, while they definitely exist, are extremely unstable. Again we have a duality (second and third generation) matched by a singularity (first generation), making a trinity (the three generations of matter). There is no scientific explanation for why there should be three generations of matter, but they can be seen as part of a larger pattern of trinities throughout the structure of the universe.

The pattern of trinity is also found in the heavens. When we think of "heaven," there's the heaven that God made, the empty space, and then there's the heaven where the angels are outside the universe as we know it, and then there's the heaven, which God formed on the second day. So there are three heavens: the first heaven (the atmosphere), the second heaven (outer space), and the third heaven (the spiritual realm where God and the angels are experienced directly, where God and the angels dwell). This delineation seems to find Biblical support in 2 Cor 12:2: "I knew a man in Christ above fourteen years ago, (whether in the body, I cannot tell; or whether out of the body, I cannot tell: God knoweth;) such an one caught up to the third heaven."

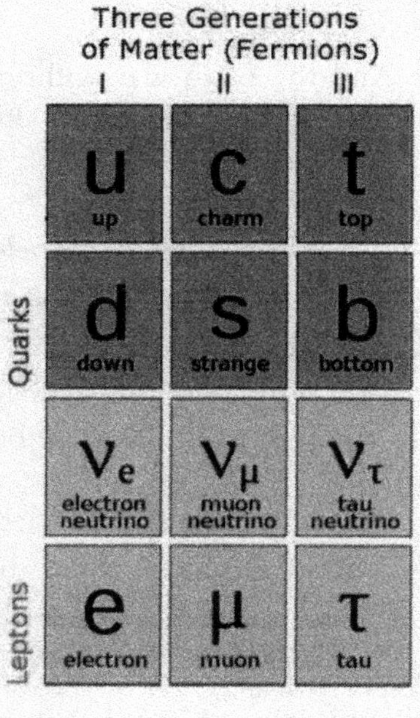

Figure3. The three generations of matter

Now on the first day what God created was the heaven and the earth and then also light. "And God said, Let there be light: and there was light." That means energy because that's what light is. This is interesting because the evolutionary myth of creation says that energy is more basic than matter.[2] But the Bible gives us the very distinct impression that God first created matter when He created the earth and then created energy when He created light. It could work either way: we can think of matter as very densely packed and highly organized energy, or we can think of energy as diffused matter. If we picked matter apart down to its individual atoms and took every atom and picked apart its electrons from its nucleus and picked apart the nucleus, the protons and neutrons, and then picked apart the protons and neutrons to their individual quarks (which we can't really do because quarks can't exist separately, since each quark only has 1/3 of an electric charge), and we just diffuse those out, stop them from being so dense and packed, they would just vaporize into energy; an enormous amount of energy, but just energy.

"And God said, Let there be light: and there was light." That also means that light existed without any source (except God making it). So God had light and darkness and He split those up so that there was light always in certain areas of the universe and darkness always elsewhere. And the earth could just rotate on its axis and produce the first day and night.

> And God called the light Day, and the darkness he called Night.
> And the evening and the morning were the first day.

That means theoretically there could have been any amount of time between the time that God first created the heaven and the earth and the time that God first created light. Not that this would support theistic evolution in the least. No matter how much time passed between those two events, we couldn't make any of this fit the evolutionary model of the universe where energy precedes matter, where the sun and other stars are created before the earth, where light always has to have a physical fire or source. It's simply a fact that the Bible doesn't start counting days until after light is created. "And the evening and the morning were the first day." And therefore you have the first evening and morning, the first day.

Then God says, "Let there be a firmament in the midst of the waters, and let it divide the waters from the waters." We know that word "firmament" means an expanse in the midst of the waters. And God made the "firmament," [the expanse] "and divided the waters which were under the firmament from the waters which were above the firmament: and it was so." That's the first heaven. We

---

[2]Matter and energy are said to have been generated simultaneously in the Big Bang. However energy *is* seen as more basic because it is less organized and energy *did* come before atoms (even before baryons), and therefore elements.

already have the second heaven and the third heaven that God made. These names "first", "second", and "third" heaven refer to their proximity to the human perspective, not to the chronological order in which God made them. God made the first heaven last. He made the second heaven in that first verse: "In the beginning God created the heaven and the earth." Actually in Hebrew that word translated "heaven" is really dual. That's why in most modern translations it's translated "the heavens". So that may actually be the two heavens that are material. What we call the third heaven, where the angels are, where just souls go when they die, that may have been created at the same time as outer space that we see.

But now this thing we call the first heaven because it's closest to us, God made that on the second day. And it was an expanse to separate the water in vapor form from the water below it.

> And God said, Let the waters under the heaven be gathered
> together unto one place.

Before the sky was made, the vaporous water and the liquid water were all together and it was hard to tell when one started and one began. But God separated the two with a clear expanse, literally cleared the air and created this atmosphere that separated the water above from the water beneath.

> And God said, Let the waters under the heaven be gathered
> together unto one place, and let the dry land appear: and it was
> so.

That day God shaped the earth's crust to rise above the water and form one land mass.

"And God called the dry land Earth." Many times when you read "earth" in the Bible it's not talking about the planet Earth, including the oceans and the atmosphere, but simply the dry land.

> And God called the dry land Earth; and the gathering together of
> the waters called he Seas: and God saw that it was good.

The dry land appeared in one land mass, what today is called Pangea, and the "seas" may be a poetic plural, but it may be an allusion to what is hypothesized in the hydroplate theory (see Chapter 10), that there was originally a body of water under the earth's crust roughly equal in volume to the body of water above it.

> And God said, Let the earth bring forth grass, the herb yielding seed, and the fruit tree yielding fruit after his[3] kind, whose seed is in itself, upon the earth: and it was so.
>
> And the earth brought forth grass, and herb yielding seed after his kind, and the tree yielding fruit, whose seed was in itself, after his kind: and God saw that it was good.
>
> And the evening and the morning were the third day.

So on the third day, the same day that He brought all the waters together in one place and made the dry land appear, He made the earth bring forth all kinds of plants including aquatic plants as well. Again, notice that all plant organisms—from ferns, to algae, to fruit trees—were all created on the same day.

---

[3]The word *his* in King James English here is really the word "its".

4

God's Clock

And God said, Let there be lights in the firmament of the heaven to divide the day from the night; and let them be for signs, and for seasons, and for days, and years:

And let them be for lights in the firmament of the heaven to give light upon the earth: and it was so.

We see from the above text two reasons for creating the sun and the moon and the stars. One is to give light, but notice that's the secondary reason. The primary reason given, is to divide the day from the night and to be for signs and for seasons. In other words, with the sun and the moon, there was not just simply light shining on the earth half of a twenty-four hour period and the other half being dark. But by having specific shining objects that move in paths across the sky in our vision, we can actually divide the day and night into hours, and say which time of day it is. Time management is so important to God that the fourth day of the universe was actually done with us in mind to help us manage our time the best way we can. We could have just had light, but instead He created specific objects that would make it possible for us to tell what time of day or night it is, what week it is, what month it is. All of these objects, not just the sun and the moon, but the constellations in the sky can actually tell us what season of the year it is. Which part of the horizon the sun rises out of can also tell the season, whether it's summer, winter, spring, or fall. So we can mark off every division of time because we have specific objects in the sky, but the secondary reason is to give light upon the earth, which of course the earth already had anyway.

Incidentally, this is another contradiction of the evolutionary myth: sun and stars are all supposed to have come about billions of years before the earth was even in existence. So the earth is actually supposed to have been spawned by the stars, in a sense. In the Genesis view, however, it's totally the other way around (which is the accurate way): the earth came first and then the sun and moon and stars all came afterwards.

But this raises a problem: how is it possible for the stars to be made after the earth when we see there are stars that are billions of light years away, which means it's supposed to have taken billions of years for their light to have reached us? Furthermore, there's another, more exegetical question, having to do with the sun and the moon being placed in the "firmament of heaven." That phrase, like our phrase "first heaven," always refers to the atmosphere. Why does the Bible say that God placed the sun and the moon in the atmosphere?

Let's start with the age of the stars. The reason why stars are billions of light-years away and yet not billions of years old is simply because the speed of light has been slowing down. I can say that confidently because this is a discovery made, not by creationist scientists, but by a "secular" scientist named V.S. Troitskii[1] who collected evidence that the speed of light has been slowing down. This discovery has been repeated three times: after Troitskii, first by Prof. John Moffat of the University of Toronto in 1993, then in 1998 jointly by Dr. Joao Magueijo at Imperial College, London, and Dr. Andreas Albrecht, of the University of California at Davis. This is a discovery that was ignored or completely repudiated by evolutionary scientists. Ironically, the idea came to solve a scientific problem with the evolutionary myth: that the universe is so uniform in radiation in a way that it shouldn't be, given its size and the speed of light[2] . Calculations have been made backwards in time to find that the fact that the speed of light has been slowing down means that at the time of creation, the speed of light was so fast, that light from stars billions of light-years away could still have reached us by now, right from the beginning because the speed of light was almost infinite. So the

---

[1] V.S. Troitskii, "Physical Constants and the Evolution of the Universe", *Astrophysics and Space Science*, 139.2 (1987):384-411.
[2] Popular science journals reporting the findings in more detail:

- Steve Farrar, "Speed of Light 'Slowing Down'" London Sunday Times 15 Nov. 1998. Print.
- Bruce Rolston, "Speed of Light May Not Be Constant, Physicist Suggests." Science Daily [Universlty of Toronto] 6 Oct. 1998. Print.
- Scarlett Lee, "Faster than light", *Varsity Publications*, 1999
- Nigel Hawkes, "Is Einstein about to Be Dethroned?" The London Sunday Times 5 Apr. 2000. Print.

great distances between the stars and galaxies is not really a problem.[3] Now, what caused the slowing down of light? Lambert Dolphin has suggested[4] that God caused the extremely high speed of light by stretching out space of the second heaven at the creation of the universe. The fall resulted in a series of contractions of the universe which resulted in the slowing of the speed of light. It's speculation, of course, but that's one possibility. The effect on radioactive dating is something that also needs to be addressed. If light is slowing down, that actually affects the calculations of radioactive isotopes in such a way that makes half-lives much longer than they should be, which means that, for example, Carbon-14 dating, *even when done in a technically precise manner,* will yield much, much older dates than it should. Something might date from 60,000 years ago when it's only 5,000 years old. Once we go back further than three or four thousand years, the slope of difference between the current speed of light (and dating based on that) and the actual speed of light (and actual dates) starts going up exponentially. The speed of

---

[3]It also suggests that we can see everything that there is. If the speed of light had always been the current speed, we might wonder if there's something out there so far out that the light hasn't reached us yet. But if the speed of light was once nearly infinite (compared to the current speed, anyway), then no matter how far out things are, light from the most distant objects in the universe should have reached us.

[4]"The nature of space as a medium is as much a mystery to us as ever, yet from Maxwell's equations we know space possesses electrical permeability, mu0, and permittivity, epsilon0, from which a propagation velocity, c, for electromagnetic waves is derived,

c = [1 / mu0 epsilon0]1/2, and also a "characteristic impedance", Z = [mu0 / epsilon0]1/2.

These electrical properties of space and matter govern reflection and refraction of light and radio waves. The velocity of light drops in a dielectric medium by a factor of the square root of the dielectric constant of a material, for instance.

The stretching out of the fabric of space, "like a tent" (Jer. 10:12, Psalm 104:2) seems to have also required the additional investment of energy from the Creator's hand. The whole of space was stretched out to a fixed, maximum "diameter" either in a matter of hours, or perhaps instantaneously, on Day Two. Any subsequent shrinkage of space (as a result of the fall of man and the angels, or as a result of judgments from God) would require space to give up its excess energy, presumably resulting in dissipative, destructive events. Or, additional input from the "vacuum" (i.e. from God) may be flowing into the universe now as the sustaining energy spoken of in the New Testament. (See What Holds the Universe Together?) Although it may require a radical change in our current thinking, it is Biblically reasonable to think of the universe as not now expanding, but perhaps having shrunk from its initial size or else remaining static in size since Day Two. Stretching out space on Day Two would lower both mu and epsilon to minimum values, and this could mean that the initial velocity of light at the end of Day Two was higher than it is now by many orders of magnitude."
Lambert Dolphin, "The Uniqueness of Creation Week"
http://www.ldolphin.org/Unique.html

light is indeed constant everywhere in the universe at any given point in time, but over long time spans the speed has been slowing down.

As far as the sun and the moon being in the firmament, i.e. in the atmosphere, in the sky, that's just a semi-phenomenological reading of Genesis 1:14,19. Instead of saying the earth turns, we say the sun rises and the sun sets, and we're not being ignorant fools for saying that. That's what the sun does from our vantage point. The image of the sun in the sky rises and sets as does the moon. There's nothing incorrect scientifically about saying that. That's what is meant by a phenomenological statement: you're saying how things look from your vantage point.

But in another sense this statement is literal, not merely phenomenological: they were placed in the firmament insofar as their function existed solely in the firmament. The sun and moon were created primarily to mark off minutes, hours, days, months, seasons, years. There's only one place where that works: on the earth looking up into the sky. Once you leave the atmosphere of the earth, you can't tell what day it is. Looking at the sun won't tell you what day it is because you've left the clock system of the sun, the earth, and the moon. Those three objects (and also the stars) work together as a kind of clock. While the physical objects exist in the second heaven, the images of them as timekeeping pieces only exist in the first heaven, the firmament.

That's why we say this is a semi-phenomenological reading; in one sense it's phenomenological (describing the sun and moon from our point of view), but in another sense, it's literal: the sun-moon-earth system really only functions in the atmosphere or surface of the earth. It's not at all inaccurate or inappropriate to say.

> And God set them in the firmament of the heaven to give light
> upon the earth,
>
> And to rule over the day and over the night, and to divide the
> light from the darkness: and God saw that it was good.

Another little factoid to back this up is the fact that the diameter of the sun is 400 times the diameter of the moon, yet the sun is also 400 times further away than the moon, so if you're in the earth's atmosphere the sun and the moon are exactly the same size. That's what makes total solar eclipses possible.[5] This is not a

---

[5]There's also such a thing as an annular eclipse when the moon is slightly smaller than the sun in the sky.

coincidence. It is a reflection of the fact that God set the image of the sun and the moon in the sky to be timepieces. Every timepiece and calendar we use now is based ultimately on the sun and the moon and the stars.

James Dwyer, formerly a computer systems programmer with the U.S. Geological Survey, has lead research on the sun-earth-moon system and has found numerous indications that this system is so well arranged for keeping time from earth's point of view that the odds against such an arrangement by chance strongly suggest that these three objects were intentionally designed to function in this way.

> A most remarkable mystery concerns the Moon and its rotational period.
>
> The sidereal orbital period of the Moon around the Earth completes in 27.321666 days while the rotational period of the Moon also completes in 27.321666 days!

The result of this is that the side of the moon that we see lit is always the same side.

> Because both rates--the sidereal orbit and the rotation--are exactly the same, the Moon can be predicted to progress throughout its orbit with the same face of the Moon showing toward the Earth at all times.

There is also the phenomenon of solar eclipses, a phenomenon which requires a very improbable combination of unusual circumstances.

> The phenomenon of equal Moon and Sun sizes--whereby both orbs appear to have the same angular size--is integral in the periodic formation of a solar eclipse. It is here significant that the orbit of the Moon happens to be tilted at only 5 degrees with the Sun. The peculiar angle of the Moon orbit (in close alignment with the Sun) is ultimately necessary for the formation of a solar eclipse on the Earth. (If the orbit of the Moon did not closely align with the Sun then the Moon would never move into direct position between the Sun and the Earth; and consequently, a solar eclipse would never occur).

It is then most unusual that in order for a total eclipse of the Sun to be observable from the Earth, the Moon's apparent diameter must equal or exceed the Sun's apparent diameter (and this is so-- as explained above). In addition, the angle of the Moon's orbit must uniquely align with Earth's orbital plane around the Sun (and this also is so!).

There is also the interrelationship of different time periods clocked off by the sun-earth-moon system.

A cycle of 7 synodic months--when cycled 7 times--can be recognized to revolve into rather perfect alignment with the same spin-phase of the rotating Earth. Essentially, a rate of whole days (1447 solar days) appears to precisely align with or come into conjunction with 7 sets of 7 lunar months (or 49 synodic months).

Note that 1447 solar days divided by the rate of the synodic-month cycle, or 29.53059 days, is equal to 49.0000 lunar months.

The following diagram attempts to more fully illustrate that a cycle of 7 lunar months (cycled 7 times) very closely interfaces with the rate of the rotation of the Earth:

THE INTERFACE OF 49 SYNODIC MONTHS *							Number Of Earth's Rotations
1	2	3	4	5	6	7	206.714
8	9	10	11	12	13	14	413.428
15	16	17	18	19	20	21	620.143
22	23	24	25	26	27	28	826.856
29	30	31	32	33	34	35	1033.571
36	37	38	39	40	41	42	1240.285
43	44	45	46	47	48	49	1446.999

* -- Earth's rotation aligns with 49 lunar months.

The four phases of the moon which indicate times of a given month, can also be used to corroborate seasons of the year:

The four distinct quarter phases of the Moon can be predicted

*to appear throughout the four seasons of the year (as
described below):*

1.   *New phase (rides high in sky in summer and low in winter, and it reaches
an intermediate height in spring and fall).*

2.   *First-quarter phase (rides low in the fall and high in the spring, and it
takes a middle course during summer and winter).*

3.   *Full phase (rides low in summer, the same as the Sun at noon in
midwinter; and rides high in winter, comparable with that of the Sun at noon in
the summer; and it takes an intermediate height in spring and fall).*

4.   *Last-quarter phase or third-quarter phase (rides high in the fall and low
in the spring, and it follows an intermediate height in summer and winter).*

There are many other features of the earth-moon-sun system in addition to
those stated here, which reflect that the sun and moon were arranged relative to
the earth in a special way precisely as a mechanism for marking "times and
seasons". Dwyer and his associates have literally written a book (and several
articles) on the aspects of the earth-moon-sun system that demonstrate a
functional time measuring mechanism by design. Reference to their work is
necessary for further study on this subject. For now, we leave the astronomical
realm for one even more amazing: the realm of living organisms.

5
Life begets life

"All the efforts of the human mind cannot exhaust the essence of a single fly."
— Thomas Aquinas

Now from the fifth day things get complicated.

> And God said, Let the waters bring forth abundantly the moving creature that hath life, and fowl that may fly above the earth in the open firmament of heaven.
>
> And God created great whales, and every living creature that moveth, which the waters brought forth abundantly, after their kind, and every winged fowl after his kind: and God saw that it was good.

Incidentally, by moving creatures in the water, this means anything that lives in the water, whether it's mammal, reptile, amphibian, fish, invertebrates, whatever. As far as the "fowl" were concerned, we know that the Hebrew word translated "fowl" ('owph) really means 'flying creatures'. One of the so-called "fowl" that the Israelites were prohibited from eating in the Law of Moses was bats.[1] Bats obviously aren't birds, and the Israelites weren't so foolish that they didn't recognize that they didn't have beaks and so on—bats are mammals—but they fly and anything that flies was created on this day. And only those things that fly, along with those things that swim, were created on that day.

But He didn't just simply say, "let there be moving creatures and let there be fowl...." It says, "Let the waters bring forth abundantly." Again, here's where we intersect with scientific theories; and those are not necessarily permanent, because they are not revealed truth. But the best light we have on this, seen from genetics and molecular biology, seems to indicate that what happened here is something very similar to what is proposed by the so-called Independent Birth of Organisms (or IBO) theory of biology: that organisms fall into categories separated by

---

[1]Leviticus 11:13-19. Verse 20 uses *fowls* to refer to flying insects, further proving that the word means 'flying creatures' rather than the narrower sense of 'bird'.

insurmountable bio-molecular barriers, each life-type had a separate origin, and all organisms are genetically, but not necessarily organismally related. That is, originally there was literally a common pool of genes and these genes were arranged in different ways to form different genomes which in turn were arranged in "seed cells" that grew into different types of organisms. So we all have the same kinds of genes—we all come from a common gene pool—but we don't come from a single ancestor that reproduced by sexual or asexual reproduction; rather every group of animals that has a unique genome all had a separate origin, but that origin came from a common pool of genes. This explains why different groups of organisms have genes that they share with other groups of organisms, but at the same time also have genes that are unique to that group of organisms. This theory was developed by Dr. Periannan Senapathy from his work at the National Institutes of Health and at Genome Incorporated in Madison, Wisconsin. Tom Mattox, an engineer, summarizes the IBO theory of biology this way:

> The primordial pond (or ponds) produced not just one or two, but millions, perhaps billions of "seed cells" which are analogous to a zygote (a fertilized egg). These seed cells were formed in the pond by the random assembly of: (1) new genes, (2) parts of previously-made viable genomes, and (3) other biochemicals, all of which existed in the pond. Very few of these seed cells grew into viable creatures, and only a few that did were capable of reproducing -- and of surviving long enough to do so. The reused pieces of previously-made viable genomes accounts for the similarities we see today in supposedly "evolutionarily related" organisms.

> The test of whether two creatures were born independently is: does either have any unique genes or body parts? If so, they are not related by evolution. For example, all birds might be related, but a fish and a whale are not. No new species are formed today, other than slight variations of existing organisms. Existing organisms can adapt and change, but only within a closed framework. This is what Darwin saw.

> "A toad can become a frog, but never a rabbit."

> A fundamental aspect of the new theory is the high probability of finding complete split genes in the random DNA of the primordial pond. Split genes contain "introns" (pieces of junk

DNA) and "exons" (the coding parts of genes). Split genes are found in all eukaryote organisms (e.g., plants and animals). On the other hand, the genes of prokaryote organisms (single-celled bacteria) do not have introns. The probability of finding a relatively short exon in a long run of random DNA is much greater than that of finding a complete gene or a prokaryote gene.

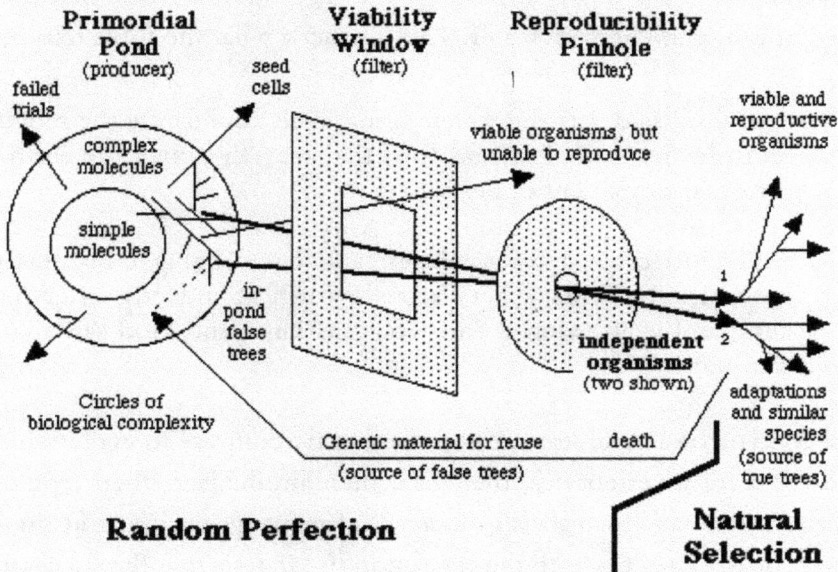

Figure 4: schematic summary of Senapathy's IBO theory

In fact, Senapathy shows that practically any exon (and hence any eukaryote gene with exons and introns) can easily be found in the large amount of random DNA available in the primordial pond.[2]

The appearance of eukaryotic cells before prokaryotic (bacterial) cells runs counter to the evolutionary myth, which claims that bacteria, or something very much like bacteria was the first life and eukaryotes evolved from them. This proves to be a very significant point as we will see in Chapter 8.

There are also, of course, very significant differences between this theory and the Genesis account. First of all, the IBO theory is completely materialistic. And the timescale is the same as for evolution with the appearance of virtually all organisms around 600 million years ago. But these differences also cause problems

---

[2]Mattox, Jeffrey. "The Independent Birth of Organisms." -- Senapathy. 31 Jan. 1998. Web. 07 Apr. 2015. http://www.mattox.com/genome/

for the theory — problems which don't exist for the Genesis account. Likewise the theory without hundreds of millions of years provides a very good model for how life could have arisen according to the Genesis account. The solution within the framework of Genesis seems to be that Senapathy got it right about eukaryotes first, but these first seed cells were designed and produced by God.

Even in the IBO theory of biology the suggestion is made that the seed cells formed in water and grew in water. This is exactly what the Bible tells us:

> And God said, Let the waters bring forth abundantly the moving creature that hath life, and fowl that may fly above the earth in the open firmament of heaven.

> And God created great whales, and every living creature that moveth, which the waters brought forth abundantly, after their kind, and every winged fowl after his kind: and God saw that it was good.

Every type of animal was created then, again contrary to evolutionists who say first there were invertebrates, then fish, then amphibians, then reptiles and then birds and mammals. Instead, all of those different types appear at the same time. The web theory thus fits with the revelation of Genesis that the successive order in which animals appear is not according to Linnaean class, but according to habitat. Animals in every kind of class, every type of phylum that lived in the water and those that fly were all created on the same day, the fifth day.

> And God blessed them, saying, Be fruitful, and multiply, and fill the waters in the seas, and let fowl multiply in the earth.

> And the evening and the morning were the fifth day.

Then we get to the sixth day; this says that God made all land animals. Again, this is all invertebrates, reptiles, mammals, and birds, and possibly amphibians, too. There are birds that neither fly nor swim, but which are simply land roaming beasts and those were also made on the sixth day.

> And God said, Let the earth bring forth the living creature after his kind, cattle, and creeping thing, and beast of the earth after his kind: and it was so.

> And God made the beast of the earth after his kind, and cattle
> after their kind, and every thing that creepeth upon the earth after
> his kind: and God saw that it was good.

I don't think "kind" is necessarily supposed to be a technical term, but the point is made: different types of animals with different genomes had different creations, but all made on that day. But if the seed cells had to form in water, how would these cells get on earth?

It's far from certain, but one very real possibility exists which would also explain how seed cells of plants appeared on land on the third day. The second chapter of Genesis has this statement: "But there went up a mist from the earth, and watered the whole face of the ground." It could be that perhaps this mist that went up would certainly go up from the water evaporating and if that could carry the genetic material with it and then water the ground, the ground would be saturated with this genetic material. The seed cells could form on the land and land animals appear.

Again, God didn't just say "let there be every living creature," but He said "let the earth bring them forth." Clearly some kind of process generated plants and animals out of the earth; God didn't just speak them into existence. That certainly seems to be the case, based on the words of that verse. And at present the IBO theory seems to best describe that process. It really does seem to paint this picture that this genetic material soaked into the earth and then God shaped them into seed cells and then the animals literally grew out of the earth.

While Senapathy's IBO theory brilliantly analyzes the molecular biology of speciation, the other aspects of the theory, such as the origin of chromosomes and cells, are outside his area of expertise and suffer accordingly. His scenario of origin by random chance does not give an adequate account for the origin of the complex structure of chromosomes (Figure 5) or the more complex organization of cells (Figure 6).

Another challenge to the IBO theory could be, "Well, after the seed cells began to grow, how could these fetuses survive for weeks and weeks just on the bare ground or floating on the water?" That *would* be a problem, but it's not a problem at all if all these animals were created within a twenty-four hour period.

God just directed first the sea, then the earth to produce these plants and animals. "Let the earth bring them forth."

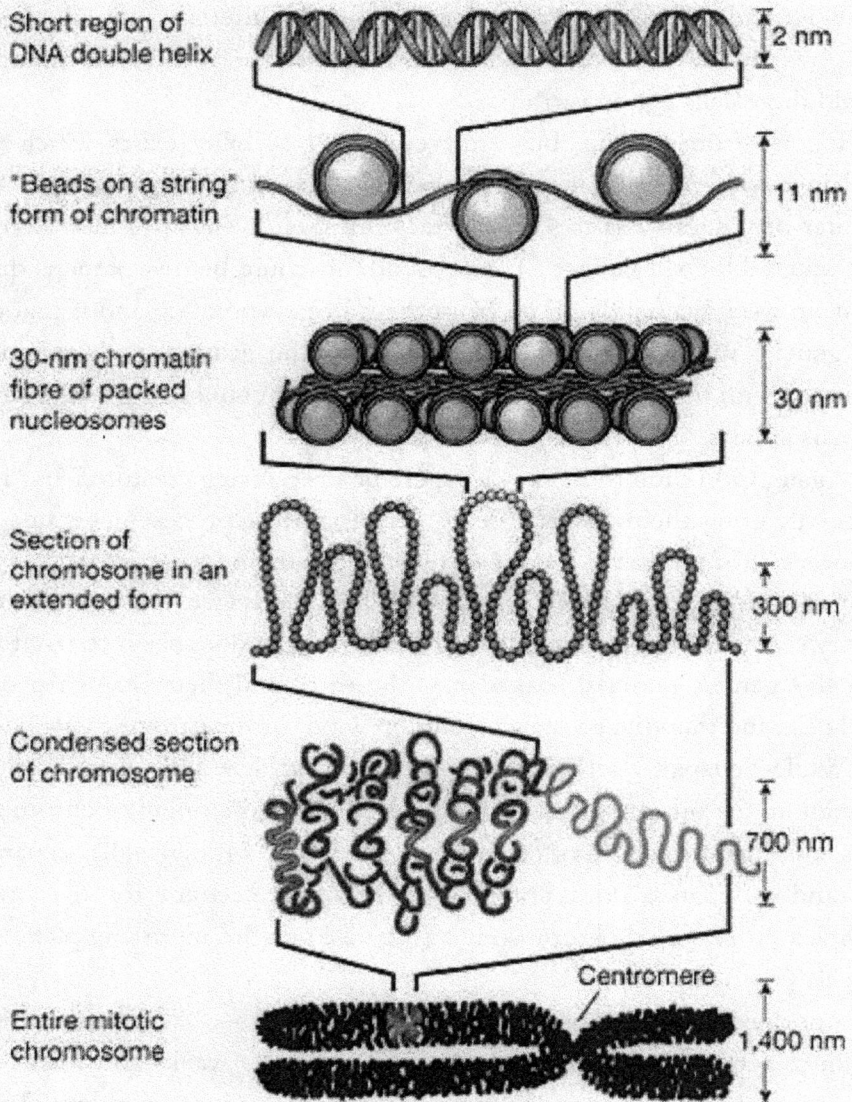

Figure 5. Complex structure of the chromosome

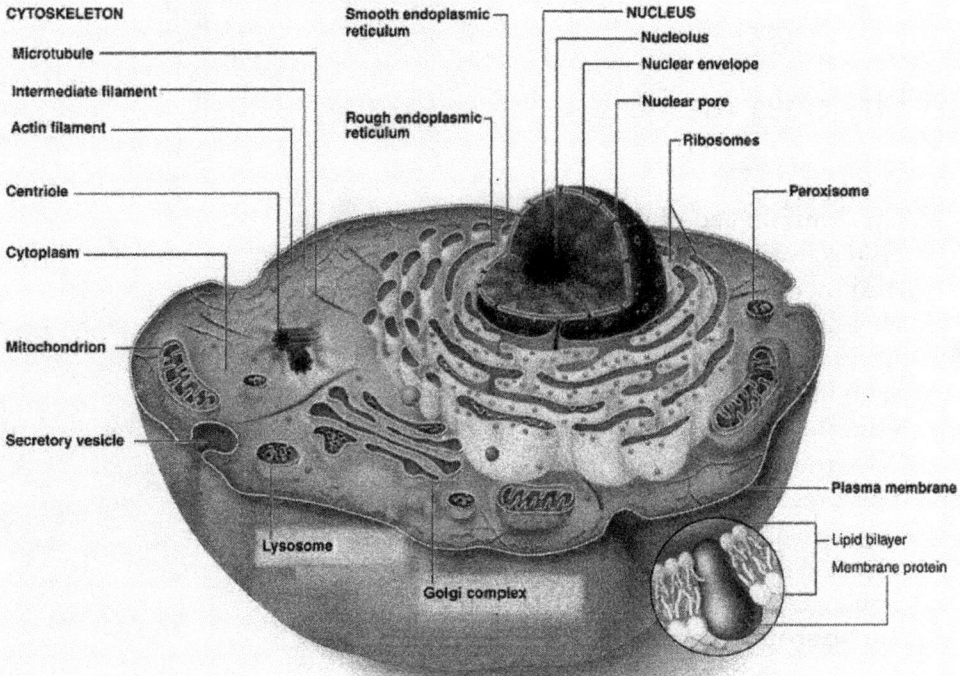

CYTOSKELETON
Microtubule
Intermediate filament
Actin filament
Centriole
Cytoplasm
Mitochondrion
Secretory vesicle
Lysosome
Golgi complex
Smooth endoplasmic reticulum
Rough endoplasmic reticulum
NUCLEUS
Nucleolus
Nuclear envelope
Nuclear pore
Ribosomes
Peroxisome
Plasma membrane
Lipid bilayer
Membrane protein

Figure 6. Structure of an animal cell (top) and a plant cell

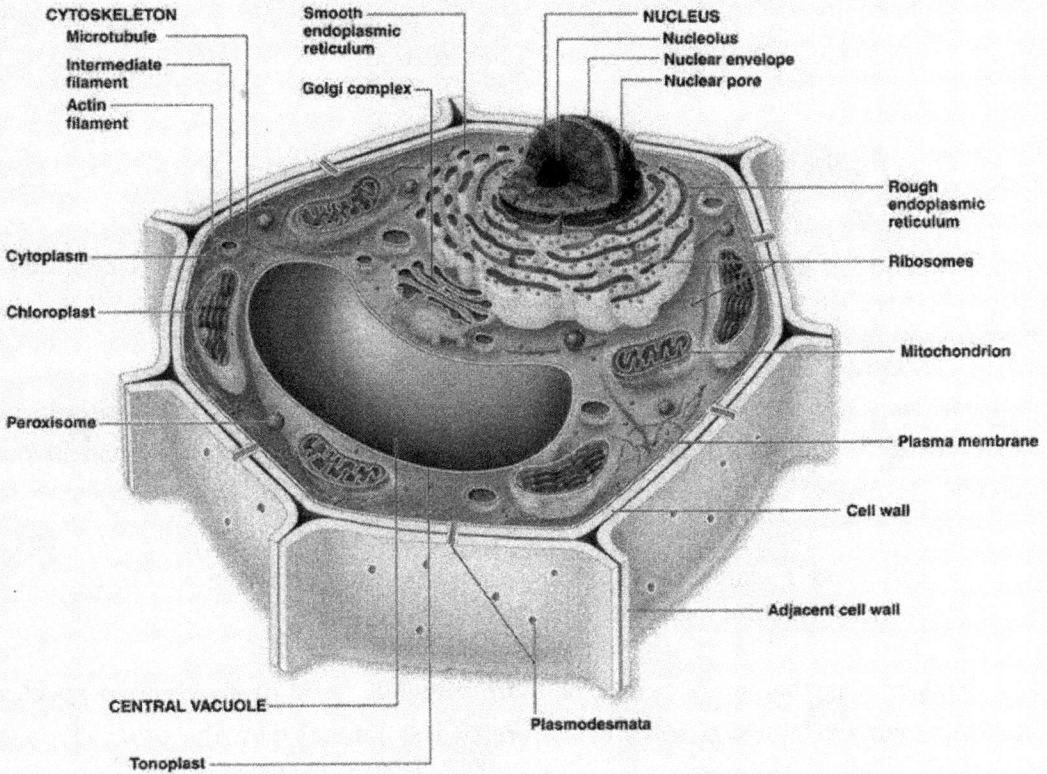

CYTOSKELETON
Microtubule
Intermediate filament
Actin filament
Smooth endoplasmic reticulum
Golgi complex
NUCLEUS
Nucleolus
Nuclear envelope
Nuclear pore
Cytoplasm
Chloroplast
Peroxisome
Rough endoplasmic reticulum
Ribosomes
Mitochondrion
Plasma membrane
Cell wall
Adjacent cell wall
CENTRAL VACUOLE
Plasmodesmata
Tonoplast

6
In His own image

Up from the bed of the river
God scooped the clay;
And by the bank of the river
He kneeled him down;
And there the great God Almighty
Who lit the sun and fixed it in the sky,
Who flung the stars to the most far corner of the night,
Who rounded the earth in the middle of his hand;
This great God,
Like a mammy bending over her baby,
Kneeled down in the dust
Toiling over a lump of clay
Till he shaped it in is his own image;

Then into it he blew the breath of life,
And man became a living soul.
Amen. Amen.

– James Weldon Johnson, "The Creation"

Then finally, still on the sixth day,

And God said, Let us make man in our image, after our likeness:
and let them have dominion over the fish of the sea, and over the
fowl of the air, and over the cattle, and over all the earth, and
over every creeping thing that creepeth upon the earth.

Notice, God doesn't say, "Let the earth bring man forth," "Let the water bring
man forth," or anything like that. It specifically says, "Let us make man in our
image." Exclusive to human beings God makes man in His own image.

So God created man in his own image, in the image of God
created he him; male and female created he them.

This means that male and female are integrally part of the human species,
neither male or female is somehow more or less human than the other. They're

58

both necessary halves of the human being and both in God's image and likeness. As for the phrase "in the image and likeness," there are a lot of ways in which we have His image and likeness. We have an immortal soul (more about that later). We have a free will. We have a conscious choice. And we're a trinity.

God is a triunity, a unity of three, and every human being is a unity of three. In fact, by looking at ourselves we can better see a reflection of God and the whole concept of trinity; it doesn't seem such a mystery at all. It does not represent something like a pagan belief in three gods as it has been misrepresented by people with erroneous ideas. There are no more three gods than I am three people named Charles Owen Schleicher, but there are three distinct aspects of my being: my body, my spirit, and my soul.

Notice not only are humans three-in-one beings, but there's also this duality matched by a singularity making a trinity, that same pattern: $3=1+2$. This is because there are two sides to the human being: the physical side and the spiritual side. But the spiritual side is itself a duality: it's made up of both spirit and soul. Then you realize a human being is made of body, spirit, and soul, so there's actually three, a threeness.

And of course the three parts are completely unified; if a fellow punches me on the shoulder, I won't just say, "Oh, you didn't hit me, you just hit my body." He hit me! This is because my body is an integral part of me. The way Adam and Eve were originally created, the body was created to be just as immortal as the spirit. It was just as eternal as the spirit. This is why the resurrection of the body is so important: matter was not something that was originally inimical to the spirit. Human beings will never be complete, will never be what God wanted them to be until they have bodies. We are trinities; we are body, soul, and spirit. Every human being who has died and whose soul has gone to heaven is incomplete—alive, but incomplete. They only have two of the three parts of them. The Bible doesn't refer to them as having gotten rid of their body, or evolved past their body, or shed their body, but rather their body has fallen asleep and they've been separated from their body. They're waiting for the reconciliation of all things which includes being united with their bodies—bodies that will then be eternal and therefore be a part of this eternal being that God has created called human beings. In His own image and likeness.

Another part of God's image and likeness that needs clarifying is the distinction between the human spirit and soul. To understand this distinction we first need a biblical understanding of spirit. If we look at the many scriptures about spirit we see it repeatedly associated with what we might call 'mind' or 'understanding'. For example, the Book of Exodus records an event at Kadesh-Barnea where all the different Israelites rejected God's promise and did not want to go into Canaan. There God judged the ten wicked spies that murmured and He said,

> But my servant Caleb, because he had another spirit with him, and hath followed me fully, him will I bring into the land whereinto he went; and his seed shall possess it. (Numbers 14:24)

In other words he had a different attitude, he had a different understanding and a different mindset that's referred to as his 'spirit'. Over and over again the scriptures connect the spirit with understanding or information.

> And I have filled him with the spirit of God, in wisdom, and in understanding, and in knowledge, and in all manner of workmanship, (Exod.31:3)

> I said, Days should speak, and multitude of years should teach wisdom.
> But there is a spirit in man: and the inspiration of the Almighty giveth them understanding. (Job 32:7,8)

> Turn you at my reproof: behold, I will pour out my spirit unto you, I will make known my words unto you. (Prov.1:23)

> He that hath knowledge spareth his words: and a man of understanding is of an excellent spirit. (Prov.17:27)

> The spirit of man is the candle of the LORD, searching all the inward parts of the belly. (Proverbs 20:27)

> And the spirit of the LORD shall rest upon him, the spirit of wisdom and understanding, the spirit of counsel and might, the spirit of knowledge and of the fear of the LORD; (Isa.11:2)

Forasmuch as an excellent spirit, and knowledge, and understanding, interpreting of dreams, and shewing of hard sentences, and dissolving of doubts, were found in the same Daniel, whom the king named Belteshazzar: now let Daniel be called, and he will shew the interpretation. (Dan.5:12)

For what man knoweth the things of a man, save the spirit of man which is in him? even so the things of God knoweth no man, but the Spirit of God.
Now we have received, not the spirit of the world, but the spirit which is of God; that we might know the things that are freely given to us of God.
But the natural man receiveth not the things of the Spirit of God: for they are foolishness unto him: neither can he know them, because they are spiritually discerned. (1Cor.2:11,12,14)

For to one is given by the Spirit the word of wisdom; to another the word of knowledge by the same Spirit; (1Cor.12:8)

That the God of our Lord Jesus Christ, the Father of glory, may give unto you the spirit of wisdom and revelation in the knowledge of him: (Eph.1:17)

Other passages could be cited to add to the biblical connection between spirit and understanding, between spirit and knowledge. The idea of spirit is very much connected to the idea of information, much as matter is connected to the idea of energy.

Matter, in a sense, is just very intensely condensed energy. But more than that, it's highly organized. Not only are electrons, baryons, and the quarks that make up baryons incredibly compacted concentrations of energy, but there's organization to a proton being made up of two up quarks and a down quark while a neutron is made up of two down quarks and an up.

Those protons and neutrons, in turn, combine to form the nucleus of an atom. The nucleus of an atom itself is so tiny that comparing it to the size of the entire atom, is like comparing a flea to the size of a baseball stadium. Then that nucleus combines with an electron, which is much smaller than the nucleus of an atom, spinning around it. An atom therefore is mostly empty space. Those atoms in turn combine with other atoms to form molecules. Then molecules collect together in the billions to form the tiniest form of matter, whether a gas or a liquid or a solid. That shows that matter is not just densely condensed energy, but is very, very tightly condensed energy that is very highly organized.

Furthermore, various substances can be very simple like the elements, or they can be more than one element combined, or they can be complex substances that combine with other complex substances to make even more complex substances. Very complex substances can be organized into very complex structures, organelles, cell membranes, and so forth to form cells, which take in matter, convert it to energy, and reproduce themselves. Then we have life, a living thing; and cells can be independent or we can have a multi-cellular organism. The same thing is true of spirit and information.

Information, by the way, is totally non-material. If we look at a very simple formula: 2+2=4, that's information. There's nothing physical about that. Now, we can try to make it physical by saying, "Oh, sure it's physical: two fingers plus two fingers is four fingers. Two apples plus two apples is four apples." But the fact remains that the concept 2+2=4 all by itself is completely non-material. The patterns by which things organize themselves (or are organized), no matter how small or big, is information. It's not the thing itself, it's not the atom itself, or the molecule itself, it's the pattern, the information, and it's totally non-material.

That's why the Bible is totally true in the statement, "The fool hath said in his heart, There is no God. They are corrupt, they have done abominable works, there is none that doeth good." (Psalm14:1) People say there is no God, generally, because they believe there is no such thing as spirit, there's no such thing as anything non-material. They believe the material world is all there is. That's totally foolish. Because even the most atheistic materialists have to admit there's such a thing as information. Likewise they have to admit that information is not something physical—it's not energy, it's not matter. It's not an opinion, it's a fact.

So in the same way that matter is not only highly condensed but highly organized energy, in a sense we can also imagine information being highly condensed (whatever it means for information to be condensed) into "particles" (I can't even imagine what this actually means), but in other words there's a compacting and an organizational structure to information, parallel to the way energy is compacted and organized in matter, that forms experience.[1] Information

---

[1] Perhaps a more accessible metaphor would be based on the theory of physics that the most elemental particles of matter are made of intersecting waves of space. Thus information, too, could be seen as waves that intersect and thus form particles of information that can

is compacted, or intensified, in a tiny, tiny "particle" like a quark and then, just as quarks are built up into subatomic particles and atoms and molecules, so there's a hierarchical organizational structure that builds into something called experience. And just as matter has many levels of complexity from elements to more and more complex substances, so there can be simple experience and there can be more complex experience. Likewise, just as complex substances can be organized to form living cells, experiences can be organized in extremely complex ways to form spirit, something that's alive. And there can be very simplex spirits or complex spirits that could even entail a certain amount of emotion and awareness.

We have to understand that the life of an animal has a spirit connected with it. We see that most explicitly stated in that rather instructive verse of Ecclesiastes 3:21, which says, "Who knoweth the spirit of man that goeth upward, and the spirit of the beast that goeth downward to the earth?" This tells us that animals have spirits, but that they're qualitatively different from the spirits of people. God just called the earth to bring the spirits forth. The earth brought forth the animal bodies and the animal spirits. This is why the animals living on earth are not going to go to heaven—or hell, for that matter—because their spirits belong in the earth. If somehow you could make an animal spirit be in heaven, then that spirit wouldn't be comfortable because it doesn't belong there. The reason why hell is torment and horror for human beings, or for anything else, is not just because there's fire—because God made fire, there's nothing inherently evil in that—but because it's not where we belong. We're made to be with God in heaven with the angels. That's where we belong. Hell doesn't just mean being eternally separated from God, it means being eternally separated from home: from our source, from our point of origin, from the substance wherefrom we were made in our spirit. So going to God is where human spirits belong and going back to the earth is where the animal spirits belong; everyone in their proper place.

This brings us right back to Genesis 2 where God said, "And the LORD God formed man of the dust of the ground, and breathed into his nostrils the breath of life; and man became a living soul." God formed man from the dust of the ground, made his body from the earth, just like the animals. In fact we read, "I said in mine heart concerning the estate of the sons of men, that God might manifest them, and that they might see that they themselves are beasts." (Eccl.3:18) Some people might be shocked to see that in the Bible, but it goes on to say in the twentieth verse, "All go unto one place; all are of the dust, and all turn

---

combine to form increasingly complex forms of information until these layers of information form experience.

to dust again."

Then comes the twenty-first verse: "Who knoweth the spirit of man that goeth upward, and the spirit of the beast that goeth downward to the earth?" There's the difference. Human beings are physically animal, but there's a qualitative difference in our spirit. He breathed into the first man the breath of life. There's nothing like this with the animals. But God Himself instilled that breath of life from Himself into man. And that's why man became a living soul.[2]

Soul is identity. We have our spirit directly from God Who is the source of all identity and God said He would make us in His image and likeness. There are a number of aspects to man being in God's image and likeness, but one of them is we have a sense of individual identity. God named the first man Man and bequeathed that name, in a sense, to all of us, to the whole human race. But the first woman also had a name of her own. The first son, Cain, also had his own name. Each human being has their own name.

That's not true of the animals. If you domesticate an animal you might give it a name, but when Adam was naming the animals he wasn't saying, "Okay, you're Bob, you're Steve, you're Julie, you're Janice." Rather he would just say, "I'll call you 'deer,'"and that name applied to the whole species of that animal. If you get a domesticated dog and call him Bob, that dog knows he's there, he's aware of himself, but he doesn't have a sense of "Bob-ness", a sense of individual identity. There's a sense of being a part of a larger entity, a pack, or a herd, or a flock, but there's no sense of individual identity. And it's not just a sense of identity, it's a reality of identity.

The spirit I have is a human spirit, it's from God; the soul I have is just strictly my own. It's from God, because it's from the spirit that came from God, but it's a unique identity all my own. It's also non-material: the spirit and soul are both spiritual, whereas the body is just physical, but there is a distinction that can be made between the spirit and the soul.

Now, having said all that, we can see in the Bible a hierarchy of plants, animals, and people based on body, spirit, and soul. There's nothing in the scriptures that ever makes any reference to plants having spirits. We further notice that the plants were formed on day 3 with the dry land and not in any sequence with the animals. Plants are totally separate from all of the animal life. They only

---

[2]There is one very important difference, of course, not mentioned here: God said, "Let the earth bring forth" the bodies of animals, but of the first man's body we read, "The LORD God formed". That is, the eternal God personally formed the first human body himself from the earth, rather than merely calling the earth to bring it forth.

have bodies. And maybe this is why cross-culturally, in widely geographically different cultures, there are tales about trees being an abode for different spirits, different gods, different deities. Because a tree is this great, massive body with no spirit, a big empty shell just waiting to be inhabited by some disembodied spirit.

Be that as it may, the fact is, plants don't have spirits. They're just bodies: mechanical, organized, cellular, but no spirit, no experience. Animals, on the other hand, have not only bodies, but they have spirits. Animals have a body and a spirit, but they don't have a soul. And humans have bodies, spirits (a different kind of spirit than the animals), and souls. We have souls, because when the source of all identity comes into that body, that person gets their own little identity, their own soul.

	body	spirit	soul
plants	✓		
animals	✓	✓	
human beings	✓	✓	✓

So we're three in one: we have body, spirit, and soul. That's another respect in which we're made in the image and likeness of God.

Because of the materialistic worldview of Western Civilization today, many academicians take the view that only the physical is factual and true, and therefore consciousness does not really exist. Interestingly, though, at least one philosopher, David Chalmers, proposes that experience is not derived from anything physical, but is a fundamental part of the universe on its own, like mass, energy, space, and time.

He makes a distinction between experience and "awareness" which he defines as having the following traits:

- the ability to discriminate, categorize, and react to environmental stimuli;
- the integration of information by a cognitive system;
- the reportability of mental states;
- the ability of a system to access its own internal states;
- the focus of attention;
- the deliberate control of behavior;
- the difference between wakefulness and sleep.

These processes can all be explained in a mechanical, and therefore materialistic way, as the process of neurons firing in the brain. But experience is another matter:

> The really hard problem of consciousness is the problem of *experience*. When we think and perceive, there is a whir of information-processing, but there is also a subjective aspect. As Nagel (1974) has put it, there is *something it is like* to be a conscious organism. This subjective aspect is experience. When we see, for example, we *experience* visual sensations: the felt quality of redness, the experience of dark and light, the quality of depth in a visual field. Other experiences go along with perception in different modalities: the sound of a clarinet, the smell of mothballs. Then there are bodily sensations, from pains to orgasms; mental images that are conjured up internally; the felt quality of emotion, and the experience of a stream of conscious thought. What unites all of these states is that there is something it is like to be in them. All of them are states of experience.
>
> It is undeniable that some organisms are subjects of experience. But the question of how it is that these systems are subjects of experience is perplexing. Why is it that when our cognitive systems engage in visual and auditory information-processing, we have visual or auditory experience: the quality of deep blue, the sensation of middle C? How can we explain why there is something it is like to entertain a mental image, or to experience an emotion? It is widely agreed that experience arises from a physical basis, but we have no good explanation of why and how it so arises. Why should physical processing give rise to a rich inner life at all? It seems objectively unreasonable that it should, and yet it does.
>
> If any problem qualifies as *the* problem of consciousness, it is this one.[3]

Chalmers' answer to the hard problem of consciousness is that experience can't be reduced to a mechanical, material process. He argues that experience is different from anything else in the material universe.

He states that it would be "hard to see" what kind of non-phyiscal feature experience might be derived from. Not that it matters, but this would not be

---

[3]David Chalmers, "Facing up to the Problem of Consciousness." *Journal of Consciousness Studies* 2.3(1995):201-2.

contradicted by relating experience to information. Electromagnetism is a form of energy, yet is fundamental. Matter is relatable to energy, and vice versa, yet matter and energy are both fundamental.

In fact if consciousness is the same as spirit, the Bible reveals something Chalmers' studies have not: that there are two kinds of consciousness. Not two states of consciousness, but two qualitatively different species of consciousness: natural consciousness, which can exist without identity and consciousness which entails independent, individual identity. The former can be related to what Chalmers writes about and what the Bible refers to as the "spirit of a beast". It comes from the earth which brought it forth with the body. Hence it is not of supernatural divine origin, but is as natural as the body. This is just what Chalmers writes about his idea of experience:

> Nothing in this approach contradicts anything in physical theory; we simply need to add further *bridging* principles to explain how experience arises from physical processes. There is nothing particularly spiritual or mystical about this theory—its overall shape is like that of a physical theory, with a few fundamental entities connected by fundamental laws. It expands the ontology slightly, to be sure, but Maxwell did the same thing. Indeed, the overall structure of this position is entirely naturalistic, allowing that ultimately the universe comes down to a network of basic entities obeying simple laws, and allowing that there may ultimately be a theory of consciousness cast in terms of such laws. If the position is to have a name, a good choice might be *naturalistic dualism.*[4]

That fits for animal spirits. But the human spirit *is* spiritual, supernatural, and comes directly from God Who is the ultimate irreducible fundamental.

With all this talk of consciousness and thought residing in our spirits, a Westerner might well ask: where does the brain fit in all this? One possibility is that the brain is a connecting organ. An analogy can be found in the muscular and skeletal systems of the body. These are two systems that cannot function fully without the other. A limb cannot move without both a bone and a muscle. But they are two different things that therefore need to be connected. Tendons perform this function. Likewise the brain may be the organ that connects the body with the spirit. And, surprisingly, at least one biologist has made a similar

---

[4]Chalmers, 210.

argument.

Rupert Sheldrake is a British biologist who has spent years studying the connection between behavior and biology. One of his conclusions is that the brain is not the temple wherein the mind resides. He explained his view of the brain's role in consciousness and thought in an interview, an excerpt of which is given below:

> SHELDRAKE: Memory is indeed one of the great unsolved problems. How you or I remember what we did yesterday, or how we remember people's names, and how we recognize people—all the ordinary facts of ordinary, day-to-day memory are profoundly mysterious. It's usually assumed that all these things are stored inside our brains as physical traces of some kind. Now, none of us has ever seen a physical trace inside our brains, and scientists who've spent many years looking for them inside the brains of people and especially rats and monkeys, have failed to find them too.

> MISHLOVE: Now, I know Wilder Penfield found he could stimulate memories by putting electrodes on different parts of the brain, but as I recall he was never able to get the same memory twice that way.

> SHELDRAKE: No. And you see, even if he could evoke memories by stimulating part of the brain, it doesn't prove they're stored there. For example, if I stimulate the tuning knob of your TV set and it tunes on to a different channel, it doesn't prove that all the programs on that other channel are stored inside the bit that I've stimulated, namely the tuning knob, and it could be that it's just simply part of the receiving or tuning system. I think the brain is like a tuning system, and that we tune in to our own memories by a process of morphic resonance, which I believe is a general process which happens throughout the whole of nature.

> MISHLOVE: Let's define for our viewers what you mean when you use the terms morphic resonance or morphic fields. What does morphic mean to you in this sense?

> SHELDRAKE: Morphic comes from the Greek word for form, morphe, and a morphic field is a field of form, or field of pattern or order or structure. Such fields organize not only the forms of living organisms, but also the forms of crystals, of molecules.

> Each kind of molecule, each protein, for example, has its own kind of morphic field -- a hemoglobin field, an insulin field; each kind of crystal, each kind of organism, and each kind of instinct or pattern of behavior. So these fields are the organizing fields of nature. There are many kinds of them, because there are many kinds of things and patterns in nature. And I think our own mental life depends on just this kind of field.[5]

The "organizing fields" are essentially information at various levels of complexity. So information and "spirit" are related.

An important warning needs to be made here about Sheldrake's thought: since beginning his research, Sheldrake has been profoundly influenced by Hinduism, a belief system that involves deeply and genuinely dangerous spirituality. Sheldrake has expanded his idea of morphic resonance to argue, for example, that telepathy is a natural process that all organisms perform. The statements made in the above excerpt are the result of observations in biological experiments and not the result of his New Age beliefs. These are all blended together, however, in almost anything written by him so his writings are not commensurate with a Christian worldview by any means. If anything, they are antithetical to it.

Nevertheless, Chalmers', Sheldrake's, and Wyller's work is interesting because it demonstrates that even scholars who were originally trained in the materialistic worldview are coming to grips with the fact that there is something beyond the material world that can't be explained by physical laws. If they do not call it "spirit" it is "spirit" they are talking about nonetheless. The materialistic worldview that arose in the last two hundred years is showing itself deficient while the Bible is showing itself superior in explaining the real world. Three thousand years ago the Bible had the answer to the hard problem of consciousness worked out better than the cutting-edge thinkers of our day.

So we do reflect the identity of God, the image of God. He's three-in-one and so are we. We have a free will as well as an identity; so does God. We're made to be eternal. We're made in God's image and likeness in all of those ways.

Finally, there's the creation of the first woman. That's in the second chapter which amplifies that part of creation. The first chapter tells the whole story of creation, including the making of the first man and woman:

> So God created man in his own image, in the image of God created he him; male and female created he them.

---

[5] Jeffrey Mishlove, *Thinking Allowed* (Tulsa:Council Oak Books, 1992) 65-74.

> And God blessed them, and God said unto them, Be fruitful, and multiply, and replenish the earth, and subdue it: and have dominion over the fish of the sea, and over the fowl of the air, and over every living thing that moveth upon the earth. (Gen. 1:27,28)

It also mentions in the first chapter that they were given plants to eat, not meat; there was no animal death whatsoever.

Chapter two puts sort of a magnifying glass on the creation of man and it segues from a summary of the first chapter to a time when

> the LORD God had not caused it to rain upon the earth, and there was not a man to till the ground.
>
> But there went up a mist from the earth, and watered the whole face of the ground.
>
> And the LORD God formed man of the dust of the ground, and breathed into his nostrils the breath of life; and man became a living soul.
>
> And the LORD God planted a garden eastward in Eden; and there he put the man whom he had formed.
>
> And out of the ground made the LORD God to grow every tree that is pleasant to the sight, and good for food; the tree of life also in the midst of the garden, and the tree of knowledge of good and evil. (Genesis 2:5b-9)

Those last two trees are not just for ordinary food. Notice that they go together: the tree of life and the tree of the knowledge of good and evil; more about that later.

> And the LORD God said, It is not good that the man should be alone; I will make him an help meet for him. (Genesis 2:18)

This may seem a little bit unusual, but God then brings all these different animals to Adam to give them names, which he did. Why did God do that when He said He was going to give him a help that was a complement, that was appropriate for him? God knew that those animals wouldn't fill the bill, but He wanted Adam to see that for himself so that when God made the first woman, Adam would appreciate the fact that he had needed this woman from God.

So God took a rib, a portion of Adam's side out and He somehow grew that out into a complete human body, with her own spirit and her own soul. And He closed Adam's side with flesh in the place of what He took out. This, by the way, is called parthenogenesis. It exists in nature. We can see that kind of reproduction to this day (not in people, of course). If we take a starfish, cut off one of it's "points" not only does the starfish grow that point back, but the point grows another starfish. That's how God created Eve, although it was miraculous not just because parthenogenesis is normally not something people can do, but because it wasn't just a clone of Adam. He changed that genetic structure so that the sex chromosomes were not an X and a Y chromosome, but two X chromosomes: a real woman. And Adam said, quite accurately,

> This is now bone of my bones, and flesh of my flesh: she shall be
> called Woman, because she was taken out of Man. (Genesis 2:23)

God wanted one body to be derived from the other so they were truly one, instead of creating two separate bodies. He wanted to illustrate the unity of Christ and His church, Christ and His body.

Calling the church the Bride of Christ is not a metaphor for based on the relationship between a husband and a wife. Rather, calling a man and woman husband and wife is a metaphor based on the relationship between Christ and His Bride. The relationship between Christ and His Bride is the original marriage.

Obviously if God created one body from another, one of them would have to come first, but there's more to it than that. There's a lot to be learned from the fact that woman is derived from man—if you will, that the feminine is derived from the masculine—even genetically. You can get two X chromosomes from cloning a male cell, but you can't get a Y chromosome from cloning a female cell.[6] So woman is derived from man, female is derived from male, and feminine is derived from masculine, in a sense.

> but the woman is the glory of the man.
> For the man is not of the woman; but the woman of the man.
> (1Cor 11:7b,8)

---

[6] It may be worth noting here, for the record, that evolutionary scientists believe that the Y chromosome evolved from the X chromosome.

That which is feminine is the rarification of humanity. That which is human, good and bad, is seen in modulated form in the man and in intensified form in the woman. That was the perfect complement for man.

It goes on to give further description of the institution of marriage in verse 24:

> Therefore shall a man leave his father and his mother, and shall
> cleave unto his wife: and they shall be one flesh.

This teaches us that spouses are to be more devoted to one another than to their parents. It even seems to suggest physically leaving the parents' household to start their own. And it closes with this statement: "And they were both naked, the man and his wife, and were not ashamed." (Genesis 2:25), reflecting the pure innocence of that time.

7
Our first home

"Apocalypse may see a symmetry in history, as it were, history in reverse, from Abraham to our 'Abrahamic minority'; Israel to Israel, if it becomes, in Martin Buber's word, Zion; ultimately, Eden to Eden"
      – Christopher Nugent, *Masks of Satan*

Now let's consider the geographical location of the garden of Eden. This obviously does not seem to be a significant issue, but it's an interesting topic and it is an important part of these Genesis studies (for reasons that will shortly be made clear) so I'm going to put my own two cents' worth in here. In the second chapter of Genesis we're given a location for the garden of Eden and it's based on the rivers connected to that place. It says

> And out of the ground made the LORD God to grow every tree that is pleasant to the sight, and good for food; the tree of life also in the midst of the garden, and the tree of knowledge of good and evil.
> And a river went out of Eden to water the garden; and from thence it was parted, and became into four heads.
> The name of the first is Pison: that is it which compasseth the whole land of Havilah, where there is gold;
> And the gold of that land is good: there is bdellium and the onyx stone.
> And the name of the second river is Gihon: the same is it that compasseth the whole land of Ethiopia.
> And the name of the third river is Hiddekel: that is it which goeth toward the east of Assyria. And the fourth river is Euphrates. (2:9-14])

Now first of all, clearly, verse 10 is not talking about the river splitting up into four rivers moving downstream, but moving upstream. Either the "heads" mean sources of the river, or (as apparently is more in line with how the word is used in Hebrew) it refers to the place where the rivers merge into a single river. So in other words, moving upstream it splits into four tributaries. And the four tributaries are those four rivers the Pison or Pishon, the Gihon, the Hiddekel, and the Euphrates.

Now apparently the first syllable of Hiddekel is from a Semitic definite article (like *ha-* in Hebrew) and the basic name of the river is Deqel, or Diglath as it is known in Aramaic. Not only is it the Tigris river, it's where the name "Tigris" comes from. The word root *dgl* was borrowed into Greek with the straightforward change of *l* to *r*: Tigr-. The final *-s* is simply the nominative singular suffix (a grammatical ending) in Greek.

In the name *Euphrates* The first syllable is the Greek prefix *eu-* 'good', but the rest *phrates*, minus again the nominative singular ending *-es* is *-phrat-*, the original name of the river: Parat.[1] So we have the Digel and the Parat, and these names go all the way back to Sumerian times. Additionally, it's pretty well agreed they're not Sumerian names, which means these go back to pre-Sumerian times, which guarantees that these are antediluvian names, names of rivers that have an antediluvian origin.

Ken Ham and the folks at *Answers in Genesis* think that the flood so totally reshaped the earth that there's no way those river beds could be the same before the flood and after the flood. They surmise that these verses in Genesis 2 must be referring to completely different rivers than the Tigris River that we know and the Euphrates River that we know.

I have tremendous respect for Ken Ham and he has done a lot to strengthen the idea of a genuinely biblical worldview, but I disagree with him about these rivers. While it's true that people reuse place names—Athens, GA and Bethlehem, PA to give two American examples—it doesn't seem to match the scripture because the scripture specifically gives geographical locations for these rivers. It says the Pishon river is the river which compasses the whole land of Havilah. It says the Gihon river is the river that compasses the whole land of Ethiopia, the whole land of Kush. The Hiddekel, the Tigris River, goes toward the east of Assyria. And the fourth river is Euphrates. Now, of course we could say that Havilah and Assyria and Kush were all also antediluvian place names, which just happen coincidentally to exist in the post-diluvian world, and the postdiluvian place names refer to places which actually relate to each other in the same way as the corresponding antediluvian places, but I think that's stretching it. There's absolutely no question in my mind that this was written primarily for people who lived after, not before, the flood.

We have already seen convincing evidence for the hypotheses that the source

---

[1] The Greeks frequently changed the consonants of borrowed words. This fact will be explained further when we look at the Table of Nations.

texts for the first chapters of Genesis were written on clay tablets and are therefore very ancient. This doesn't necessarily mean they were of antediluvian origin, with a copy kept on Noah's ark and handed down. But even if that should be the case, I'm not convinced that the second chapter of Genesis *in its current form* was actually written before the flood. As near as I can tell, Abraham came out of an idolatrous background that did not have this scripture, and Moses wrote it by the inspiration of God.

Even if this part of the Bible had been written on a tablet before the flood, it was edited by Moses. And if Moses wrote this for the people of his day, then the Kush that he would be referring to would have been the Kush that we know in the postdiluvian world. The Assyria he wrote about would have been the Assyria we know about in the postdiluvian world. The Havilah he wrote about would have been the Havilah we know in the post-diluvian world. So when he wrote that there was a river Hiddekel which was to the east of Assyria, and there is today the Tigris River which is east of Assyria; that's not coincidence. That's not just people giving antediluvian names for completely different places that just all happen to correspond.[2] It's most likely that the land of Havilah is the land of Arabia and that there was gold there and that there was a river that flowed through there before it became a desert.[3] So there was a river that flowed through postdiluvian Havilah, there is a river that flows to the east of postdiluvian Assyria, and there was a river that encompasses the whole land of postdiluvian Cush: it's called the Nile. It doesn't flow into the river Euphrates today, but these are the rivers that fit the descriptions in Genesis 4.

The significance of this is to show that Eden is not a mythical place, but a real geographic place, by giving references that we *can* identify with. This passage in Genesis enables the reader to say, "Look, I can tell where Eden is today! It's located by those four rivers and I can tell where those rivers flow today." If Ken Ham is right, the message of these verses is, "Here's how you locate Eden: you just find these rivers, but you can never know where they are and you can't possibly tell where they were or what they referred to." This would not just be the message of those verses today. This is what these verses would have meant *ever since the flood,* to Moses, to Abraham, to the builders of the Tower of Babel. Since

---

[2] In Kentucky there is a town called Paris and a town called Versailles, both named after famous cities in France. But Versailles, KY is over 30 mi away from Paris, KY, unlike their French counterparts.

[3] Archeologist Juris Zarina was the first scholar to make this discovery. See Dora Jane Hamblin, "Has the Garden of Eden been located at last?" *Smithsonian*, 18.2 (1987):127-135.

we believe this book was written or at least edited by Moses by inspiration of the Holy Spirit, this seems absurd. So I believe that these rivers—Wadi al-Batin, Nile, Tigris, and Euphrates—are the rivers that flowed into Eden. That would mean that Eden is somewhere around southern Iraq today.

All the foregoing presents us with a problem: how do you square that with flood geology? As it turns out, it's not necessarily a problem. I would really want to see proof, first of all, that all these rivers flow on top of miles of sedimentary rock. Secondly, every calculation—and calculations vary widely; they seem to be based on whether one is biased in favor of the validity of the Bible or not—whatever the calculation, every one seems to be in agreement that the continental plates absorbed a great deal of energy in shifting the way they did. If granite, which is the bedrock of the continental shelf, is heated up and cooled again slowly, it becomes layered, like stratigraphic rock. How much of the stratigraphic rock that we see in the world is sedimentary, built up by sediments, and how much of it is the result of melted and recooled granite may still remain an unresolved question as of now.

Clearly the rivers have somewhat changed their course; what is now the Arabian peninsula is the Arabian *peninsula*. It's no longer "attached" to Africa; it has separated, leaving a gulf between Arabia and Cush, and

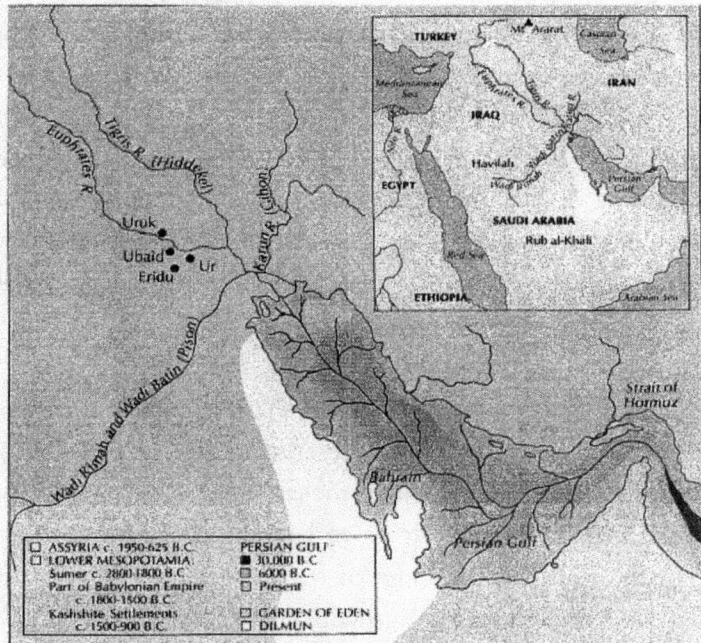

Figure 7: possible location of the rivers of Eden (the Gihon is not equated with the Nile on this map).

consequently because of its separation and buckling there are mountains now between Egypt and Israel where there didn't used to be, which of course keep the Nile from flowing in that direction. It has to flow straight into the Mediterranean because of that change in terrain. If in our mind's eye we reattach the peninsula and get rid of those mountains we can see that river flowing into the Euphrates and Tigris rivers along with the river bed we see is buried under tons of sand in the Saudi Arabian peninsula. Moreover this river bed, the Pishon river bed as we'll call it, flows for awhile under the sand and then it goes down underneath the rock. So that riverbed has at least partly been buried under sedimentary layers of rock, and partly not.

Okay, so then why weren't the Tigris and Euphrates rivers buried under sedimentary layers of rock? I think if enough money were available to research the flood as it deserves, we'd find it's not nearly as simple as it's portrayed. The flood was a global catastrophe. So think of a very local catastrophe, like a tornado: a tornado hits and there are two houses that are demolished and leveled, yet one house in between them is untouched. How does that happen? It shouldn't be possible, but it happens. I suspect that something like that is the case with the flood. I think there are places where the crust and the contour of the earth was really demolished and buried under rock or what have you, and then there were places where it was largely untouched. I think the riverbeds for the Nile River, for the Euphrates, for the Tigris, for the Pison River, had been deeply cut in the ground at creation to such an extent that if sediments were later piled on top of them there would still be a depression where that notch in the earth was. Then, when water started flowing through it would cut right through that buildup again. The rivers were just "re-cut", except that they flowed differently.

This was especially in the case of the Nile, which couldn't flow over the postdiluvian mountains so it flowed straight on up north through Egypt and then out into the Mediterranean sea. And if someone did geological work on that I suspect that they would find that hypothesis confirmed: there would be a difference in the geology of the river bed close to the river delta than there would be, say, close to Lake Victoria, or near the juncture of the Blue Nile. Maybe before the flood the river flowed in the opposite direction it now does, *up* the Blue Nile over to what is now the Arabian Peninsula. We don't know, but the point is, those rivers were a part of the Garden of Eden and they're still there today in altered form. One of them, the Pison, is just gone completely.[4]

There's just one more topic to consider about the Garden of Eden. In the midst of the garden there were the tree of life and the tree of the knowledge of good and evil. And that brings us to the fall. I believe those two trees were put there literally as a gateway; not exclusively for that, but first of all as a gateway.

---

[4]Another possibility is that what I'm calling the Pison river bed is actually what's left of the original path of the Nile River.

God made Adam and Eve and put them in the Garden of Eden, but that's not the end of the story. God didn't just make them to brainlessly frolic about in the garden. He made them there to worship Him, to have fellowship with Him, to be *joined* with Him. And I believe that's what those trees were there for, as a kind of gateway: To truly love God, they had to choose Him, even when they had the freedom to choose not to serve Him.

As God said to the Israelites through Moses: "I have set before you life and death, blessing and cursing." He literally, physically set before Adam and Eve life and death; the tree of life was life, and the tree of the knowledge of good and evil was death—spiritual and ultimately even physical death. He set those two trees before them so that they could choose: by choosing the tree of life, they would be choosing God; by choosing the tree of the knowledge of good and evil, they would be choosing to separate from God. If they had the opportunity to choose to separate from God and they didn't, even when the devil tempted them to, then everything would have stayed hunky-dory. Then after a thousand years, multiplying, filling the earth, people would have moved out of Eden, and settled in other places. God could then have just replaced or transformed the earth, or the whole universe for that matter, into what we will experience in the new heavens and the new earth and all the human beings would have just been joined with God forever (see discussion on the Millennial Hypothesis in Chapter 9) . We know that, tragically, that's not the choice they made and subsequently the whole course of history was changed. They made the wrong choice and the consequence was the fall: the fall of man, the fall of humanity, the fall of the whole universe with it.

8

The fall

"You do not think men love death more than life? It happens very often. It is the sickness of sickness."
— Thomas S. Klise, *The Last Western*

The fall is, in a sense, the beginning of history. At least, it's the beginning of a need for scriptures and a need for a messiah, a need for a savior, any need for redemption. That doesn't mean that up to the fall there was no need for God. There was, but that was God as Father, in a sense God as Mother because it was God who nourished our first parents and all of creation through them; nourished them not only with physical life, but with spiritual life as well. The idea has been advanced that the tree of life was not a one-shot deal.[1] That is to say, you didn't need to eat just one piece of fruit and then, wham-o, you live forever, but rather it was a constant supply of life.

An analogy one could make would be something like this: think of a baby growing in a mother's womb. The baby has a placenta, an organ which is really the baby's, since it is not actually fused with the mother's tissues, only entangled with them. The placenta makes a connection with the mother's body at the wall of the uterus, where nutrients from the mother's blood supply are passed to the baby's blood supply in the placenta. The mother's blood never actually passes into the placenta, the blood vessels are not fused with the blood vessels in the placenta; only nutrients pass through the membranes of the mother's blood vessels and through the membranes of the baby's blood vessels. And through the placenta it flows through the umbilical cord into the baby's body and thus nourishes the baby. We can think of creation before the fall as a baby. Adam was the lifeline

---

[1] Glenn Morton, "Death Before the Fall: The Theology", http://www.oldearth.org/death_theology.htm. I find this idea quite enlightening, but I should point out that Glenn Morton is a theistic evolutionist who would passionately disagree with most everything else I write here about Genesis. His referenced article in part attempts to argue that if ceasing to eat from the tree of life would mean death, even after one had eaten from it, that means Adam and Eve were made physically mortal. This is part of his larger argument that animal death existed in God's creation from the beginning (a necessary part of an evolutionary view). I use the baby analogy to show that dependency on the tree of life is not inconsistent with saying that Adam and Eve were originally immortal.

between God and creation. Adam was, in a sense, the umbilical cord between God (the mother, the womb) and creation (the baby). The tree of life was the transmitting vehicle of physical life (the placenta) from God to Adam. Somehow God's life, even manifesting itself as physical life—the nourishment of the human body and even of the animal and plant life, and maintaining cohesion in the physical creation of the rocks and the stars—all of this was transmitted into creation by means of the tree of life.

Don't ask me how. All of creation was directly linked with that third heaven in a way that we don't understand today. If you go up into the sky, that's the first heaven. If you travel far enough upward, at escape velocity, you'll leave the first heaven and go into the second heaven. But you don't bump into anything along the way, there's no wall between the first heaven and the second heaven. There's no sign saying, "Now leaving the first heaven and entering the second heaven. Come again." The first heaven fades into and blends in with the second heaven. When you're well into the second heaven you can look back and see the first heaven and know that you're not there. And vice versa. But you cannot exactly pinpoint a specific spot where one ends and the other begins. This is because they all blend together. I believe that this is exactly how it was before the fall with the third heaven as well, what we think of as the place of God's throne and the place where the angels dwell—this was all blended together with the rest of creation. This is why we read about God communing with Adam walking through the garden in the cool of the day. There was as much communion with God on earth as there was in the third heaven. We can imagine everything from the third heaven passing in and out of God's creation rather freely and, for that matter, things from God's creation passing freely into the third heaven.

Now, it's not that the third heaven was all right there on earth. They weren't the same thing, just as outer space is not the atmosphere. But in those days the third heaven blended smoothly with the rest of creation. So right there from earth you could blend smoothly into the third heaven; there was a real link.

Today, of course, it's not that way. The only way to make it into heaven is to die. To some degree, all of creation is separated from God, spiritually as well as physically [2]

But with the link that originally existed between the third heaven and all of creation, God's life could somehow pass freely into the tree of life. Then Adam

---

[2] The Bini tribe in Nigeria even has a legend about a golden age when the sky was physically close to the earth, but after humanity fell from grace the sky moved far away as it is today.

and Eve would eat the fruit of that tree and that life from God would pass into them, into their bodies. From them it would pass freely, mystically, into all of creation.

That's just the physical life. The spiritual life, feeding Adam's spirit and therefore strengthening his soul (and the same for Eve), involved communion with God. I talked about God walking through the garden in the cool of the day. That passing through just as freely as if Adam was in the third heaven, was Adam's spiritual tree of life, so to speak, for feeding his spirit in the same way as the tree of life would feed his body. When Adam and Eve were in that perfect communion and that eternal life was constantly flowing through them from God, then all of creation was nourished.

So, yes, God was always necessary, but He was not known as the Savior, because there was no sin, danger, or destruction to save humanity from. He was not known as the Redeemer because there was no sin to be redeemed from. There was only need for God as a perfect Parent, as a perfect Father and a perfect Provider, a perfect Nourisher, a perfect Master, Companion, Friend.

But Adam and Eve made the wrong choice and they chose to follow the serpent and to eat from the tree of the knowledge of good and evil. When and how the serpent came into the picture is mysterious because the Bible is our way of knowing and the Bible is silent on this question. What we do know is that the serpent was already there at the time of the fall. It has been advanced, and I think persuasively, that since the Bible tells us that when God made everything He said it was very good, everything was perfect. That suggests that even the angels had not fallen. After all, the three heavens were all together; there was perfect union between God and His creation. So when God is talking about His creation, He's not divorcing what we know as the physical universe from the spiritual universe. It's all "very good." There had been no fall. It was only after God created everything, including Adam and Eve, that Satan fell.

What exactly was the origin of Satan is a considerably mysterious subject, but what is clear from the Bible is that an active, independent, agent of evil doesn't fit in with the picture of creation until after the creation of Man. Evil is not a creation of God; it's not a creation at all. There is no substance inherent in evil. Evil is not a thing. Evil is a technique. Evil is an event. Evil is taking that which is perfectly good and twisting it.

Another way of approaching this is: the devil, being incapable of destroying God, sought instead to attack God through His children. And Adam and Eve were unquestionably God's children.

Yet another way to look at it is this: Satan's great master plan is to overtake God's throne. Since this was impossible with a direct assault, the next step was to take what Jesus called God's footstool: the earth. If he can't take the throne, he'll take the footstool and maybe then, once he has taken mastery of the footstool, he can launch a new, fresh assault then up to the throne of God itself and this time, win.

Deep down Satan knows he can't do it, but as Christopher Nugent wrote in *Masks of Satan*, "the *devil* is schizophrenic." He's detached from his own reality. His oldest trick, as Baudelaire pointed out, is to make people think that he doesn't exist. His oldest trick is to deny his very own existence. How schizophrenic can you get? So there's a part of him that knows he has already lost, and yet there's a part of him that still insists on believing in the ultimate delusion: that he can win against God. In any event, he's got nothing else to do but try and so he does. There's no rest for Satan. And so he toils in this great twisted plan without end and without rest.

So he appeared in the garden as a serpent, the most alluring of creatures, to get Eve's attention and to tempt her. Now as we talk about the fall, about the tree of life, I have given, frankly, a rather spiritual description of the tree of life. One author once described the fruit of the tree of life as having an extra high dosage of B vitamins.[3] Well, I can tell you right now an extra dosage of B vitamins may be healthy for you, but it won't keep you from aging, and it certainly won't make you live forever. So I don't buy into that. It's so crassly, strictly physical. This was the union of spiritual and physical life. It was the glory of God which is Man fully alive.[4] As such the tree of life was as much a spiritual tree as it was a physical tree. If that's so, and its fruit was as spiritual as it was physical, then the same is probably to be said for the tree of the knowledge of good and evil. No mere apple tree, this was something very, very different, something whose fruit literally put you into spiritual contact with evil, with the separation from God. I am here

---

[3]The book by said author appears to be out of print; but more recently on the website for "Elijah's Health Network" is this statement: "Then again, when in the garden of Eden, they had the tree of life to eat which had all the vitamins, minerals and supplements they needed to live forever." (http://members.fortunecity.com/elijah_web/ehtn001.htm)

[4]This statement inspired, of course, by the famous words of the second-century church leader Irenaeus, *Adversus Haereses* IV, 20, 7. It is very appropriate to include his famous quote here in its fuller context: "The glory of God is man fully alive, and the life of man is the vision of God. If the revelation of God through creation already brings life to all living beings on the earth, how much more will the manifestation of the Father by the Word bring life to those who see God."

suggesting something that has been advanced by Christopher Nugent from his book, *Masks of Satan*. In the first chapter of this book, he writes (p.24):

> The mention of hallucinogens prompts a not entirely gratuitous or fanciful digression. We refer to what John Milton, in Paradise Lost, called 'those fair apples' of the Garden of Eden. Milton's Satan volunteers that, after plucking and eating one's fill, 'ere long I might perceive strange alteration in me'. In other words, this is to advance a drug hypothesis for the Adamic Fall which might claim biblical and even anthropological support. For example, the Book of Genesis proscribed eating from the tree of the knowledge of good and evil, 'for on the day you eat of it you shall surely die' (Genesis 2:17). But our faulted first parents did not immediately die. The reference was apparently to spiritual death, perhaps disguised as an illuminated life. Again the serpent, who from the internal evidence knew what he was about, entices Eve:

> > God knows in fact that on the day you eat it your eyes will be opened and you will be like gods, knowing good and evil. [Genesis 3:5]

> And this sounds like a formula for instant divinization, and one perennially associated with hallucinatory drugs. The most revolutionary if delicate reinforcement of this conclusion can come out of the Rig Veda of ancient India. The Rig Veda, the raw if poetic beginning of Hindu religious thought, is essentially magical, and it contains over a thousand references to the wondrous drug Soma. For over three thousand years Soma was unidentified, but a recent scholarly article has convincingly demonstrated that it was the Amanita muscaria mushroom, the fly-agaric.[5] The Soma was considered divine, 'father of the gods', and some of the most famous verses of the Rig Veda ring disturbingly familiar to those of Genesis:

> > We have drunk the Soma, we have become Immortals,
> > We are arrived at the light, we have found the Gods.

---

[5]See R. Gordon Wasson's illustrated article, 'The Soma of the Rig Veda: What was It?', Journal of the American Oriental Society 91 (April-June 1971), 169-86, esp. 175, 181 and 186 for quotes. For the orgiastic and violent use of the mushroom see [John G.] Bourke, [*Scatalogical Rites of All Nations*, Washington, (D.C.) 1891, p.]74.

This mushroom was taken by Siberian shamans until recent years. Interestingly, it was associated with a sacred 'Tree of Life', the birch, which enjoyed the patronage of a serpent. There are variations on this story in the Gilgamesh of ancient Sumeria, which goes back beyond the third millennium before Christ. The very word 'Druid' is an amalgam of tree of knowledge. And, curiously, a mushroom is a miniature 'tree'. Moreover, we know from another account that the mushroom could be productive not just of 'divinization', but of orgies and violence. Whatever their remote origins, the three go well together as common elements of the demonic.

The main objection to the so-called drug hypothesis might be, "Why would God create something destructive like drugs, something that was hallucinogenic, something that would destroy people?" That's kind of a specious argument to make; after all, we're talking about the tree of the knowledge of good and evil. This was *bad* for you. It would result in your death. It's the exactly the same question as saying, "Why have the tree of the knowledge of good and evil at all?" To eat from it was to commit rebellion against God. Of *course*, it was bad for you. Unlike the erstwhile popular children's version of the story of the fall of Adam and Eve, these were not apples. It wasn't God just saying, "See that apple tree? Don't eat one of those apples." And it may very well have been some kind of hallucinogenic drug, in which case this would certainly explain why certain hallucinogens (such as the mushroom discussed in Nugent) have proved a literal connection to the demonic—a spiritual connection. That is to say, the actual ingesting of these drugs leads one's spirit to be connected to the spiritual realm in a demonic way. And this brought not only physical death, but spiritual death. As Eve related, God had said that even if they touched the fruit they would die. So there was something bad in the Garden of Eden. Or to be more precise, there was something *potentially* bad; it was only there so that they could choose to serve Him or not to serve Him. Thus having that opportunity and choosing life, choosing God, they would truly express their love for God and be ready to spend eternity with Him without any temptation because they had declared their love once and for all. But they didn't; they chose the tree of the knowledge of good and evil.

The spiritual death was instant. The physical death came later, because as Adam and Eve first found themselves in spiritual death—and this is manifested first of all in the fact that they knew that they were naked— it produced something called shame. What the knowledge of good and evil meant was the knowledge of evil. They already knew good. To know good and evil was to know good from the perspective of evil—and that requires, of course, knowing evil. Knowing evil means knowing what it is to twist God's creation. God's creation was first twisted when Adam and Eve took the fruit and ate the fruit of the tree of the knowledge of good and evil. When they thus ingested the knowledge of evil, ingested the knowledge of twisting God's creation, the first creation they saw twisted was themselves.

'Strange alteration' in them, psychically, spiritually? Perhaps. But what the Bible first tells us is they knew they were naked. They saw that they were naked—which, in a sense, they didn't see before. Not that they were blind, or unaware, but because their naked condition was just normal. What else do you do when there's no such thing as clothing? The very concept of clothing was totally foreign. It wasn't something they had rejected, but something they were simply completely ignorant of. Walking around in just the bodies God gave them and nothing else was just normal and they didn't know anything else.

But 'naked' means '*unclothed*'. They didn't see themselves as *naked* before in the sense of the body *minus* the clothing. They knew they looked the way they looked, but up to that point they hadn't seen themselves as being deficient. Naked essentially means 'deficient', 'lacking something you're supposed to have.' What they really saw after the fall was that they were *un*clothed, that something was uncovered that wasn't supposed to be uncovered. In other words, God's creation looked perverse, wrong, and embarrassing, a perspective that still inspires both humiliation and lust. And they immediately started to cover it up.

The part they were most ashamed of, the part that was most twisted was the part of their bodies that was to bring forth life. Isn't that interesting? They didn't cover their shoulders, they didn't cover their ribs, they felt ashamed of that part of their bodies that God had created to produce new life. They felt ashamed of the instruments of new life because they had partaken of that which loves death: the knowledge of evil and knowing good only through the twisted perspective of evil – the knowledge of good and evil. So they wove leaves together and made loin cloths (the 'aprons' of the KJV). That was the first thing.

Secondly, the next time they heard God they experienced something else that was new: fear. For the very first time, hearing God's voice inspired fear. It had never inspired fear; it only brought nourishment before. But they felt the stirring of God. They felt His presence. They didn't immediately hear His voice, but they knew He was there and they ran and hid from God's presence. The presence of God's Spirit felt odious to them, like something awful, dangerous, something that might hurt them. That was the result of spiritual corruption.

Now as yet there was no hint that anything physical had gone wrong with the universe. But spiritually, they had already been severed from God. Their spiritual life has been severed from the third heaven. But physically, they could still be united to God's life as long as they ate from the tree of life. This would mean that at least their bodies would be alive, but their spirits would be dead. It's not clear what all that implies; some have suggested that their spirits would be incapable of being redeemed. Perhaps, but it's also possible that even their bodies would begin to age and rot (decay had already entered the world through the original sin), but as long as they ate from the tree of life they wouldn't die. No matter how you slice it, to take part in God's physical life while completely divorced from His spiritual life is horrifyingly grotesque. And it was as much out of mercy as out of punishment that "the LORD God sent him forth from the garden of Eden, to till the ground from whence he was taken." (Genesis 3:23)

God drove Adam and Eve out of the Garden of Eden for precisely one reason: to keep them from eating the fruit of the tree of life. He actually went to the extent of putting cherubim at the east of the garden (apparently the place where Adam would enter it) and a spinning, flaming sword to keep the way, that is, to guard the way *of the tree of life*. In the terms of our baby-in-the-womb metaphor earlier, that severed the umbilical cord from the placenta. It prevented God's life, manifested in physical life, from ever coming into Adam's and Eve's bodies ever again and thus all of creation was separated, not just from God's spiritual life, but from His physical life as well.

All this happened after God pronounced the curses on the serpent, then the woman, and then on the man. Of course much has been said about how Adam and Eve passed the buck, first Adam passing it onto the woman and the woman passing it onto the serpent, and so God curses the serpent and the woman and then Adam. The serpent's curse:

"And the LORD God said unto the serpent, Because thou hast done this, thou art cursed above all cattle, and above every beast of the field; upon thy belly shalt thou go, and dust shalt thou eat all the days of thy life." (v.14) That could have a spiritual meaning to it, but I think it also speaks of the result of what the devil did having an effect on the serpent. Everything that the devil touches, withers and is twisted. That's what happened to the very body of the serpent. Perhaps God did it in part because the serpent was so alluring and so fascinating, so God made it so that serpents would never again be so alluring and fascinating, but rather repulsive. But of course He's talking to the devil also because He continues, "And I will put enmity between thee and the woman, and between thy seed and her seed; it shall bruise thy head, and thou shalt bruise his heel." (v.15). Romans 16:20 makes it clear that this verse in Genesis is referring to the devil. The fact that the seed is referred to as "his" indicates that we're not dealing with Eve's collective seed or her descendants generally, but a particular individual. As the Apostle Paul would write later in a different context, "Now to Abraham and his seed were the promises made. He saith not, And to seeds, as of many; but as of one, And to thy seed, which is Christ." (Gal 3:16). In summary, the curses are:

- For the devil: that seed, Christ, would crush his head even as he tries to strike His heel. Crushing his head would of course be defeating him completely, by His self-sacrifice and resurrection, the devil striking His heel by His crucifixion, by His temptations. If a serpent strikes someone's heel that's one thing, if that someone crushes the serpent's head, that serpent is finished. That's exactly the image that God was communicating here.

- For the woman: giving birth would be physically painful, and that she would be turning to her husband instead of to God for her source, for her identity, for her comfort and meaning of life, and that her husband would lord it over her— something that we find as a human universal so it really does come from the first woman and the first man, a curse on all of humanity.

- For the man: that thorns and thistles would grow up, that the ground would be cursed for his sake, the first hint that all of creation, not just their physical selves, would be harmed by this. They would eat of it in toil, in sorrow, it would not be satisfying or pleasurable, and he would have to work hard, "in the sweat of his face" until he died and his body would turn back into dust. This is the first mention of death. And of course sickness and everything else that goes with it: disease, pain, suffering, sorrow, all of these were part of the curse. God did not make them happen; rather, they were the natural result of what happened when God was separated from creation by the sin of Adam and Eve.

And yet, at the end of all that, it said, "Unto Adam also and to his wife did the LORD God make coats of skins, and clothed them." (Genesis 3:21) In all this mess God was still ready to show mercy, and pity, clothing their now shameful nakedness. And in that there is also a first reference to sacrifice because for Him to make coats out of skins, animals had to die. By the death of those animals and the provision of those animal skins, God was showing that the sacrifice of those animals clothed their sense of shame. That began to communicate the concept of sacrifice which would be fulfilled in the sacrifice of Jesus Christ.

Now, having said all this, there are some arguments by people who say both that they believe the Bible and that death did not come from the fall, but was always a part of life. Humans may have been intended to be immortal before the fall, but there was already death in the world and the world in the Garden of Eden was not that different from the world we have today. Of course such statements are promoted as part of the theistic evolutionary position because one can't say that the world is billions of years old and say that nothing died in all those years. The position taken is that, not only did animals die, but they were killing and eating each other, which is not communicated at all in the book of Genesis. All Genesis says on the subject of eating is that God gave plants for food, to people and animals. Nothing else is given or sanctioned until after the flood. But of course in an evolutionary perspective animals have been killing and eating animals all along.

Probably the most articulate spokesperson against a literal reading of Genesis is Glenn Morton, a theistic evolutionist whose biblicism sometimes seems questionable from what he writes. In his article, "Death Before the Fall: The Theology" He gives five reasons for saying there had to be death in the Garden of Eden.

- First of all, plant death was necessary; eating plants means killing them.
- Cellular death was inevitable and in effect necessary. The epidermis (the outermost layer of skin) is a layer of dead cells.
- Rapidly reproducing organisms like bacteria and cockroaches would quickly take over the earth if there were no death to kill them off.
- The impossibility of no death by violence is an absurdity. If an animal ripped off another animal's leg would the animal go on living without the leg? If a meteor comes crashing to the earth and hits a fox on the head does the fox just bounce back like in a cartoon and go its way?
- Organismal death by accidental ingestion was inevitable. A cow eats a blade of grass that has an ant crawling on it.

It turns out none of these are really convincing points and some of them are pretty poor.

To answer the first two points: the only death recounted as absent in the Garden of Eden is death of creatures with the breath of life (animals). Recall that plants have a body, but no spirit. Animals only ate plants so there wouldn't have been animals ripping the legs off other animals.

The impossibility of no death by violence is not an absurdity when we realize that this universe was totally under God's control. There was no separation whatsoever between God and His creation, between the third heaven and the first and second heaven, and the earth. We can't even imagine a universe like that, except that everything would be perfect; everything perfectly orchestrated by God.

Organismal death by accidental ingestion was not inevitable, for two reasons. First, every detail of creation was in line with God's will, even at the level of sub-atomic particles. Certainly where each cow stepped and where each ant stepped fit perfectly with everything staying alive. But more than that, if human beings could live forever, who knows how things were for animals before the fall? Some insects may have had the power to survive ingestion. In fact there are some organisms to this day that *require* ingestion by animals in order to reproduce![6] Of course those animals now are parasites, but this pre-fall survival of ingestion could be the origin of parasitism. Some parasites that live in animals' guts and so on may be a perversion, brought on by the fall, of an original 'device' by God to keep animals that were accidentally ingested from being killed by ingestion and digestion. So it just goes in one end and pops out the other, crawls out of the dung and goes on it's merry way. That's not absurd because it actually happens among some organisms today.

What about bacteria? Would bacteria (or cockroaches) swamp the earth? Again, based on the IBO theory of biology, bacteria are biochemically and genetically more advanced than any independent organism and if bacteria had existed before any other organism, they might have consumed the genetic material.

---

[6]One (perhaps extreme) example: "The human liver fluke, *Clonorchis sinensis*, has a life cycle that requires two intermediate hosts, snails and fish. The eggs pass out of humans via the feces. They survive if they are deposited in water and eaten by snails. The larvae invade the soft tissues of the snail from the digestive tract where they pass through several stages and reproduce asexually; they emerge from the snail as free-swimming larvae. If they manage to encounter fish, they penetrate into the flesh and encyst; if the raw fish is eaten by humans, the young flukes are released in the intestines. They then crawl up the bile duct, attach by their suckers, mature, reproduce sexually, and begin to shed eggs."
"Fluke", article on *encyclopedia.com*

That all points to the conclusion that bacteria were the last living things to appear on the earth. That in turn would indicate that bacteria appeared after human beings. And if bacteria are associated with rot and decay, it would fit in perfectly with Genesis that bacteria would first appear after the creation of human beings because rot and decay first happened *after* the fall, after the creation of man.

In fact, bacteria are nearly structurally identical to the mitochondria of animal cells while blue-green algae are structurally identical to the chloroplasts of plant cells. And eukaryotes had to have had those from the beginning. A eukaryotic cell cannot respirate properly without the mitochondria or chloroplasts. Eukaryotic cells were here first, and if those existed before bacteria, then one very logical explanation for the origin of bacteria is that they originated from the mitochondria and chloroplasts of eukaryotic cells. As things (including biological organisms) literally, physically fell apart, the mitochondria continued to live on their own and developed into bacteria. That's another example of the fall producing a perversion of God's original creation.

So we end up with bacteria, which as it turns out, apart from just producing rot, turn out to be essential in a world where things die. Where there's death there needs to be rot or else you have a bunch of dead bodies piling up all over the place. They have a lot of positive functions in this world even though they primarily exist to facilitate decay and produce a lot of disease. This scenario of bacteria appearing as a *result* of the fall certainly answers the question about bacteria taking over the world when there was no death.

So to recap: Adam and Eve were given the two choices of life or death, the tree of life, the tree of the knowledge of good and evil. They chose the tree of the knowledge of good and evil at some point when the devil tempted them as a result of which they sinned, cutting off their spiritual life from God, losing fellowship with Him, and thus severing all of creation from communion with God and the connection to God, both physically and spiritually.

That was manifested in the conviction, the fear they felt when they heard God's voice. It resulted in the curses which God pronounced, which as much as anything were simply the natural consequences of Adam and Eve's severing themselves, and thus the rest of creation, from God's life. God sealed this by casting them out of the Garden of Eden where they could no longer eat from the tree of life and He went out of His way to put cherubim and a flaming sword by the way of the entrance to the Garden of Eden so that they could not go there any more. They could never have access to the tree of life again and therefore they would not be able to live forever; they would ultimately die.

The whole creation started disintegrating—bacteria arose, diseases arose, viruses arose, all these things arose to pervert life. All of these things had some sort of function. The ability of some small invertebrates to survive being accidentally consumed changed them into parasites, which carry disease, especially disease born by bacteria, and viruses. All of this death, disease, and corruption echoed out through the whole physical universe because Adam first severed his spiritual connection with God, and then God severed Adam's physical connection. As it is written in the first letter of Paul to the Romans, "For we know that the whole creation groaneth and travaileth in pain together until now." (Rom 8:22)

That was the beginning of the fall. It was the beginning of history as we know it because the world before then was so perfect, we literally can't imagine what it was like. What was it like to live in a world that needs no bacteria, needs no rot, needs no decay, has absolutely no death? Everything was so perfect it's physically impossible for a meteor or any other rock to hit an animal because everything was so perfectly in harmony between the free will of human beings and God's orchestration that nothing went wrong, ever. It was literally heaven on earth. It's impossible to imagine that, but it existed once. Then, when Adam and Eve fell from grace, it was over.

But the promise was also given to Adam and Eve that the seed of the woman would strike the head of the serpent (Satan) even as Satan would strike at the heel of that son of Eve.[7] That was the promise that Jesus would come, even as the devil would strike Him by persecution and ultimately by killing Him in crucifixion. By His self-sacrificial death and resurrection Jesus Christ the Messiah, the Redeemer, for His part would strike and crush the devil's head, destroy the power of death, and start everything going backwards, ultimately back to Eden. That promise of redemption was given and the beginning of that promise was already seen when God killed animals (the first thing to die) and provided animal skins from them.

> Unto Adam also and to his wife did the LORD God
> make coats of skins, and clothed them. (Gen 3:21)

Because now Adam's and Eve's bodies were truly covered, that gave them the understanding that what felt so shameful could be covered if animals were killed and coats of skins were made to them. That spoke of the first inkling of the concept of animal sacrifice and the idea that something has to die to cover up the shame and destruction that Adam and Eve produced. That was probably as far as

---

[7]To verify this understanding of Genesis 3:15, cf. Romans 16:20.

they understood it at that point, but it was made known to them. It was the first instruction for survival in a fallen world.

9
Antediluvia

"Much that once was is lost, for none now live who remember it."
– Galadriel's prologue from the film *The Lord of
the Rings: The Fellowship of the Ring*

So now we enter the world *sort of* as we understand it. Still the world was very, very, different. All the land was still in one place, the single continent which today people would call Pangaea. All the water was in one world ocean. People still lived a whole lot longer than they do today. And maybe this would be a good place to mention the Millennial Hypothesis.

Death came from the fall. Life became finite. And the life span for human beings was reduced to under a thousand years. If we look at almost every antediluvian person written about in the Bible, they lived for over nine hundred years. Adam himself didn't die until he was nine hundred and thirty nine years old. And the oldest human being on record was Methuselah, who lived to be nine hundred and sixty-nine years old. That's very close to a thousand years, but it's not a thousand years. And the fact that just about every person up to the time of Noah lived to be almost a thousand years old, but not quite, suggests something. Consider the fact that when Jesus comes back to restore this world to Eden, He will rule for a thousand years. After that thousand years the whole universe is going to be destroyed and replaced with a perfect New Heavens and New Earth. (1 Cor 15:23-28; Rev. 20:4-21:1)

Now consider the fact that, if they hadn't fallen, Adam and Eve would have kept having children while they continued to live forever. Eventually the world would have been filled with people. They were told, "Be fruitful, and multiply, and replenish [fill up] the earth, and subdue it" (1:28a). Eventually the world would have been filled if people had kept having children and nobody had died. So while we don't have to worry about the world being smothered by bacteria or cockroaches taking over the universe, there is reason to ask what would have happened when people kept having children and we would have had billions and billions of people and there would be no place for anybody to stand on this earth.

One possible answer seems to be what we can call the Millennial Hypothesis, which says that God originally had some sort of cosmic alarm clock to go off when human beings reached a thousand years. When that happened they would go up to the next level, from this kind of universe to the New Heavens and the New Earth and everything would be perfect. Tragically, as it happened they didn't choose to stay with God and so when God kicked them out of the Garden of Eden, the alarm clock was put on perpetual hold. That's why when human beings started dying after the fall they died just short of a thousand years—just enough to keep that alarm clock from going off. So even if someone lived to be 969, they didn't live to be a thousand and the New Heaven and the New Earth never happened. It's sort of a message that no matter how long people live they can never get to the New Heavens and New Earth until the Redeemer comes, turns everything around, restores Eden, and then holds it there for a thousand years. Then we get to the New Heavens and New Earth. But more than that, it's also the first example of what we read in that very famous verse from the Epistle to the Romans: "the wages of sin is death." (Romans 6:23)

Sin brought death into the world. But not only did sin bring initial death into the world, sin also continued to bring death into the world, ever after the fall.[1] Anytime the whole world united in sin and turned it's back on God, the life span of human beings shortened dramatically. Now the life span of any individual human being may shorten dramatically if that individual human being lives an especially sinful life. But when the whole world is joined in the same sinfulness, that actually has effected the human species in a dramatic way.

- The first sin event was the fall.
- After the fall human beings died, but they still lived to be over nine hundred years old *on average*, until the flood came.
- The next major sin event was the sin of the whole world that was judged in the global flood. After the flood, human beings only lived an average of about four hundred years.
- After that the next major sin event was when the whole world built the city of Babel and tried to leave God out of their life and out of the whole world's history and said, "We no longer need God in the history of the human species, we're going to chart our own destiny and make ourselves

---

[1]"In the final analysis, I would see the divine love as that which breathes life into the cosmos—by which it is energized and sustained—and the demonic as ultimately anything that dams up this current. It is movement away from love, movement away from life." (Nugent, p.183)

God, as it were." God confused their languages and scattered them abroad. Not only were they scattered abroad, but the human life span was dramatically shortened from four hundred years to just under two hundred years on average.

After that, the human life span pretty much stayed right around a hundred sixty years or so, on average, and then there was no other major sin event like that where the whole world sinned. Eventually, however, after that time, God started creating His own special nation, His people, something that had never existed before, a People of God. God Himself had created from scratch an actual nation, who were all completely consecrated to God, to be the light for the rest of the world. When they were ushered to the land of Canaan and rebelled against God's plan at a place called Kadesh-Barnea, Moses, who was there at that time, wrote down in his psalm, the 90th Psalm, that because of God's wrath the human life span once again was cut short by more than half to where the average life span is seventy years. Now it's true that some people since then have lived to be a hundred years, a hundred and twenty years, a hundred and twenty-two years. But so what? Abraham's father lived to be over two hundred which was a lot older than the average lifespan of his day. There are always some who live longer than average, but that average has been shrinking. And about seventy years is where it stays today.

The original sin of Adam and Eve, the sinfulness of man before the flood and the desire to build the city of Babel: these three sin events break up history into four ages of mankind, each one of which is worse than the one before. The historic memory of four ages is found in cultures all over the world. We see it, not just among ancient cultures like the Sumerians and ancient Greeks, but we see it in India, with the Hopi, the Mayans, the Aztecs, the Germanic tribes.[2] And some traditions even say that the life span of human beings got shorter at each point. The fall of man was the beginning of that and it shortened to just under a thousand years.

That brings us to the next age, if you will, of humanity, between the time of the fall and the time of Noah. Of that time we know very little. We are not hardly even capable of knowing what the world was like before the fall. It was so totally perfect, and there is no history of it because there is no history when there is no sin.

---

[2] See Appendix 1 for detailed list of global versions of the four ages of the earth.

There are other examples of this in the Bible. In the Book of Judges, there is no history given for the periods when the Israelites served the Lord as they should. There is only history written for the times when Israel was backslidden. Likewise, when Solomon reigned, after he built the palace and the temple, he reigned perfectly for over thirty years. In that time, there was no war, no famine, unimaginable prosperity. There was also no history. After the dedication of the temple, the queen of Sheba visits him, and there is a brief account of his riches. Then the Scripture flashes forward to Solomon's backsliding in his old age. Then history resumes again (1 Kings 10:14-11:4). History is something that goes hand in hand with sin.[3]

History is a story; the word 'story' comes from the word 'history'. And we can't have much of a story if we have no ups or downs, everything is just this perfect daily cycle. There is no story to tell and so there is no history. There's an old tradition that says that Adam and Eve lived in the garden for eight years before they sinned[4] and maybe they did. The fact that we don't see eight years of history recorded between creation and the fall doesn't really mean anything because what would the writer say? There's eight years of living in total perfection, totally perfect fellowship with God—there's no story to tell. So who knows how long they lived before the fall? We know it was less than a hundred thirty years because we know that Adam was one hundred thirty years old when Eve gave birth to their son, Seth. Seth was at least his third son so it definitely was less than a hundred thirty years. But that's all we know; it could have been a long time (from our point of view).

That means after they sinned, that's really the beginning of history, the beginning of where there's a story we could tell. But the fact is, between the time of the fall and the time of the flood, of well over 1500 years, we have very little recorded history.

While we may be incapable of knowing about life before the fall, we are capable of imagining what the world was like between the fall and the flood. But it was a world very alien from our own. For one thing as we've already noted, people lived for over nine hundred years! There were no continents as we think of them; all the dry land was in one place still. There was one world ocean and one world continent, what people today would call Pangaea. Most, or maybe all, of the

---

[3]"To live in history is to live in sin. Upon this both Marxist and Judeo-Christian ultimately agree: history begins with evil, and if it ever ends it will be with the end of evil." (Nugent, p.7)

[4]Book of Jubilees 3:8-13.

sedimentary rocks didn't exist at that time! So we've got soil on granite in a lot of cases. No fossil fuels in the ground. The meteorology may have been different: there's no mention of rain before the flood. That doesn't necessarily mean there was no rain; there probably was no rain before the fall, just because scientifically it doesn't seem like that would work[5] and we really read in the second chapter of Genesis that there was no rain on the earth before Adam was created:

> for the LORD God had not caused it to rain upon the earth, and
> there was not a man to till the ground.
> But there went up a mist from the earth, and watered the whole
> face of the ground." (Genesis 2:5b,6).

There may have been rain between the fall and the flood, but there's no mention of it.

That's quite a remarkable world; a very strange, very different world from the one we live in, one which piques our curiosity. There's something in our human nature that would stir us up and say, "I wonder what it was like. What kind of stories are there from that strange world? Were there civilizations? What were they like? What kind of lives did people live? What did people say about God? Were there prophets? Were there houses of worship? How did people worship God? Did people worship God like they do today? What was life like?" For better or for worse, we just really don't know at all. But we'll review a little of what we do know.

Part of what we know is how little we know. That is to say, from the time of the fall to the time of the flood there are two chapters in the Bible. That's it. And half of that is taken up with the story of Cain and Abel. What that says is, Adam and Eve had a son. It gives us the impression that Cain was the first son and possibly the first child that Adam and Eve had ever had. She called him Cain, which means 'I have gotten'; she said, "I have gotten a man from the Lord." (Genesis 4:1) She later bore his brother Abel. Now Abel may have been their second child, or their second son; but we don't know that. All we know is that it says, "And she again bare his brother Abel." (Genesis 4:2a) Maybe she had other children between the two of them; we don't know. All that we know for sure is that Abel came after Cain and Seth came after Cain and Abel and those three children were not the only children that Adam and Eve ever had. We know that because, skipping ahead to the fifth chapter of Genesis, it says in the fourth verse,

---

[5]See Brown, p.174-179.

"And the days of Adam after he had begotten Seth were eight hundred years: and he begat sons and daughters" (Genesis 5:4).

So he had other sons, he had daughters. How many did they have? We don't know, but do the math and you'll probably reason that it's likely that they had lots and lots of children. That's how Eve got her name, by the way. *Adam*, we know, just means 'Man'. Eve's original name (in Hebrew) was *Ishshah*, which simply means 'Woman'. It makes sense that that would be her first name. But we know her as Eve because Adam gave her that name when she had children, referring to her as the mother of all the living. *Eve* is from the Hebrew name *Hawwah*, which is derived from a Hebrew root *hay* 'life'. She was called Mother-of-all-the-living, She-from-whom-life-comes, something like that. (We'll revisit all these Hebrew names in Chapter 11.) They probably had lots of children because we know that Seth was born when Adam was a hundred and thirty and he lived a long time after 130. But, at first, we only know two by name: Cain and Abel.

We also know that Abel was a keeper of sheep and Cain was a tiller of the ground. That tells us this fact about humanity: animals and plants were domesticated right away. It wasn't something that human beings came up with after tens of thousands of years of living in caves the way the evolutionary tale would have it, but right after the fall.

When Adam and Eve had a few children and they were old enough to do it, they started domesticating animals, taking herds of goats and sheep, keeping them locked up, and either using their animal skins for clothing or learning how to weave their hair to make cloth, milking them, perhaps, but not using them for meat. All God had given them for food was plants and they didn't even think about eating animals; that probably would have grossed them out. But they used them to make sacrifices. Abel made an offering up to God. Cain did, too. But he didn't offer one of the sheep; he culled his offering from the domestic plants he grew.

That probably doesn't mean that they practiced agriculture because they didn't need to have crops of a size such as is produced by a farm. Adam's family was horticultural, growing just enough food to live off of. Cain was the horticulturist and Abel was the keeper of the sheep. There's something to be said for the idea that Cain's offering could not be for sin, not being a blood offering. But that's not to say that it was no legitimate gift that Cain offered. To offer something from the ground could be appropriate, but it could not be pleasing to God if his heart was not right. Cain's heart needed to be made right like Abel's heart was made right. But how did Abel's heart get right? By repentance.

Cain's heart needed to be made right by repentance. God had already very clearly illustrated to Adam and Eve that sins are not covered without killing an animal and taking its skin. Maybe the animals themselves they offered and the way that sacrifice was made was very different from the way it was done in Moses' time. There's no reason why it would be just the same. Maybe there was some sort of ritual that they did with the skin to show they had repented and God had forgiven them.

Regardless of how precisely a sacrifice for repentance and forgiveness was made, Cain did not present such an offering to God. Abel offered a gift, Cain offered a gift. But Cain didn't offer it up with a true heart so God didn't accept his offering. He was upset and God told him very plainly, "Look, I'll accept you if you do the right thing. Isn't it obvious that if you do the right thing I'll accept you? So if you're not accepted then there must be something you're doing wrong. It's not My fault. If you're not doing the right thing, then sin is crouching at your door. And you can be it's master. Sin's desire is toward you."

He chose not to be sin's master, not to overcome the sin. Instead he went the other direction and became downright demonic. He did not openly wreak his wrath on his brother Abel, but he hated him with a murderous hatred. He wished Abel was dead like those animals he was killing. That by itself is a progression of the demonic right there.

The commentary in the New Testament on this story tells us very plainly the bottom line of why Cain hated Abel: he hated Abel because he was good. That's it. Period. As it's also written, "he that is upright in the way is abomination to the wicked." (Proverbs 29:27) Just by being evil, Cain's nature had fellowship with evil and therefore was out of fellowship with good. Good looked ugly and evil looked beautiful.

It's true to this day: People who love sin hate people who love righteousness just because their righteousness looks disgusting: "Eww, ick! They go to church! They pray! Eww, how disgusting!" What's wrong with that? What's wrong with being loving and patient and forgiving? They hate to see love, patience, or forgiveness in others. Cain hated Abel for this very reason. And instead of being honest he was deceitful and called him out.

> And Cain talked with Abel his brother: and it came to pass, when they were in the field, that Cain rose up against Abel his brother, and slew him.

> And the LORD said unto Cain, Where is Abel thy brother? And
> he said, I know not: Am I my brother's keeper? (Genesis 4:8,9)

No social responsibility. This is always a fundamental characteristic of those who cherish sin. "It's not my problem to worry about other people." Sinners can pretend to have a sense of social responsibility in order to get something for themselves. But they never really, genuinely have a care over someone else's welfare for its own sake.

> And he said, What hast thou done? the voice of thy brother's
> blood crieth unto me from the ground. (Genesis 4:10)

It still does whenever the innocent are killed.

> And now art thou cursed from the earth, which hath opened her
> mouth to receive thy brother's blood from thy hand. (Genesis
> 4:11)

This was the first murder and God compounded the curse of Adam onto Cain. So not only does he have to till the ground and earn his bread by the sweat of his face, He says now when you till the ground it won't even bring you plants.

> When thou tillest the ground, it shall not henceforth yield unto
> thee her strength; a fugitive and a vagabond shalt thou be in the
> earth. (Genesis 4:12)

Notice what this means. The hunter-gatherer mode of existence is the *last* one to be followed. The evolutionary idea is that all human beings were hunter-gatherers and then eventually became horticulturists and then eventually became pastoralists, and so forth. But according to the above passage, people were first pastoralists and alongside that horticulturists, and only *after* that did somebody become a nomad, a hunter-gatherer. Cain was not a hunter, since people were still strictly herbivorous, but he did have to gather. He had to forage off the land. That happened only after people learned horticulture and animal husbandry.

Cain said, "My punishment is more than I can bear." God actually heard that cry from his heart and said, "Okay, I'll be merciful to you," because Cain was scared that "anyone who finds me will slay me." Some say this proves there were other people besides Adam and Eve, that there were not just two original people. That's nonsense. As we've already seen, Adam had other sons and daughters. They were the "anyone" Cain was referring to.

"And the LORD said unto him, Therefore whosoever slayeth Cain, vengeance shall be taken on him sevenfold. And the LORD set a mark upon Cain, lest any finding him should kill him." (Genesis 4:15) We don't know what that mark was, but He set a mark on him to identify him as the man God would avenge seven times over if anyone killed him. That's the kind of mercy God had on Cain. Cain didn't deserve it for a second. Neither do we. Cain deserved death, but instead God spared him and set him out. Cain started wandering east of Eden "in the land of Nod," which literally means the land of wandering.

"And Cain knew his wife; and she conceived, and bare Enoch: and he builded a city, and called the name of the city, after the name of his son, Enoch." (Genesis 4:17) And people say, "Where'd she come from?" Once again, Genesis 5:4: "And Adam begot sons *and daughters.*" So there's no mystery there, it was his sister, and because we've never heard of her before this means absolutely nothing. We know for a fact that the patriarch Israel had daughters (Genesis 46:15). But we only hear of one by name: Dinah. Her own identity would also be unknown to us were it not for the tragic fact that she was raped and significant consequences developed from that. We would think Israel had nothing but sons. But we know he had sons and daughters. The only reason why you never hear about Cain's wife is because she wasn't significant to the story up until now.

So he took one of his sisters, she became his wife, she conceived and gave birth to a son. She called him Enoch (which is another word for 'man') and Cain built a "city" naming it after his son. One may ask, "Why would he build a city if there weren't that many people alive then?" The Hebrew word that's translated 'city' can mean anything from a city to a village.[6] It can mean a cluster of huts. So now we start having towns with names. Right from the time you have the first village, people start giving villages place names.

Next we have the whole genealogy of Cain all the way down to Lamech, where it says Lamech took to him two wives. This is the first instance of polygamy, specifically bigamy. Adam didn't have two wives. Cain didn't even have two wives. Nobody had two wives. That never happened. The only case of bigamy up to this point is Lamech, who, as we'll see, was a wicked man.

No righteous man up through Noah—up to the case of Jacob—took more than one wife at a time with God's approval. In a sense Abraham took more than

---

[6]The Hebrew word is *ŷr* (עִיר) and is almost the only biblical Hebrew word for a permanent independent dwelling (e.g. the same word used in Deut 3:8 is translated as an unwalled town).

one wife when he took Hagar, but God told him to send her away. Never did any righteous man legitimately have more than one wife at a time, or divorce his wife and have another. This backs up what Jesus said millenia later, when He told the scribes and Pharisees, "Moses because of the hardness of your hearts suffered you to put away your wives: but from the beginning it was not so." (Matthew 19:8) From the beginning marriage was one man and one woman, for life. That the first recorded instance of bigamy was committed by a transparently wicked man is established in verse 23. I say that because in verse 23 we read,

> And Lamech said unto his wives, Adah and Zillah, Hear my voice; ye wives of Lamech, hearken unto my speech: for I have slain a man to my wounding, and a young man to my hurt. (Genesis 4:23)

He killed a man. So clearly this man is not a righteous man. That's why he's got two wives.

Furthermore this gives us the tiniest little glimpse into civilization between the time of the fall and the time of the flood. Adah, Lamech's first wife, bore a son named Jabal (Genesis 4:20); he was a pastoralist. Not just raising domesticated animals in a settlement, but actually being a pastoralist, being a nomad with cattle, with flocks. "And his brother's name was Jubal: he was the father of all such as handle the harp and organ." (Genesis 4:21) So there you see the first reference to music and musical instruments. "And Zillah, she also bare Tubal-cain, an instructer of every artificer in brass and iron: and the sister of Tubal-cain was Naamah." (Genesis 4:22) Now, we think it's not until about David's lifetime that we start reaching the iron age, when, indeed, the Israelites had no knowledge of how to make iron, but the Philistines did. Yet, thousands of years before what we call the iron age, before the flood, people were making iron.

Now, this is not to say that the archeologists have got it all wrong. When they say that in 1300 BC human beings began to make iron, they're right. That was when human beings first learned to make iron *after the flood*. But before the flood, people had known it, too. That knowledge was lost with the civilization(s) that was/were destroyed by the flood. But this brief passage does give us a little insight into that world.

No hut-dwelling, neolithic primitives, the people of antediluvia had all the components of advanced civilization. They had most of the technology we have today. They knew how to build settlements and later, as the population grew, cities; and thought to name those cities, just as in our day. They knew how to work every kind of metal. They knew, not only how to produce bronze, how to make things out of stone, but also how to fashion objects out of iron. They composed and played all kinds of music, every different kind of musical instrument. They practiced husbandry at an advanced level. Furthermore it is likely that the multitude of societies of the time exhibited the same degree of cultural diversity that exists today: pastoralists, urban societies, agricultural societies all flourished. In short, everything we have in our modern world today they had. They had the technology and the smarts to do everything that we do in our modern world today, with one notable exception: the internal combustion engine.

We can say, with a great deal of certainty, that there was no such thing as the internal combustion engine in the world before the flood. It's fairly certain because the internal combustion engine is run by fossil fuels. There was no oil, there was no coal, there was no natural gas in the days before the flood. Why not? Because it was the flood that produced fossil fuels in the first place. They were produced by billions of dead things being buried in rock layers laid down by water all over the earth. And billions of dead things had not yet been buried in rock layers laid down by water all over the earth before the flood.

All other technologies that do not necessarily depend on the internal combustion engine, were possible. They could produce indoor plumbing, flush toilets, septic tanks, sewage systems, multi-storied buildings, the works. They had a lot of the amenities of the world after the flood up to the industrial revolution—say, the beginning of the eighteenth century. Anything that people could do or make, up through the seventeenth century, people could do or make in the antediluvian world—and possibly more. We don't read that much about multi-storied buildings in the ancient world, or even the medieval world, but there were multi-storied dwellings in Noah's day. And there was iron.

All of this suggests there was a lot of intellectual activity going on, a lot of inventing going on, a lot of culture going on because of the proliferation of music, musical instruments and different musical forms. And that seems to be what is meant by someone being the "father" of people in a certain skill. Now, it is possible that Jabal "was the father of such as dwell in tents" in the sense that his descendants became pastoralists and Jubal's descendents became musicians as crafts and trades are handed down from father to son. But it could also be in the more generic sense that Jabal came up with the pastoral lifestyle, Jubal invented musical instruments or formal musical notation and performance and thus became the "father" of all those who do it, just as today we talk of the father of modern medicine, or the father of modern chemistry. Similarly, Tubal-cain was the father of metalworking or metallurgy, although it doesn't use the word "father" for him, it just says he was the founder of it.

> And Zillah, she also bare Tubal-cain, an instructer of every artificer in brass and iron: and the sister of Tubal-cain was Naamah. (Genesis 4:22).

So ultimately everyone who ever learned metallurgy could trace their apprenticeship, directly or indirectly, ultimately to Tubal-cain. And then finally, we come to the time when Lamech makes his proclamation about having killed a man.

I want to say a little bit more about antediluvian civilization. It was so complete except for the amenities of modern industrial civilization, no factories as we think of them, no internal combustion engine, no cars. But there is the possibility that there was a good deal of magic. There are a couple of reasons why I say that. First, because there was so much corruption and so much evil that God decided to destroy the whole earth. Second, because God says that the days of the return of Jesus would be like the days of Noah. And there's a lot of magic, a lot of occult, in our day; that suggests there was a lot of occult in Noah's day. If there was bad spirituality, bad religion (and there was religion in those days as we saw at the end of chapter four), then there was bound to be the demonic. If people leave God out of their lives, the devil will quickly jump in.

It seems plausible—I won't commit to it—that people had the ability to do some of the things that they did through magical power. Achievements that today we accomplish strictly through the use of fossil-fueled technology (such as building very large complex structures or communicating over very long distances) they used psychic or magical powers to accomplish. When we look at the kind of occult powers that people have in places of the world like West Africa; people do things like "shorten the path" for example, transmogrify things, change the shape of things, make things appear or disappear. For example consider an article published as recently as 1995 in the National Geographic Magazine, a publication not known for sensationalism, on Voodoo practiced in Ghana. They documented in writing and photography the voodoo celebration in Kokuzan:

> We were distracted by a man teetering on the edge of possession. Grabbing a wooden mortar, he dropped to the sand and braced the vessel on his chest. Four men in turn slammed a pestle into the container (left). We wondered if the man's chest would be

badly injured from the blows. Yet he sprang up, flung the mortar aside, and danced away unharmed.

We were even more mystified when four men drew knives from the calabash fetish and pointed them at a chicken held atop a boy's head. Within seconds, the bird collapsed, snatching a few shivering breaths before dying. When the chicken was cooked in a calabash, the flammable gourd did not catch fire.

How can we explain what we witnessed? We can't. Yet for voodoo followers, explanations aren't needed. Faith is enough.

All around us the celebrants at Kokuzan seemed to push the limits of pain: A woman splashed sand into opened eyes, a man cut his belly with shards of glass but did not bleed, another swallowed fire.

Nearby a believer, perhaps a yam farmer or fisherman, heated hand-wrought knives in crackling flames. Then another man brought one of the knives to his tongue. We cringed at the sight and were dumbfounded when, after several repetitions, his tongue had not even reddened.

"The gods protect us," explained Doavu Hayibor Atsivi, the chief priest presiding over Kokuzan. "They direct our actions and tell us which medicines to take so no harm can come to us."[7]

People in Africa use those kinds of occult demonic powers for very petty, foolish, selfish ends. "So-and-so hurt my feelings, so I'm going to go make a knife drop out of their ceiling to kill them." "I want his house so I'll make a potion that will make him drive his car over a cliff without knowing it." That's not exactly the kind of activity that will advance civilization. But supposing that someone had that kind of power and used it in a constructive, albeit an evil, way. In other words, this is to suggest that the antediluvian world used such powers as a kind of occult spiritual technology to actually achieve things. Someone could connect between their city and another city a hundred miles away, they could walk there in two hours by the magical power of "shortening the way". Transportation could have been affected very easily. One could communicate with someone else long distance by reading their minds. One could use these very same powers to substitute for almost all the different types of technology that we enjoy today.

One of the reasons why I hint at this is because in the 1870's a Jesuit named

[7]Carol Beckwith and Angela Fisher, "The African Roots of Voodoo." *National Geographic* 188.2 (1995):102-13.

Ignatius Donelly wrote a book about the legendary island kingdom of Atlantis. Titled, *Atlantis: the Antediluvian World*, it was the book that revived interest in Plato's ancient work on Atlantis. While scholars agree that Atlantis was probably inspired by the island of Thera, Donelly had his own ideas. Synthesizing Plato's writing with the Book of Genesis, he imagined that Atlantis was a great majestic kingdom that existed before the flood and imagined, as have those who have been his successors, that it was this great kingdom with all kinds of occult powers. There seems to be a sense among those interested in the paranormal that there was an ancient time when there was a kingdom where magic ruled, whether they think of this ancient time as the antediluvian world or not.

While occultish visions of the world definitely do not fit in with a biblical worldview, one wonders if there might not be something to a connection between the antediluvian world and magic power. Definitely there was an antediluvian world that was buried under the sea. It wasn't Atlantis—it was the whole world. Maybe that was part of the evil that God judged: this incredible occult explosion, such as we see today, actually put to pragmatic use.[8] Ultimately, all this is speculation. It's what we can think based on what we believe. But we don't know for sure.

One thing we do know for sure, from what we read in the scriptures: people were involved with the occult and people did have a very advanced technology and civilization. And we also know this, that a lot of that civilization is credited to the descendants of Cain, who was wicked and begot people who were wicked! These three men, Jabal, Jubal, and Tubal-cain, were all the sons of Lamech and we've already seen how wicked he was. Specifically, his wickedness is not just in the fact that he killed a man, but in that after he confessed this to his wives he said, "If Cain shall be avenged sevenfold, truly Lamech seventy and sevenfold." (Genesis 4:24). This does not bode well for mankind.

When people start saying that mercy is something they have coming to them, this shows how abusive they are toward the mercy of God. God was merciful toward Cain, in warning him to overcome sin in the first place before he killed Abel. And after Cain murdered, before even pronouncing judgement, God first showed mercy to that murderer. Subsequently people reasoned, "Oh, okay, then God *owes* me mercy." In which case mercy is not treated as mercy at all, of course,

---

[8]To a considerable extent, this has happened in the 20th century, not so much as a substitute for technology, but to acquire and maintain control over people's minds for political, and ultimately spiritual, purposes. Detailed discussion on this can be found in Nugent Chap. 5, "A Century of Satan". Dave Hunt's book *Peace, Prosperity, and the Coming Holocaust* deals with this subject in even greater detail as well as broader scope.

but as justice.

In practice, such a standard of justice is, that murderers should get off the hook. That, in fact, if one punishes a murderer, it's the punisher who's guilty; the murderer is innocent. That's a complete upside-down perversion of God's standard of justice, but it's exactly what human beings came up with. That's why, after the flood, God insisted on teaching people the law and keeping with the law for well over a thousand years before He introduced the gospel of mercy. Because when people start saying that mercy is justice and confusing mercy and justice, they're in for a world full of abomination and wickedness, with impunity.

By the way, that's another thing our world has in common with the world of Noah: people see evil as perfectly okay; it's punishing evil that's wrong. Fair is foul and foul is fair. That's the ethic of Satan, of the demonic. We shouldn't be surprised therefore that the very first thing that we read in Chapter 6 of Genesis is that the world was completely corrupt.

But actually the very next thing that we read after Lamech's statement that mercy equals justice, is that Adam had another son, named Seth, and Eve said, "Oh, now God has given me another in the place of Abel, whom Cain slew." This tells us that Seth was probably the first son born to them after Abel had been killed. That means Abel probably died not too long before Adam was 130 years old. He was a grown man when Adam was 130 years old so he was probably born a good deal before that. So Adam had another son, named Seth, "And to Seth, to him also there was born a son; and he called his name Enos: then began men to call upon the name of the LORD." (Genesis 4:26) It gives the genealogy from Seth, but first it stops for a minute and says, "when Enos was born, Seth's son, Adam's grandson, that was the time when people began to call upon the name of the Lord."

There has been some debate about this. Some people think this to be something of a mistranslation and say this means some people started to take the name of the Lord in vain, or people started cursing God, or using God's name as a curse. That seems a bit of a stretch for the translation. It certainly goes against our principle of taking the Bible at face value. Other people say that's when people started praying. That doesn't make a whole lot of sense either, because presumably Abel was already praying. People were in communication with God before that. But it may mean this was the beginning of formal worship. After all, up to this point it's everybody out for themselves.[9] Originally each person offered sacrifices

---

[9] There is also the possibility that this is referring to taking oaths to discern conflicting witnesses., which would be a sign of an increasingly dishonest society.

on their own. Maybe this was the beginning of people gathering together to worship in a body with some sort of worship leader. Notice that none of this is instituted by God. But people are gathering together to call upon God in a formal, ritualistic way. In other words, this marks the birth of religion. And by all accounts, comparing Seth's lineage and Cain's lineage, it would seem that Seth's son Enos would have been born a long time before Lamech. So religion came along pretty early.

And speaking of lineages, there's a rather interesting comparison to be made between Seth's line and Cain's line. Seth's son was Enos. Enos' son was Cainan; that's a lot like the name Cain. Cainan's son was Mahaleel; that's very close to the name Mehujael. Mahaleel's son was Jared, which is very similar to the name Irad. Jared's son was Enoch; that's of course identical to the name of Cain's son. So if you transpose the names of Enoch and Mehujael/Mahaleel, the two genealogies are completely homologous. The similarity in names is even more apparent in Hebrew where the vowels are omitted in the script.

What's the point of this parallel? It seems more than coincidence. One possibility is that Cain's line had the potential of continuing God's truth and failed, concentrating instead on earthly progress over against spiritual progress. Cain's genealogy gave us civilization, that is to say, the beauty of the world. Cain's descendants gave the world technology, city building, metallurgy, as well as the

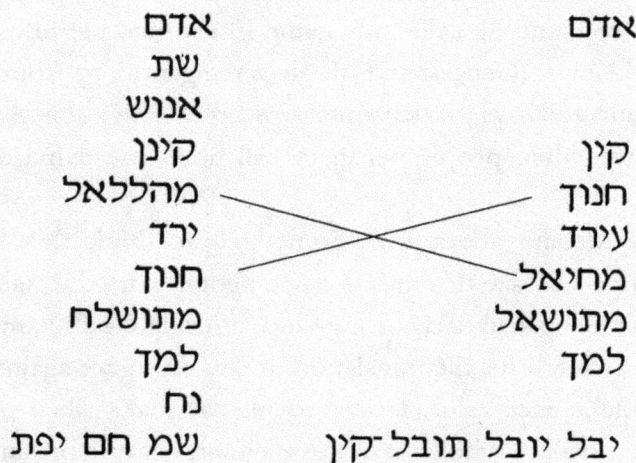

אדם	אדם
שת	
אנוש	
קינן	קין
מהללאל	חנוך
ירד	עירד
חנוך	מחיאל
מתושלח	מתושאל
למך	למך
נח	
שם חם יפת	יבל יובל תובל־קין

Figure 8. Genealogies of Cain and Seth in the original Hebrew

fine arts, music, vocal and instrumental, even orchestral, and so on. Maybe Cain's descendants even came up with the idea of formal, liturgical worship. But from Cain, that same lineage that gave the world so much civilization, also gave us polygamy, injustice, deceit, delusion, dishonesty, hardness of heart, rebelliousness, corruption, and violence on a global scale. From none of that civilized line came holiness. The holiness, rather, came through the line of Cainan. The parallel starts with Cainan[10] in Seth's line and Seth was born after Cain slew Abel. We know that Seth was a hundred and five years old before he even begot Enos, and then Enos lived another ninety years before he begot Cainan. It was therefore a hundred and ninety-five years after Abel was dead before Cainan was even born. Then Cainan lived seventy years longer before he begot Mahaleel. Although we don't know how old Cain was when he got his wife, Cainan probably begot Mahaleel, close to the time of Lamech's birth. So Cain's genealogy progresses almost down to Lamech when Cainan's genealogy begins.

It's as though God had given Cain and his descendants the chance to do something right and they failed. They did a lot of good things for this world, but not for the world to come. It's almost as though in the line of Seth and Cainan, God started over again: "Let's do a version of Cain's lineage this time that will do the right thing." So we have a lineage that's parallel in many ways to Cain's line, except this line stays with the truth. Enoch the son of Cain was the first person to have a city named after him in this world. Enoch the son of Cainan was the first person to be translated out of this world into the heavenly city. And while the people of that time could say the world as they knew it came from the genius of

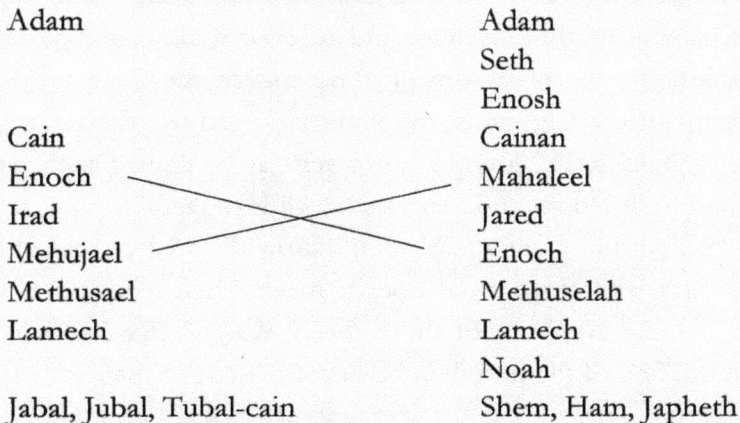

Adam	Adam
	Seth
	Enosh
Cain	Cainan
Enoch	Mahaleel
Irad	Jared
Mehujael	Enoch
Methusael	Methuselah
Lamech	Lamech
	Noah
Jabal, Jubal, Tubal-cain	Shem, Ham, Japheth

Figure 9. Genealogies of Cain and Seth in English

Jabal, Jubal, and Tubal-cain, their genius died with them in the flood; but Shem, Ham, and Japheth started the world we know today after the flood. It was their

---

[10]Semantically, it actually starts at Enos(h), which, like Adam, means "man".

generations that would inherit the world to come.

Methuselah lived 969 years and thus had the longest life span ever recorded. It also happens to extend right to the year of the flood. He died the same year the flood happened. We don't know why that was. It could mean that he himself was not righteous and died in the flood.[11] It could mean that he died just before the flood and that's the only reason why he wasn't on the ark. We don't know either way. The name of Methuselah is difficult to interpret and some have interpreted it as meaning in Hebrew 'in his death it will be sent,' his name being a prophecy that the flood would be sent in the year of his death, that he simply died of natural causes and that was the year that the flood happened. That's a very real possibility, but it's not something we can say that we know.[12] His own son Lamech, died young at the tender age of 777 years. We don't know if there's some special spiritual significance to that, either. But definitely it was very young for that time. Noah was five hundred years old when he had his children.

Now, we read in the Bible that Noah begot Shem, Ham, and Japheth. This is the first instance of something that occurs more than once in the Bible: that is, a list of brothers in a genealogy is not according to birth order. In fact we know that's not the birth order because Japheth is referred to as the elder (Genesis 10:21). He was certainly older than Shem and he may have been older than Ham, but he's the last one on the list, not because they're done in reverse order of age, but because it's done according to the significance of the sons. So Shem, being the ancestor of Abraham, of the Israelites, and of course ultimately of Jesus Christ (physically speaking), is by far the most important of the three brothers. Ham, being the ancestor of the Egyptians, the Philistines, and the Canaanites, is a very significant person in sacred history. He's not quite as significant as the ancestor of the Israelites, so he's listed second. And last of all is Japheth because he's just the ancestor of all those other Gentiles. We don't know the relative ages of Shem and Ham. They weren't triplets, so what does it mean when it says Noah was five hundred years old and Noah begot those three? Was he five hundred years old when he begot the first of them? When he begot the last of them? It's not certain, but the evidence tips in favor of it meaning that he was five hundred years old when he began to beget those three. So he could have been a lot older by the time all three of them had been born. In any case, he was probably five hundred years

---

[11]Unlikely if he was part of a sacred genealogy and sacred history.

[12]But consider that his name was given 969 years before the flood, if he was so named at birth, while God Himself does not pronounce that judgment until 120 years before the flood.

old when he begot Shem because

- Shem was one hundred years old when he begot his son
- Shem's son probably wasn't born in the ark (no mention of his birth is made in the flood account)
- Noah was six hundred years old when the flood started.
- Shem was not the oldest son

So Noah couldn't have had his sons first before reaching five hundred years. And that will fit in well when we talk about the genealogy of Abraham, but that's later on.

Of course this brings us to the end of the fifth chapter of Genesis and all we can know about the antediluvian world. So it's all still very much a mystery. What kingdoms existed? What nations existed? What peoples existed? What did they look like? We know there was a much greater genetic diversity than after the flood, since the world's population was reduced to eight people. What kinds of body types, what kinds of facial features, what kinds of hair textures, what combinations of all those things existed before the flood? It's very tantalizing isn't it? It really stirs the imagination. But it's just going to have to be our imagination because we have no word on any of those things. It's just a mystery.

That world really was lost. God could have revealed all kinds of stuff about that world, but it's as though God is saying, "I'm not going to tell you about that world because I want to forget it myself. I wiped it out to be remembered no more. That world is gone forever. I want it to stay forgotten." That's how much God hated the way the world was.

The God of the Bible says that the world had gotten so bad that God repented that He had made man. He regretted that He had made human beings. That's one of the most powerful statements in the whole Bible. That almost ranks alongside John 3:16: "For God so loved the world, that he gave his only begotten Son, that whosoever believeth in him should not perish, but have everlasting life." We stand in awe of that verse. But before then, way back in the days of Noah, the Bible says God so hated the world, or the condition of the world, that He regretted that He'd ever made it.

But people had completely earned that wrath. The Bible says, "And GOD saw that the wickedness of man was great in the earth, and that every imagination of the thoughts of his heart was only evil continually." (Genesis 6:5) But what really sealed the doom of mankind was, not the wickedness of Cain, not the wickedness of Lamech, not even the fact that people began to take wickedness for granted and take mercy as something that was owed to them as a basis of justice, and therefore took true justice as wickedness. What really sealed the doom of humanity was what begins Chapter Six.

> And it came to pass, when men began to multiply on the face of the earth, and daughters were born unto them,

> That the sons of God saw the daughters of men that they were fair; and they took them wives of all which they chose. (Genesis 6:1,2)

Those are dire verses, simply because of the first words of verse two: "the sons of God." These are not just any people; we already knew that people were taking wives of all which they chose. Lamech took two wives, Adah and Zillah. But when sons of God started doing it, when the children of God were acting the same as Lamech—this is what it means—it got to the stage where people who had been sons of God were no better than Lamech. And if they were no better than Lamech about their wives, and about the way they started their homes, if they left God out of the absolute bedrock foundation of society—the forming of their marriages and their households—that meant they left God out of everything else. They left God out of every part of their lives. That meant we can be sure if they were as wicked as Lamech about picking their wives, they were as wicked as Lamech about insisting that mercy was something that was owed to them. And that changed their whole attitude toward God. "God owes me something. God couldn't send anybody to hell. I can sin every day in word, thought, and deed, and God is duty bound to take me to heaven." Sound familiar? "As the days of Noah were, so shall the days of the Son of Man be."

"The daughters of men" here does not refer to the daughters of sinners. It simply means women in general. But precisely because it means women in general it includes sinners. It means they weren't even paying attention. They weren't going out of their way to marry daughters of God, they weren't even going out of their way to marry sinners. The spiritual aspect didn't even enter into the equation at all. They married whoever they jolly well felt like marrying. Just based on what? Oh, they saw that they were beautiful.

> That the sons of God saw the daughters of men that they were fair; and they took them wives of all which they chose. (Genesis 6:2)

The whole basis for marriage was just, "Hey, she's hot! I'm takin' her. And if I find another one who's hot, maybe I'll take her, too." And these are the people who called themselves children of God. When that happened, *only* when that happened, it says, "And the LORD said, My spirit shall not always strive with man, for that he also is flesh: yet his days shall be an hundred and twenty years." (Gen 6:3). What modus operandi is God responding to here? "Mercy is owed to me." "If Cain shall be avenged sevenfold, truly Lamech seventy and sevenfold." (Gen 4:24) And even the sons of God were adopting that. "God has to be merciful to me. If I sin, it's God's duty to defend me against just punishment." God stands up and says, "Mercy is me striving with your spirit, telling you to repent. Not sticking up for you and helping you, defending you and protecting you so you can commit more wickedness, lewdness, and injustice. That's not mercy. Mercy is striving with you. And I'll tell you about mercy: I'm not always going to strive with your spirit. Because you're flesh. You children of God are just as much flesh as the children of Cain. I don't answer to you. I made you. I could wipe you out in a second if I wanted to." But He spared them a little longer. At this point, He said, "yet his days shall be an hundred and twenty years." (Genesis 6:3b) That means there were a hundred twenty years left. The clock was ticking.

Children of God, in any age, are the gatekeepers of hell. They are the ones who keep the way of hell from being the way of the earth. No unregenerated person, no organization or nation of unregenerated people has the power to stop evil from taking over the world. Children of God alone have that power and the responsibility is finally theirs. But when once the children of God stop being the children of God, when the people who have been taking up the cause of God start adopting the ways of hell, what's to stop evil? There is nobody else. Evil goes unchecked and it sweeps like a flood. Only God is left to intervene.

It says there were giants in the earth in those days. Notice that it does not say that those giants were born as a result of the sons of God marrying the daughters of men. Contrary to popular misunderstanding it just simply says giants existed in those days. That's another cultural universal: people know that in ancient days, there were giants. We're not talking about children's fairy tale story type giants that are a hundred feet tall. We're talking about giants the way there is giantism today: giants that are seven feet tall, or even eight or nine feet tall.

> There were giants in the earth in those days; and also after that,
> when the sons of God came in unto the daughters of men, and

> they bare children to them, the same became mighty men which
> were of old, men of renown. (Genesis 6:4)

That shows that the giants were around before the sons of God ever came into the daughters of men. There were giants *when* the sons of God first started coming into the daughters of men. After that happened, their children became the mighty men of old.

Samson was certainly like these mighty men of old mentioned in Genesis 6, though he lived centuries later. He was perhaps the only true, non-fictional superhero in the history of the world. But he was, to put it charitably, very morally ambivalent, mostly using his supernatural powers for pride even though his parents were very godly. Samson seems like the kind of person that would come from a spiritually ambivalent kind of family.

That's what happened shortly before the flood. There were these very religious backsliding children of God, who picked whatever wives they wanted, did whatever they wanted with their lives, and thought God owed them everything. Those sons of God who went into the daughters of men weren't raised that way, but they changed the doctrine for themselves to believe that God owed them everything.

When their children grew up in that kind of doctrine from the beginning, they really thought they could do anything. They were full of pride, conceit, and overwhelming self-confidence, which in fact gave them the strength to do all kinds of exploits—not *good* exploits, but amazing exploits. And to this day there are legends about these heros, mighty men of renown. That age of heros comes from this historical event before the flood.

Most likely some of those same mighty men were the ones who perpetuated the violence and the wickedness all over the earth; constantly trying to beat each other out, constantly competing, ruthlessly, brutally, more and more. Imagine a whole race of people, so to speak, who are full of power-lust sweeping over the world, conquering and showing no mercy, expecting everything to be owed to them. It says there that "GOD saw that the wickedness of man was great in the earth, and that every imagination of the thoughts of his heart was only evil continually." (Genesis 6: 5) That's when God regretted

> that he had made man on the earth, and it grieved him at his
> heart.
> And the LORD said, I will destroy man whom I have created from

the face of the earth; both man, and beast, and the creeping thing, and the fowls of the air; for it repenteth me that I have made them.

But Noah found grace in the eyes of the LORD. (Genesis 6:6-8)

The only holy man at that time. We know he was holy because it says,

Noah was a just man

which means he was righteous,

and perfect in his generations,

which means he was holy.

and Noah walked with God.

Now before I go on to talk about Noah and the flood, there's this one other thing I would like to point out about the age between the fall and the flood. In archeology there are certain gaps that exist in the archeological record. I'll give an example of one of these: Neanderthal cultures and Cro-Magnon cultures in France, where is located the actual site where Cro-Magnon Man was so named by archeologists. There are also Neanderthal sites beneath that. There's a description of the way that record looks, that has been aptly described as follows:

> Using the earlier analogy of stone tools as a radio broadcast across the years, imagine the following chain of events: the one station the receiver picks up has an announcer chatting away about normal topics in his normal tone of voice; suddenly he begins to sputter and yell; then he goes off the air altogether, and the radio is ominously silent for a moment; then a new voice comes on the air, talking rapidly in a totally different language. It would be only natural to believe that the radio station had been attacked and taken over by invaders.[13]

That's the way the archeological record looks. That scenario was given in part to suggest that Cro-Magnon Man took over Neanderthal Man's settlements. But

---

[13] George Constable, *The Neanderthals* (New York:Time Life Books,1973) 124.

another way to think about it is that there wasn't an invasion, but that something sudden and catastrophic occurred.

There are points like that elsewhere in the archeological record where we have some culture continuing on quite nicely, and then suddenly there's this gap. All at once the culture seems to be wiped off the face of the earth and then there's a gap and then suddenly a completely different culture takes its place. I submit that wherever we find this kind of gap in the archeological record, that's where we have evidence of the flood. We have relics of antediluvian cultures or civilizations being replaced by postdiluvian cultures. Those show up in a lot of different places and with cultures which are at different stages of technological development. For that reason they're not linked in the evolutionary scheme of things as being part of a pattern.

The idea that everybody was a Neanderthal, everybody was living in an agricultural culture, or that everybody was a hunter-gatherer, etc., etc. prevents anyone from making a connection between these gaps. Because of this prevalent way of thinking, when gaps like this show up, if there is in the archeological record a gap between two urban cultures and a gap between two hunter-gatherer cultures, scholars don't think of those as being part of the same gap. Because it is assumed that no hunter-gatherer societies co-existed with the urban societies. That's not how it really works, but that's how evolutionists think of it.

But if we just look at the gaps, as gaps, anywhere they appear you can see there's something of a pattern. The Neanderthal were one example of this.

This is further confirmed by the study sponsored by the Rhineland Museum in Germany in the late '90s which seems to show that Neanderthal are not ancestral to modern humans.[14] The study used samples of Neanderthal mitochondrial DNA to reach its conclusions. The study showed that Neanderthal are equally unrelated to modern Europeans, Africans, Asians, Americans, and Australians. In the biblical view this is what we would expect. It's true that Neanderthal are fully human and members of the same species, but they are not our ancestors because they were wiped out in the global flood.

Another example of these gaps is in the archeological record between the Halaf culture and the Ubaidian culture in Mesopotamia; in fact, there's a great deal of wet silt between the remains of the Halaf culture and those of Ubaid. That gap

---

[14]Igor V. Ovchinnikov., Anders Götherström, Galina P. Romanova, Vitaliy M. Kharitonov, Kerstin Lidén, and William Goodwin. "Molecular Analysis of Neanderthal DNA from the Northern Caucasus." *Nature* 404.6777 (2000): 490-93. See also Kate Wong. "Neandertal Genome Study Reveals That We Have a Little Caveman in Us." Scientific American Global RSS. Scientific American, 6 May 2010. Web. 07 Apr. 2015.

seems to represent the sudden disappearance of civilization in the flood. Wherever gaps like these occur they seem to be an indication that artifacts beneath the gap represent some society, civilization, culture before the flood, and above the gap are the postdiluvian societies. Looking for these gaps may be a way to identify traces of the antediluvian world. That, in turn, could give us some insight into what the antediluvian world was like.

Then we come back to the call of Noah. God called Noah to a unique calling—unique in the strongest sense of the word.

10
It's the end of the world as they knew it

Ever since the world ended
I don't go out as much.
People that I once befriended
Just don't bother to stay in touch.
Things that used to seem so splendid
Don't really matter today.
It's just as well the world ended
It wasn't working anyway.

— Mose Allison, "Ever Since the World Ended"

Noah had a calling that nobody else has had before or since. He was called to be God's human instrument for preserving life on the planet, not just human life, but animal life as well. God gave Noah the special commission to make a box—that's what the word *ark* means of course; it doesn't mean a boat, it means a box—a box which was to be extraordinarily large. The size of this box, this ark, was in biblical measurements 300 cubits long, 50 cubits wide, and 30 cubits high. Based on an 18 inch cubit, the ark would be 450 feet long. Using a 21 inch cubit the size of the ark has been calculated at 525 feet long, 87 feet wide, and 52 feet high. Even larger dimensions have been calculated, again depending on the size of the cubit to be as long as 547 feet, 91 feet wide, and 54 ½ feet high. In any event, the ark had definitely enough space for all the animals. One estimate has the ark having enough room for 7000 animals. It had at least one and a half million cubic feet of space inside.

The biggest challenge to the realism of this task is that there wouldn't be enough people to take care of all of these animals for a full year and enough food to feed them. There is a scheme for that that has been worked out in Woodmorappe's feasability study of the ark which shows that with eight people such a project could be carried out successfully, but those eight people would have to work almost round the clock. It would definitely be a difficult task taking care of all these animals, but it could be done.

That's getting a little ahead of the game here because before the ark was completed and the flood took place, building the ark itself was a process that took roughly a hundred and twenty years. God Himself had said, "My spirit shall not always strive with man, for that he also is flesh: yet his days shall be an hundred and twenty years," meaning that humanity had a hundred and twenty years to prepare themselves spiritually before the flood would inevitably come on the earth. The New Testament explicitly refers to Noah as a preacher of righteousness (2 Peter 2:5) who condemned the world (Hebrews 11:7), who warned people of the wrath that was to come. Evidently very few people harkened because by the time the flood came there was no one to enter the ark with Noah except his family. Initially, when He commanded him to build the ark, God told Noah that he should take all animals two by two:

> But with thee will I establish my covenant; and thou shalt come into the ark, thou, and thy sons, and thy wife, and thy sons' wives with thee.

> And of every living thing of all flesh, two of every sort shalt thou bring into the ark, to keep them alive with thee; they shall be male and female.

> Of fowls after their kind, and of cattle after their kind, of every creeping thing of the earth after his kind, two of every sort shall come unto thee, to keep them alive.

> And take thou unto thee of all food that is eaten, and thou shalt gather it to thee; and it shall be for food for thee, and for them.

> Thus did Noah; according to all that God commanded him, so did he.
> (Genesis 7:18-22)

This last verse, the twenty-second verse of chapter six, gives one of the most powerful testimonies of any human being in the Bible.

But apart from the fact that God told Noah to take the animals two by two, by the end of the hundred twenty years, when the flood was about to take place, we see at the beginning of chapter seven:

> And the LORD said unto Noah, Come thou and all thy house into the ark; for thee have I seen righteous before me in this generation.

> Of every clean beast thou shalt take to thee by sevens, the male
> and his female: and of beasts that are not clean by two, the male
> and his female.
>
> Of fowls also of the air by sevens, the male and the female; to
> keep seed alive upon the face of all the earth. (Genesis 7:1-3)

Some people see a contradiction in that, but it's not a contradiction. First, only those that are clean come by sevens. Secondly, it was about a hundred twenty years after people had first refused to board the ark. Some have interpreted this detail to mean that God was saying, "Since people wouldn't enter the ark, take extra animals and let animals take up the space that people could have taken to save their lives." No human being apart from Noah's immediate family— his wife and three sons and their wives— would board the ark.

Of course, the other good reason for having all those different animals in sevens was the need to have extra domestic animals. That's what I think is really meant here by *clean animals*. The law of Moses had very specific and very narrow specifications of what would constitute a clean animal. But of course this was Noah's day, more than a thousand years before the law of Moses, and what's really meant here is not so much clean animals according to the law of Moses, but clean in some other way. What would constitute clean or unclean in Noah's day? We may never know precisely. But the most likely answer is that as all clean animals were domesticated under the law of Moses, so clean animals in Noah's time were domesticated animals.

There were extra animals for sacrifices (and later for food after the flood) without wiping out an entire kind of animal. Likewise with flying animals. When Noah later released a raven and it flew away and never came back, that would have been the end of ravens, except that Noah had seven of them so they were still able to multiply after the flood was over. How Noah collected all these animals, I don't know. God may have brought them miraculously. But God did say, "thou shalt bring into the ark two of every sort of animal."

Creationists have generally asserted that the word 'kind' really is a technical term. What is a 'Genesis kind'? Since the word *kind* happens to be cognate with the Latin word *genus*, some creationists have suggested that *kind* really is the same biological term as *genus*—or the same as *family*. I take the word 'kind' to just mean "kind", i.e. every type, without being a scientific technical term. But there is a scientific basis for classifying animals other than just Linnaean classification of phyla, families, genera, and so on.

The Linnaean system really is based on morphology, sometimes deep morphology, but not on genetic code, and it hasn't always been a fair indicator of closest genetic relationship. Sometimes it has to be revised and nipped and tucked to fit what we know about genetic relationships between different types of animals. I think it probably needs to be replaced completely: we could use Linnaean classification for official purposes, but to really understand the relationship of animals probably it's best just to start over and look at what the actual genomes of different animals are. I think this is where the IBO theory of biology is very informative. Those animals that share the same genome can be classified as members of the same *kind*—regardless of how that fits, or doesn't fit, the Linnean system. If we use the term 'genome group,' there probably was one pair of animals for every genome group on the ark. From there you can get multiple species from the same genomic type, such as different species of frogs, or different types of dogs or what have you. This understanding leads to a few conclusions:

- This means that the variations we see today within each type did not exist before the flood. For example, there were no lions, tigers, or leopards in the antediluvian world; but there were big cats which also shared the earth with other varieties of that same genome type which didn't make it onto the ark and therefore became extinct in the flood.
- There was much greater variety of life before the flood, especially among land animals (while many aquatic animals died in the flood, it was obviously not as devastating to marine life as to terrestrial life).
- All fossil life from Precambrian, Paleozoic, Mesozoic, and Cenozoic eras in the evolutionary myth co-existed on the earth before the flood.
- "Transitional forms" were actually co-existing variations or genome types or distinct organisms with closely related genomes. Mastodons, mammoths, deinotheres, etc. would be an example of this; horse "ancestors" would be another example.[1]

Even after they went in, they stayed in there for seven days before the flood actually occurred. We can imagine that it must have been very tense, wondering "What's happening? Nothing's happening!" We can imagine the mockery that went on outside the ark when they were all inside for one week without anything

---

[1]See Appendix 2 for more on "transitional" forms.

happening. People outside would have been more confident than ever that nothing was ever going to happen. But of course after seven days the flood was upon the earth. "The fountains of the deep broke up and the windows of heaven were opened."

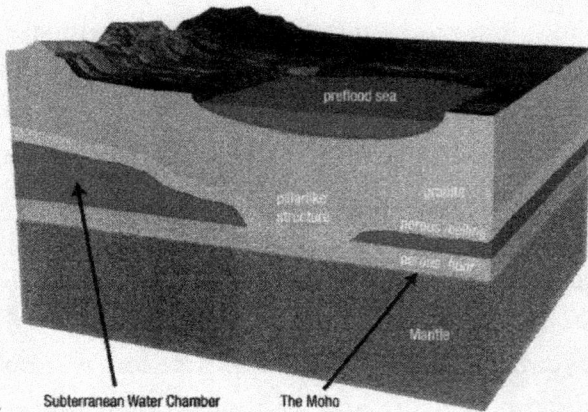

Figure 10: cut-away diagram of water chambers under the earth's crust (from http://www.creationscience.com /onlinebook/HydroplateOverview6.html)

Much has been written about that phrase, specifically about the mechanics (meteorological, geological) of the great flood. The clearest description of that to date is Walt Brown's hydroplate theory, which makes more sense than anything else does about Noah's flood. It's still science and it's subject to change, but it seems to have made a number of predictions which have since been confirmed and certainly seems to be more viable and more reasonable than, say, the water canopy theory of Henry Morris. I don't think there was a water canopy that just fell in on the earth, much less a shell of ice or anything else like that. I think the hydroplate theory is the most accurate. I'll just briefly summarize it here.

According to the theory the continental plates were once connected in one land mass. There was a large amount of salty water in interconnected underground chambers, forming a continuous layer around the whole earth (Figure 10), in the form of a spherical shell. This was about 5/8 mile (1 km) thick, lay at a depth of 10 miles (16 km) under the earth's surface and contained about half of the water which is now in the oceans. The water contained dissolved minerals and gases, especially salt and carbon dioxide. There was basaltic rock underneath this water, then the earth's mantle.

The pressure was increasing in the subterranean water layer. According to Brown, this happened naturally,[2] but it could have happened by divine intervention, like the parting of the Red Sea. This was preparing for the judgment of the flood and judgment is contingent on man's choice. If the pressure build up

---

[2] This could have been several things, for example the mantle's temperature could have been increasing due to radioactive decay, causing it to expand, therefore pressurizing the water above it.

had been purely natural, it would imply that man was doomed from the beginning to incur the judgment of the flood. On the other hand, one could conjecture that man's sin mysteriously altered nature to produce the pressure build up in the same way that sin brings more death into the world.

> In the six hundredth year of Noah's life, in the second month, the seventeenth day of the month, the same day were all the fountains of the great deep broken up, and the windows of heaven were opened.
>
> And the rain was upon the earth forty days and forty nights. (Genesis 7:11,12)

This was the moment when the earth's crust was fractured, one crack went all around the earth, and the continental plates were produced. Rock connecting the continents was quickly eroded by upward gushing subterranean water and transported worldwide.

Most of the sediments on earth were formed from this eroded rock. The continents quickly slid away east and west from the Mid-Atlantic Ridge, and moved to their present positions over a period of about a year.

> And the waters prevailed, and were increased greatly upon the earth; and the ark went upon the face of the waters. (Genesis 7:18)

Walt Brown also points out that the way the ark is described in its construction suggests that the window was close to the top of the ark. This allowed the ark to float very deep below the surface so that most of the ark was below water and that kept it very stable, kept it from capsizing. Again we can imagine being in such a huge vessel working tirelessly day and night with very little sunlight, taking care of all these animals and cleaning up after them (itself pretty much a full time job) confined under unbelievably stressful conditions, i.e. the whole world had basically come to an end.

To get a tiny bit of a feel for what that was like, imagine the following scenario. Imagine that you're locked up in a space ship that's been launched away from the earth and then the earth blows up. Now the world as you know it is gone, it doesn't exist anymore. You have no idea when you're going to stop floating. How do you feel?

God did not tell Noah in advance how long the ark would be floating before it would stop, or if it would ever stop floating at all. The tension, the stress must have been almost enough to drive Noah's sons and in-laws insane—in the literal sense of the word. They must have had to wrestle with some serious mental health issues.

Partly for this reason, it is worth considering the kind of personality that God chose to be at the helm of this project. God brought the flood, but Noah directed the goings on at the ark. He had to have leaned heavily on God for grace and assistance, but Noah would have needed a certain kind of personality to be the kind of instrument that God could use. It's fair to say that Noah must have been an

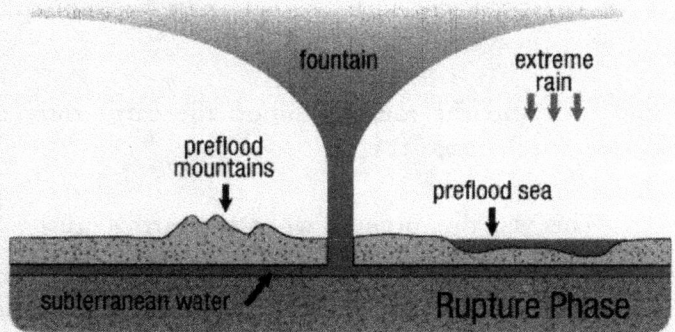

Figure 11: cut-away diagram of subterranean water bursting through the earth's crust (from http://www.creationscience.com/onlinebook/Hy droplateOverview6.html)

extremely charismatic man in the sense that he must have been able to command respect and unquestioning obedience on behalf of his children. He must have been a strong anchoring force to be able to hold his family together and keep them from going at each other's throats after just over a year of being in this box.

They entered the box a week before the flood. During the flood itself the rain fell for forty days and forty nights, but the mountains continued to be covered for another hundred and ten days (Genesis 7:24) and finally the ark wasn't able to open up again until another two hundred twenty-one days (Genesis 8:4-16). In that time all life on land was wiped out and all of the civilization that had existed was obliterated.

This extraordinary catastrophe that obviously had no parallel before or since in the history of the world was of such a nature that, according to the hydroplate theory, it produced miles of layers of sedimentary rocks all over the planet. That is to say, turbid sediments being laid down and being pressed into rock, dead animals and their carcasses being compressed until nothing is left but their carbon and carbon compounds which form vast deposits of petroleum, oil, coal, and even diamonds in some low-lying parts of the rock. Many other bodies were buried in such a way that their bones were instantly fossilized (we know they were fossilized instantly because there are fossils of animals with other animals in their stomachs, and both their skeletons and those of their prey are fossilized) because we have strong reason to think that not just so-called prehistoric animals but also human beings of all different cultures, urban cultures, rural cultures, primitive cultures, advanced sophisticated cultures, all existed at the time of the flood. There were not only human skeletons that were fossilized, there were also tools and other implements that originally would have been made out of wood, or perhaps metals, that were fossilized and just turned into stone. Any other kind of sophisticated equipment that might have existed, was for the most part fossilized or destroyed completely and lost forever.

Such unimaginable devastation did not simply kill people and animals. The flood wiped out everything from the previous world. Only vague, slight, tantalizing artifacts and human remains, but overwhelmingly the world that then was, perished. Their cultures, their language, is gone forever without any possibility of recovery.

The Bible gives this account of the end of the flood.

> And God remembered Noah, and every living thing, and all the cattle that was with him in the ark: and God made a wind to pass over the earth, and the waters asswaged;
>
> The fountains also of the deep and the windows of heaven were stopped, and the rain from heaven was restrained;
>
> And the waters returned from off the earth continually: and after the end of the hundred and fifty days the waters were abated.
>
> And the ark rested in the seventh month, on the seventeenth day of the month, upon the mountains of Ararat. (Genesis 8:1-4)

Ararat of course is not a single mountain; the name "Mt. Ararat" is of relatively recent coinage. Ararat here is the name of a region in what is now eastern Turkey and western Armenia. It corresponds to the region and city that archeologists refer to as Urartu.

Partly because of evaporation of the water, partly because newly formed mountains shot up above the level of the water,

> And the waters decreased continually until the tenth month: in the tenth month, on the first day of the month, were the tops of the mountains seen.

And it came to pass at the end of forty days, that Noah opened the window of the ark which he had made:

And he sent forth a raven, which went forth to and fro, until the waters were dried up from off the earth.

Also he sent forth a dove from him, to see if the waters were abated from off the face of the ground;

But the dove found no rest for the sole of her foot, and she returned unto him into the ark, for the waters were on the face of the whole earth: then he put forth his hand, and took her, and pulled her in unto him into the ark.

And he stayed yet other seven days; and again he sent forth the dove out of the ark;

And the dove came in to him in the evening; and, lo, in her mouth was an olive leaf pluckt off: so Noah knew that the waters were abated from off the earth.

And he stayed yet other seven days; and sent forth the dove; which returned not again unto him any more. (Genesis 8:5-12)

The world that they had known had been completely destroyed, and it was a totally new world to them. The geography and geology of the whole earth's crust, the whole planet, the earth as they knew it was totally different. Even if they looked at the whole world before and after, they wouldn't have recognized the world that they had left behind; it just didn't exist anymore.

Consider just a sketch of how great a cataclysm this was and how devastating its effects on the world:

- The entire earth's crust broke up and the appearance of the planet even from outer space changed forever.
- All (high) mountains we see today were formed suddenly
- mesas and palteaus
- Most/all islands were formed
- Ocean trenches were formed
- Fossil fuels were formed
- All sedimentary and much/all metamorphic rock was formed
- The subterranean seas were largely drained and gone forever

- The salinity of water in the oceans was drastically increased
- The asteroid belt was formed—an entire belt of asteroids that circles the sun between the orbits of Mars and Jupiter
- Comets didn't exist before—now they do
- Volcanoes came into existence—or at least the vast majority of them did
- Diversity of terrestrial life was vastly diminished
- The meteorological pattern of the entire planet was radically changed forever
- Climatic zones (tropical, temperate, arctic) came to exist

So completely was the earth transformed by this cataclysm that many of the cultures that preserve a story of the worldwide flood merged the story of the flood and the story of creation. In African and North American cultures there are creation stories about birds going out over the world covered with water and pulling dirt from the bottom up to the surface, or scratching and spreading it, and creating the first dry land. Those stories ultimately come from the Genesis 8 account of Noah sending out a bird— first a raven, then a dove— to find the first dry land after the flood.

> And it came to pass in the six hundredth and first year, in the first month, the first day of the month, the waters were dried up from off the earth: and Noah removed the covering of the ark, and looked, and, behold, the face of the ground was dry.
>
> And in the second month, on the seven and twentieth day of the month, was the earth dried.
>
> And God spake unto Noah, saying,
>
> Go forth of the ark, thou, and thy wife, and thy sons, and thy sons' wives with thee. (Genesis 8:13-16)

There's some debate about this, but on the surface of it, it looks as though Noah may have been in the ark for two months after the earth dried before he actually got out of the ark. That sounds very strange, but it has to do with something very peculiar in the beginning of the story of the flood: "and the LORD shut him in." (Genesis 7:16b)

What does that mean? How, physically, did that happen? We don't know. All we know is it's written in the Book of Revelation "he that openeth and no man shutteth, and shutteth and no man openeth." When God shuts a door, only God can open it. And when God somehow closed that door behind them, it was shut in such a way that no one could open it even if he wanted to. When people came, banging on that door, wanting to get into that ark, Noah couldn't do a thing about it. God had shut it. Of course there's a parallel there with the Rapture of God's church. When that happens, nobody's going to be able to open that door. God's going to shut the door, and nobody will be able to open it. Even when the earth was all dry, Noah could not go out of the ark until God told him to go out of it.

> And God spake unto Noah, saying,
>
> Go forth of the ark, thou, and thy wife,
> and thy sons, and thy sons' wives with thee.
>
> Bring forth with thee every living thing that is with thee, of all flesh, both of fowl, and of cattle, and of every creeping thing that creepeth upon the earth; that they may breed abundantly in the earth, and be fruitful, and multiply upon the earth. (Genesis 8:15-17)

The first thing that Noah did after he went out, was worship. In response to his sacrifice, God gave Noah the promise that He would never again flood the whole world:

> While the earth remaineth, seedtime and harvest, and cold and heat, and summer and winter, and day and night shall not cease. (Genesis 8:22)

Apart from the fact that this is the first mention of a covenant in the Bible, it is also unique in being the only covenant between God and the whole earth.

> And God said, This is the token of the covenant which I make between me and you and every living creature that is with you, for perpetual generations: (Genesis 9:12)

The covenant was that He would never again send a flood, and that the rainbow would be a sign from then on of that covenant.

God gave Noah certain commandments: he should not eat blood, or eat flesh with the blood in it, and interestingly enough He specifically says,

And surely your blood of your lives will I require; at the hand of
every beast will I require it, and at the hand of man; at the hand
of every man's brother will I require the life of man.

Whoso sheddeth man's blood, by man shall his blood be shed:
for in the image of God made he man. (Genesis 9:5,6)

Notice the difference between this and the mercy God showed to Cain, saying,
"If anyone slays Cain, Cain shall be avenged sevenfold." He saw how human
beings respond to that mercy and so now God gives very strict justice, and says,
"What's deserved is this: whoso sheds man's blood, by man shall his blood be
shed." If an animal sheds any blood, his blood will be shed, if a human being kills
another human being, that killer himself shall be killed. "By every man's brother
will I require the life of man." God started strictly with justice because justice had
not been learned and justice had to be learned for mercy to be properly learned.

And then we begin the next section of the Bible.
And the sons of Noah, that went forth of the ark, were Shem,
and Ham, and Japheth: and Ham is the father of Canaan.

These are the three sons of Noah: and of them was the whole
earth overspread. (Genesis 9:18,19)

It mentions specifically Ham as the father of Canaan, because of what's coming
up: the less than fortunate coda to the story of Noah's life.
He began to be a husbandman and he planted a vineyard. No problem there.

And he drank of the wine, and was drunken; and he was
uncovered within his tent. (Genesis 9:21)

This verse raises many questions: Did Noah intend to drink alcohol? What was
the consequence of this event on his soul? What was Noah's moral responsibility
in this incident, what was the consequence of this? Did he know what he was
doing? Was there experience with alcoholic drink before Noah's time? The fact of
the matter is, all we know is that he got drunk. But it was a problem; at the very
least he made a mistake. And it may have been a sin.

But remember, Noah was a man of intense character; he had to be or he
couldn't have pulled his children through what they went through riding in that

ark. That was no pleasure cruise—nothing, including John Huston's depiction of the event in Dino de Laurentiis' film *The Bible: in the Beginning* comes close to illustrating the horror of that event. It was not a cute little cruise. It was an extremely horrible thing to endure. And Noah had to be extremely strong and strong-willed to be able to pull his family through that.

That same intense character shows in this episode because when Noah woke up and found out that Ham had seen him naked while Shem and Japheth had avoided doing so, he cursed Ham's son. He didn't just curse Ham, but he really got to him in a way that he knew would do even greater damage, by cursing Ham's son Canaan.

> And he said, Cursed be Canaan; a servant of servants shall he be unto his brethren.

> And he said, Blessed be the LORD God of Shem; and Canaan shall be his servant.

> God shall enlarge Japheth, and he shall dwell in the tents of Shem; and Canaan shall be his servant. (Genesis 9:25-27)

In a sense all that's true. Japheth accounts for the majority of the population of the earth today. He certainly was enlarged. Noah didn't really curse Ham per se, he cursed Canaan, his son. Canaan certainly became a servant of servants. The few Canaanites that remained after the Israelites took over the land of Canaan certainly were servants of the sons of Shem, the Israelites. Anywhere else they existed among the descendants of Shem they were servants. And Shem certainly was blessed. So the story can be seen as a rationale for all that: "here's why Canaan ended up being a servant of servants," and so forth.

But more than that, what this story tells us is that the root cause of all this wickedness in the world was not taken away by the flood. The outward wickedness, the abominations, the injustice, the violence, the corruption, was taken away. But the original sin problem that had produced it all in the first place was still there, even in Noah's own family. And that showed itself when Noah's sons started having children and they multiplied and grew to a large enough number to build a city. But before we go on to that, we'll come to the concluding verses of Noah's life:

> And Noah lived after the flood three hundred and fifty years.

> And all the days of Noah were nine hundred and fifty years: and
> he died.
> (Genesis 9:28,29)

Last of the great patriarchs to live nearly a thousand years.

Noah's age by itself left a lasting impression on the new world. Remember that the flood ended in Noah's six hundred first year and He died at the age of nine hundred and fifty. That means he lived after the flood three hundred fifty years. There were probably people born after the flood who did not live that long. Most did. For example, Eber lived four hundred sixty-four years. Selah, his father, lived four hundred thirty-eight years, Arphaxad lived four hundred thirty-eight years. People lived on average over four hundred years, but Noah himself lived for three hundred fifty years after the flood. And he was already six hundred years old when the flood happened. People might have begun to get the impression that this man was never going to die. In the Sumerian story about the great flood, Noah is called Ziusudra, "length/height of life", while in Assyrian he was called Utnapishtim, "he found life". To other people alive it seemed like this man would never die.

They moved east through the mountains and eventually journeyed from the east into the plain in the land of Shinar, which we know is the same as Sumer. So they lived in Sumer and they dwelt there and came up with the idea of building a city and a tower that would reach the heaven. Now, this didn't happen overnight. It happened over generations and we get an idea of how many generations by looking at the genealogy of Shem. Shem begot Arphaxad,

> And Arphaxad begat Salah; and Salah begat Eber.

> And unto Eber were born two sons: the name of one was Peleg;
> for in his days was the earth divided; and his brother's name was
> Joktan. (Genesis 10:24,25)

The most likely interpretation of this verse is that it was divided in terms of the languages being confused and the peoples being scattered. That is the event in sacred history that is most important and that is what is referred to here. The continents had already been divided. At least physically they had been split apart. Walt Brown has publicized his own belief that it means the continents were divided in terms of borders, that is, they were isolated by water.

When the waters receded after the flood, much of it ended up being locked up in ice. Water had shot up above the atmosphere, frozen, and then come back down again, burying animals alive in ice, and producing something like what people call an ice age: huge glaciers covering a big part of the northern hemisphere of the earth. That means that the ocean level was lower than what it is today by as much as 1200 feet. And that meant that all of the continents were connected. Even Australia was connected to Asia. It was just as distant as it is now, but the sea between Australia and the southeast Asian (Pacific) coast is much less than 1200 feet deep. The continental shelf connecting Asia and Australia would have been exposed land that animals and people could walk across. But when that ice started melting and the waters of the ocean started rising, then Australia was divided as it were from Asia by the water; Alaska was divided from Asia by water and so forth and so on. According to Walt Brown, this is what is alluded to by "the earth was divided." He has even made the case, not very convincingly, that Peleg is actually related to various words like the Greek word for sea, and so forth.

If that's true, presumably people crossed all those different barriers before the ocean levels rose again. That would mean that all those continents were divided by the waters flowing back: Asia from Australia, North America from Asia, even after the Tower of Babel. And the Tower of Babel happened even earlier than Peleg's lifetime, which means even less time between the flood and the city of Babel. On the other hand, the Omission Principle[3] (see Setterfield (1999)) could mean that there was more actual time between those events than what's mentioned in the Bible. This idea seems unlikely to be correct, though, since Peleg's parents did not have access to information about the inundation of natural land bridges around the globe.

While it's unlikely that Peleg's name refers to the flooding of land bridges, flooding of the land bridges did take place. After people began to repopulate the earth, there were several catastrophic floods, the scale of which we cannot hardly even imagine today, and yet they were still small and local compared to the global flood. They are as follows:

- the Tigris/Euphrates valley, formation of the Persian Gulf
- the Great Sunda wetlands (Indonesia) now covered by part of the South China Sea
- Carpentaria Plain (joined Australia with New Guinea)
- Black Sea from the Aegean Sea

---

[3]The Omission Principle is a principle of scripture that explains the omission of 1) generations from genealogies of Israel when an individual in that genealogy died outside the faith and 2) years from the chronology of Israel's history when Israel did not serve God. This principle was first given this name in Setterfield (1999).

- Aegean Basin
- Doggerland (North Sea)
- North America (postglacial flooding which formed, among other things, the Grand Canyon, other flooding such as the Missoula of Washington

There were floods like this all over Eurasia and North America and possibly Africa as well. Massive, huge, colossally catastrophic, but still locally restricted floods that were after shocks, so to speak, of this great global cataclysm. They were floods that in part account for the reseparating of the different land masses by water (for more information on these floods, see Appendix 3).

11
The Table of Nations

"Therefore we have reason to regard the Holy Bible highly and to consider it a most precious treasure. This very chapter, even though it is considered full of dead words, has in it the thread that is drawn from the first world to the middle and to the end of all things....This knowledge the Holy Scriptures reveal to us. Those who are without them live in error, uncertainty, and boundless ungodliness; for they have no knowledge about who they are and whence they came."

– Martin Luther, *Works*, XLII, 408-9

The old saying has it, "if you don't know where you came from you don't know where you're going." Martin Luther said as much over five hundred years ago.

Only after the end of the flood do we have the beginning of the world as we know it today. This is why many cultures confuse the flood story with the creation story. This is why people have been moved for centuries to study the Table of Nations to link the lost world with our world; to see where we, all of us, came from.

The Bible does say that the multiple descendants of Noah after the flood settled in what is called the plain of Shinar, which is the same as the plain of Sumer. The people who settled that area may very well have left their traces in what is known as the Ubaidian culture, which itself experienced one of those catastrophic, but regional floods that occurred all over the world as kind of after shocks of the global flood. The one in question here was in the Tigris Euphrates plain, leaving traces behind of that Ubaidian flood that Leonard Wooley had discovered.[1] The next civilization to inhabit that area is the Sumerian civilization and the Sumerians clearly are one of the nations descended from Cush. But we're getting ahead of ourselves. Let's begin looking at the Table of Nations.

The Table of Nations, Genesis chapter 10, comes before the story of the Tower of Babel. It chronicles all the descendants of Noah down to at least two or

---
[1]See Appendix 3.

three generations and, in some lineages, further down than that. It therefore is a kind of bridge, literarily and chronologically, between the story of the flood and the story of building the tower of Babel and the confusion of tongues.

To try to trace the generations of Noah from the Table of Nations is no new undertaking. People have been doing this for centuries. People have made many mistakes in trying to discover who the descendants of Noah are. One method used was to just arbitrarily match people up. Just to say, "Well, let's just take this name and stick it together and just say these people are these people." Another method—it hardly can be called a method—is to take names that start with the same letter. So you say, Gomer equals Germany because they both start with G, or Tubal equals Turkey because they both start with T. That's not very much of a method, either. And sometimes there's an unspoken (and erroneous) assumption that each patriarch listed in the Table of Nations corresponds to exactly one modern nation state.

We need a special key to understand what the Table of Nations can tell us about the descent from Noah to the entire population of the earth. That key is found in a formula that is repeated, in more or less the same fashion, after the genealogy of each son of Noah. At the end of the list of Japheth's descendants we find this: "By these were the isles of the Gentiles divided in their lands; every one after his tongue, after their families, in their nations." (Genesis 10:5) At the end of the section on Ham, we read, "These are the sons of Ham, after their families, after their tongues, in their countries, and in their nations." (Genesis 10:20) At the end of the section on Shem, we read, "These are the sons of Shem, after their families, after their tongues, in their lands, after their nations." (Genesis 10:31) There's the formula. Side by side with "after their families," we read, "after their tongues". The word "after" here means, "according to". According to their families, according to their tongues. Apparently grouping people by language (at the time that people were scattered from the tower of Babel) was all the same as grouping people by families.

If "according to their families" is the same as "according to their tongues" then there must be one language for each family, not for each individual. It's obvious that God would not give every single person at Babel a different language, or every single individual would be alone and isolated. They wouldn't be able to reproduce and many of them would just die living on their own, anyway. That would be the end of the human race. So when He confused the languages He still left people speaking the same language within their family, clan, or tribe.

Now when we look at the Table of Nations we can actually transfer this document from a literary format to a chart, a genealogical tree. And that genealogical tree has *end points*. By *end points* I mean a point where there are no more descendants listed after that point. My understanding is that each one of those end points represents a separate people that was scattered away from every other people. Therefore each end point, each one of those families that was separated from other families had its own language.

Moreover, each one must have spoken a unique language completely unrelated to the others. So then we have three problems to solve: what were the end points, what were the languages, and which end point spoke which language?

The first two of these questions are somewhat intertwined. In the remainder of this chapter we will investigate the first question, try to use current archeological and linguistic observations, and combine them with what we think about those observations to reach conclusions about the identity of these endpoints, where they moved, and who their descendants are today. We'll begin, in the order of the genealogy of chapter 10 of Genesis, with the descendants of Japheth.

Of the seven sons of Japheth (Gomer, Magog, Madai, Javan, Tubal, Meshech, and Tiras) four (Gomer, Madai, Javan, and Meshech) are ancestors of people who today all speak Indo-European (IE) languages. IE languages can be traced back to a single language, Proto-Indo-European (PIE). Does that mean when people were scattered from the Tower of Babel the descendants of Gomer, Madai, Javan, and Meshech all spoke the same language? No, or else there would be no reason why they would have been scattered; they would have stayed together. But they didn't stay together.

In fact we know that they didn't stay together at all; they went in completely different directions. Javan, whose descendants were the Greeks, and Madai, whose descendants were the Indo-Iranians, went in opposite directions from each other. Javan went pretty much straight west or west by northwest, and Madai went straight east. They clearly were scattered from one another and it doesn't make sense to say they spoke the same language.

Of these four, Gomer is not an end point; Gomer has three end points: Ashkenaz, Riphath, and Togarmah, so we're really talking about Madai, Javan, Meshech, Ashkenaz, Riphath, and Togarmah.

One of the ways we can figure out who's who is to look at names of these peoples in history because these people have left their marks behind. Gomer, Elam, Seba, Madai, Cush, Javan, Tubal, Meshech—their names for the most part still survive in place names and even in names of different ethnic groups and tribes to this day. These names that we see in the Bible show up in world geography and in ancient history outside of the Bible. Consequently we can find these ancient peoples in ancient records outside the Bible and see what else these records say about them. We need to consult extra-biblical sources at that point because after Genesis 10 and 11 there isn't a whole lot written in the Bible about Tubal, Tiras, Riphath, or most other Gentile peoples. So we don't really know from the Bible the subsequent history of these people after they were scattered from the Tower of Babel. But we can learn it from looking at ancient history, archeological records, and so on. We'll look at each name in the order that they appear in Genesis 10, starting with Gomer.

Gomer shows up in the Armenian city of Gamir. So it shows that somewhere in ancient times there were descendants of Gomer settled in Armenia who left their name behind. The Greeks also recorded the existence of a people who were known to them as the *Kimmeroi*. The *-oi* suffix designates a plural subject and *Kimmer-* is the root, which is clearly related to *Gomer*. We know them as the Cimmerians. And they're sometimes identified with Scythians and speakers of Indo-Iranian languages (well, not exactly, at least not originally, but probably Indo-European borrowed from the Indo-Iranians which we'll get to later). But the *Kimmeroi* were originally descendants of Gomer. Now, we may wonder, if Gomer was not an end point, how there could be a united tribe of Gomer.

The simple answer is there wasn't. The descendants of Gomer did not all stick together. They were split up between these three tribes: Ashkenaz, Riphath, and Togarmah, each of which had its own unique language, its own unique identity. However, just as the people in the tribe of Judah could call themselves Israelites, because they were a tribe of Israel, so members of the tribe of Ashkenaz, or of Riphath, or Togarmah, could call themselves Gomer because they are tribes descended from the patriarch Gomer—even though they separated from one another. But the name Gomer still exists. We see the name among the Germanic peoples, among the Celtic peoples. We find it in the name of Cimbershauen in the Netherlands, and even in the national name of the Welsh: Cymru.

If we further look at the names of the three end points, Ashkenaz, Riphath, and Togarmah, their later identities are readily discernable. There's an ancient august tradition that links Ashkenaz with the Germanic peoples. It's not hard to figure out. I wouldn't be the first one to point out the connection between the name *Ashkenaz* and the name Scandinavia. It's not just a vague look-alike connection between Ashkenaz and Scandinavia. Analyzing the name by diachronic linguistics (that is, the study of how languages change) shows how *Ashkenaz* could become *Scandinavia*. If we look *Scandinavia* up in the dictionary it will tell us that it's from *Scandin* + *auja* meaning 'wetlands', but it won't tell you, can't tell you where *Scandin-* comes from, beyond saying that it's some place name. It's from *Ashkenaz*. So Ashkenaz we know is the ancestor of the Germanic peoples. Identifying the origin of *Scandin-* is an insight that the Bible uniquely provides. Identifying the unique language of Ashkenaz is another matter.

Togarmah is very straightforwardly associated with the Tokharians. The Greeks called them *Tokharoi*[2]. Now again, the Tokharians are seen as being an Indo-Iranian speaking people. Some of them may have been influenced to borrow that language, but the original Tokharoi were the descendants of Togarmah, who migrated northeast into what would now be northwestern China and became the ancestors of the various Turkic peoples. In fact, the word Turk (*Türke* in Turkish) probably derives from Tokar, the name of the descendants of Togarmah. Togarmah is historically equivalent to the Tokharians. In the last century these were identified with the speakers of Tokharian who lived in the northwestern extreme of China. Scholars are now skeptical about this, but it's probable that this is correct and that they are also ancestral to various central Asian people as well (Turks, Afghans, Kazakhs, etc.).

We know that some of the Celts, the Welsh, still use the name of Gomer in the name of their people, *Cymru*. But even aside from that, we have to account for the Celts somewhere; it makes more sense for them to be closely related to the Germanic peoples than otherwise. In fact the Celts inhabited the central belt of Europe. Right in the center of that central belt in what is now Switzerland, there was an ancient Roman province called Raetia. It was called Raetia because it was inhabited by a people called *Raeti* by the Romans.

This name *Raeti* looks suspiciously like it can be linguistically derived from the name *Riphath* (for reasons we will see in the next chapter), suggesting that Riphath was ancestral to the Celts.

Magog seems to have its closest geographic analogue in Magyar, the Hungarians' name for themselves and possibly the Mongols. This points to Magog being ancestral to speakers of Uralic languages; that is, not only to the Finnish, Estonians, Lapps, and Hungarians, but also Samoyeds and peoples of northern and northeastern Asia.

This seems to be corroborated by recent genetic research (Cavalli-Sforza

---

[2]Another example of aspiration of a voiceless stop in a borrowed word in Greek. Evidence from Tokharian suggests that there was no voicing distinction in Tokharian; hence the *Togar-* of *Togarmah* would have been *Tokar-* to the Tokharians themselves. This, in turn, was borrowed by the Greeks as *Tokharoi*.

1994:119), which shows that Northeast Asians are actually more closely related to Europeans than to Southeast Asians.

Madai is straightforwardly ancestral to the Medes. This would connect them to at least some of the ancestors, not only of Iran, but of the Indian subcontinent, at least in the north.

Tiras connects to a variety of peoples in the Mediterranean with the initial *Tir-* in their names. Turrhenians, the Greek name for the Etruscans, may be among these. And interestingly, the Etruscan name for themselves according to Ovid was *Rasna* or *Rasenna*, suggestive of the *-ras* element in *Tiras*. Some form like **Tiras(e)na* may be behind Greek Tyrsenoi and Tyrrhenoi (Τυρσηνοι and Τυρρηνοι, respectively). Another people with a similar name are the Thracians (Gk Θρᾷκες). The root Thrak- could be from Trak-, which in turn could be related to Tiras.

Tubal is attested in the ancient Anatolian kingdom of Tabal. In more recent times it is attested in the name of the city Tblisi, the captial of the Republic of Georgia, suggesting the eventual settlement of Tubal was in what is now the Republic of Georgia.

Javan is clearly ancestral to the Greeks. The authentic pronunciation of the name is /yawan/so that *Yawan* became Yōn, in Greek spelled Iōn (Ἴων), which is, of course, the root of the names for Ionia and the Ionians (Ἴωνες). The Greeks themselves wrote of a man Iōn, who was ancestor of the Ionians, and this was no doubt the preserved history/memory of the patriarch Javan. Of course the word *Ionians* referred to just a part of the Greeks, and *Ionia* refers today to a very small island of Greece; but originally, *Ion* referred to the ancestor of all the Greeks. And his sons were Elishah, Tarshish, Kittim, and Dodanim.

It is here that we find something in the Table of Nations that we're going to see more of when we talk about the sons of Ham. Two of the names listed among Javan's descendants are not names of people: Kittim and Dodanim. Why is that? Because they end in the letters *-im*, which doesn't absolutely guarantee that they're not the names of a person, but they're probably not. The *-im* is a plural suffix in Hebrew and the names *Kittim* and *Dodanim* simply mean, respectively, Kittites and Dodanites.

It doesn't mean that they were descended from somebody named Kitt and Dodan, either. *Kitt* is an ancient name for the island of Cyprus. So the Kittim refers to those descendants of Javan who lived on Cyprus and Dodanim would be associated with the island of Rhodes. Those names don't have to be from the names of people; they could have been descriptive place names to begin with. The fact that they're given in the plural—in effect, "Javan was the ancestor of the

Kittites,"—indicates that they were not descended from a single common ancestor after Javan, or the Bible would give the name of that man. Rather, these are from an assortment of different Greek clans or tribes who mixed together and gathered their identity from the island they settled on, or from the region that they inhabited, rather than from their ancestry.

But two other names are given: Elishah and Tarshish. There aren't plural endings on those names and they may actually be the names of individual sons. Elishah, of course is connected to the Greek name Elis, the city that was the home of the original Olympic games. Tarshish is related to the name Tartessos, a Greek outpost in what is now southern Spain.

So the Greeks originally inhabited much of the northern coast of the Mediterranean from southern Spain to Sicily to the Greek mainland to Cyprus. Because Kittim and Dodanim were not each from a single eponymous ancestor, that means they were not one of the original people groups that were separated at the confusion of tongues. And if they weren't, it's quite possible (though not at all certain) that Elishah and Tarshish were not as well. In fact the Greeks did maintain a cohesive identity throughout the Mediterranean and when they spread out through that region they were all speaking different dialects of Greek. So it seems as though Elishah and Tarshish, much less the Kittim and Dodanim were not speaking different languages. All of Javan had the same cultural identity. [3]

There ends the genealogy of Japheth. Now we move on to the genealogy of Ham.

Ham right away confronts us with this issue we considered earlier with the Greeks. If there is a name of descendants in this genealogy that ends in *-im*, that's either a dual or plural suffix in Hebrew. In that event, it refers to 'X-ites' and those X-ites aren't descendants of a common ancestor after the given patriarch. This presents itself in the first generation of Ham, which is very unusual.

We have in the first generation after Ham: Phut, Cush, Canaan, and then Mizraim. That last name ends in a dual suffix in Hebrew, so what we have here is the dual of *mizra. Mizra* simply means 'the border(land)' in Hebrew, referring to the fact that Egypt borders Israel. Even in Arabic up to today, the word for Egypt is *al-Misra.* So that part of it, *Mizra-* is not the name of some eponymous ancestor, it's simply the word for Egypt based on its geography. It's in the dual because there were originally two kingdoms of Egypt, the northern and the southern kingdoms which were eventually united. These verses are saying, "the sons of

---

[3]But again, this is not certain. It is possible that they were distinct culturally, if the Kittim and Dodanim appeared *after* the Indo-Europeanization of the Greeks.

Ham include Cush, and the two Egypts, and Phut and Canaan." Furthermore, Mizra is a Hebrew word and as we shall see in Chapter 12, these people weren't speaking Hebrew.

If the Egyptians did not have a common ancestor, it means the Egyptians were not one of the groups that was scattered from Babel. They were a national identity that arose after that. This falls in line with a common belief among scholars today[4] that Egypt was from the beginning a kind of multi-ethnic, multinational concern. It was never a tribalistic society; it was an international society with a global vision, which is of course very similar to the vision of Babel. The Egyptians seem to be the earliest people to preserve the high degree of technology and civilization that would have existed in the city of Babel, carried

Figure 12. Egyptian wall painting depicting the four principle classical ethnic groups of Egypt: in order of sequence from top, Egyptians, Canaanites, Nubians, and Libyans or Berbers.

over from Noah and his family leaving the ark. The immediate descendants of Noah still had memory of the original world that they had left behind. They weren't primitives by any means; on the contrary, they were very advanced in their understanding of technology and civilization. That knowledge was lost by many peoples after they were scattered, but the peoples that seemed to preserve it the best were the Sumerians and the Egyptians.

The Egyptians seemed not only to preserve the sense of civilization, but also the very global vision that the original builders of Babel had to unite all the peoples of the world into one great kingdom.

Interestingly, the Egyptians themselves left behind a painting of what they perceived as the main groups of their world.

There are four groups; and these four correspond pretty well with the four sons of Ham. Each group is represented as four men walking: one group is

---

[4]See Berlinerblau (1999). For the controversy surrounding this issue see Bernal (1987) and Lefkowitz (1996).

Nubian, corresponding to Cush; one is Lybian (or Berber), representing the descendants of Phut; one is Canaanite representing, of course, the descendants of Canaan; and the other is Egyptian. Even looking at how they're represented on that painting gives us an idea that the Egyptians were a mixture of all these other three. There were three groups: the Cushites, the Phutites, the Canaanites, and then the amalgam of these three groups was the multiethnic group called Egypt.[5]

Havilah? Sabtah? We have those names in extra-biblical Greek writings—and Raamah, too. In fact, the people Raamah were right there in the Gulf Coast; they never really moved to Africa. But we find those names Raamah, Sheba, Dedan, in ancient records there in the Persian Gulf, Raamah in the name of Ra'ma in Southwestern Arabia and possibly in the name of the town of Regma or Regina in southeastern Arabia (A.S. Fulton). Dedan is seen in the name of the island of Dadan off the Persian Gulf (James Orr, International Bible Dictionary).

The Havilahites probably are the ancestors of the inhabitants of the kingdom of Kush themselves: the Sudanese, the Ethiopians, and so forth.

Seba, we know from the writings of Josephus[6] lived roughly in the Sahara or in what is now northern Chad, and was known to the classic writers as Sabas. The only name that's conspicuous by its absence is Sabtechah.

Sabtah may be reflected in the name of the city Saubatha in eastern Yemen, but more likely, it is found in the names of multiple tribes like Sotho, Swati, Sutu, etc. Also possibly the source of the name of Sabaiticum Ostium. While also resembling Sabtechah, the -ic- here is probably the derivative adjectival suffix -ic- borrowed from Greek (as with also English Asiatic, Arctic, etc.). If this is so, Sabtah could be ancestral to peoples of Eastern and Southern Africa.

Raamah settled on the Persian Gulf and I suspect strongly that 1) they were ancestral to the Sumerians and 2) they migrated eastward and were ancestral to the east Asians. Why do I say that? First of all, Raamah, Sheba, especially Sheba and Dedan are identified there in the Persian Gulf. Also all other sons of Cush are accounted for elsewhere; Sumerians can't be from Japheth because all of Japheth's and Shem's descendants are accounted for elsewhere except for Asshur; but the Assyrians are explicitly described in the Table of Nations as different from the Sumerians. Finally, Nimrod is referred to as a descendant of Cush (more about Nimrod later). And Nimrod's name is almost unmistakably Sumerian in it's

---

[5] Of course it could also be that Egyptians were descended from two or more *other* sons of Ham besides the three others mentioned.
[6] *Antiquities*, 1.6.134,135.

phonological shape.[7] So Nimrod is almost certainly Sumerian and a descendant of Cush. The Sumerians then are evidently descended from Cush and Raamah is right there where the Sumerians were. It seems to be a pretty good fit; Raamah—and either Sheba or Dedan—seems to be the ancestor of the Sumerians. And they moved further eastward over the Indian subcontinent; there's an area between Afghanistan and Pakistan, that to this day is still called Hindu Kush. That is to say, "Kush in India," Indian Kush. This

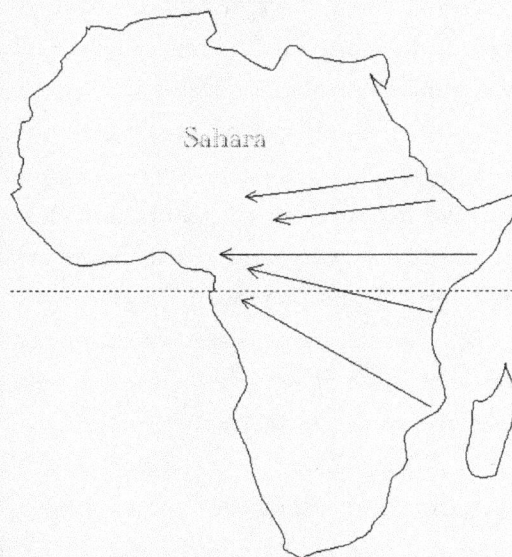

Figure 13. General map of Africa. Note how the physical shape of the continent, together with the at least eventual pressures of the Sahara compel westward migration from a wide variety of points of origin into a relatively narrow area, resulting in very complex language mixing and metacreolization.

almost certainly reflects that people there were descended from Cush, through people who had a close common ancestry with the Sumerians.

For Sabtechah there is no certain correllary—possibly (if only by process of elimination) they may be seen as ancestral to peoples of western and central Africa.

But one thing is for sure: there seems to have been a general pattern of migration from all parts of the eastern half of Africa into western Africa and the very shape of the continent acts as a kind of geographic funnel. If we continue moving westward we end up moving into the region north of the Gulf of Guinea and south of the Sahara. That's a very narrow region compared with the whole eastern seaboard of the African continent. Consequently many people from many different backgrounds, languages, and places all merged together in west Africa.

Now we return to Nimrod. After all this genealogy, it says, "And Cush begat Nimrod. He began to be a mighty one in the earth." Lots of people, too many

---

[7]Of various etymologies for this name, most convincing is William F. Albright's interpreting Nimrod as < *Ni-Marad < *Nin-Marad 'Lord of Marad,' i.e. Lugalbanda of Sumerian literature. For a more thorough treatment on Sumerian etymologies of *Nimrod*, see Appendix 7.

people in fact, have interpreted this to mean that Nimrod was a son, in the twentieth century sense, of the man Cush. And that's not true.

There are two principle reasons why that cannot be the case. First, Nimrod is not listed with the other sons of Cush. Sabtechah is the last son of Cush listed. After Sabtechah it moves on to the next generation. So Seba through Sabtechah is an exhaustive list of the first generation of sons of Cush. Second, Nimrod lived after the confusion of tongues. His name is clearly Sumerian and Sumerian is a language prime. If he had been Cush's son in the modern sense, he would not have had a Sumerian name, since the Sumerian language didn't exist at that time.

Then why does it say that Cush begot Nimrod? Because 'to beget' in the biblical sense can mean 'to be the (male) ancestor of'. For example, Matthew 1:11 says, "And Josias begat Jechonias [Jehoiachin]," when in fact Josiah begot Jehoiakim and Jehoiakim begot Jehoiachin. But this is all the same in the Bible. Jesus is the Son of David and the Son of Abraham (Matt 1:1). There is this passage in Hebrews (Hebrews 7:9,10):

> And as I may so say, Levi also, who receiveth tithes, payed tithes in Abraham.
> For he was yet in the loins of his father, when Melchisedec met him.

Other such cases abound: "And Amram took him Jochebed his father's sister to wife; and she bare him Aaron and Moses: and the years of the life of Amram were an hundred and thirty and seven years."(Ex 6:20) This statement is given when we know from other scriptures that Amram can't have been the immediate father of Moses.[8]

> "These are the sons of Zilpah, whom Laban gave to Leah his daughter, and these she bare unto Jacob, even sixteen souls."[Gen 46:18]

---

[8] If Amram had been Moses' direct father, there would have been four generations from Jacob to Moses, whereas there were eleven generations from Jacob to Joshua. Moreover there were 430 years from Jacob to Moses. If there were only four generations from Jacob to Moses (Jacob-Levi-Kohath-Amram-Moses) then Moses was born 350 years after his grandfather, a mathematical impossibility (Kohath lived 133 years (Ex. 6:18) and Amram 137 (Ex 6:20)). Moreover if Kohath was Moses' grandfather, then he produced 8600 grandsons by Moses' lifetime (Numbers 3:19,27,28), a biological impossibility. The logical conclusion is that the generations from Kohath to Moses were many more than two, but most are not recorded because of the Omission Principle.

These include Leah's grandsons.

> The sons of Rachel Jacob's wife; Joseph, and Benjamin.
>
> And unto Joseph in the land of Egypt were born Manasseh and Ephraim, which Asenath the daughter of Poti-pherah priest of On bare unto him.
>
> And the sons of Benjamin were Belah, and Becher, and Ashbel, Gera, and Naaman, Ehi, and Rosh, Muppim, and Huppim, and Ard.
>
> These are the sons of Rachel, which were born to Jacob: all the souls were fourteen.
>
> And the sons of Dan; Hushim.
>
> And the sons of Naphtali; Jahzeel, and Guni, and Jezer, and Shillem.
>
> These are the sons of Bilhah, which Laban gave unto Rachel his daughter, and she bare these unto Jacob: all the souls were seven. (Gen 46:19-25)

Again, these include Rachel's and Bilhah's grandsons as "sons".

When we read that so-and-so begot someone it means that so-and-so was the male ancestor of that person. So when it says that Cush begot Nimrod it means that Cush was the ancestor of Nimrod. It's not part of the genealogy in the previous verse; it's rather the introduction to the next passage coming up in the immediately following verses, which is the comment on Nimrod. The whole thing reads as follows:

> And Cush begat Nimrod: he began to be a mighty one in the earth.
>
> He was a mighty hunter before the LORD: wherefore it is said, Even as Nimrod the mighty hunter before the LORD.
>
> And the beginning of his kingdom was Babel, and Erech, and Accad, and Calneh, in the land of Shinar.

> Out of that land went forth Asshur, and builded Nineveh, and the city Rehoboth, and Calah,
>
> And Resen between Nineveh and Calah: the same is a great city. (Genesis10:8-12)

What's all that about? And if it's not part of Cush's genealogy, why is it in Genesis 10? It's talking about Sumer, and later Assyria. Why do they mention Nimrod in particular? Because it says he began to be a mighty one in the earth. We know from archeology that when the Sumerians first built their cities they were a kind of democracy. The people got together and they ran things. This fact fits in very nicely with what happened before the confusion of tongues when we read in chapter eleven:

> And the whole earth was of one language, and of one speech.
>
> And it came to pass, as they journeyed from the east, that they found a plain in the land of Shinar; and they dwelt there.
>
> And *they* said one to another, Go to, let *us* make brick, and burn them throughly. And *they* had brick for stone, and slime had *they* for morter.
>
> And *they* said, Go to, let *us* build *us* a city and a tower, whose top may reach unto heaven; and let *us* make *us* a name, lest *we* be scattered abroad upon the face of the whole earth.
> (Genesis 11:1-4, emphasis added)

So it was the *people* that decided that, *they* came up with that idea. There's a long standing religious tradition that links Nimrod with the Tower of Babel.[9] Nimrod had nothing to do with the Tower of Babel. The Bible says it was the people who decided to build a city and a tower, not Nimrod. Nimrod is nowhere mentioned in this story of Babel.

---

[9] *Antiquities* 1.4.1-3. Josephus' source for extra-biblical claims about Nimrod may have to do with influence from the Gilgamesh Epic. Also the most convincing etymology for Nimrod is Nin-Marad (Appendix 3) and *marad* means 'rebellion' in Hebrew. That is irrelevant of course, since Nimrod and his name were Sumerian, but before the twentieth century nearly all Jewish and Christian scholars believed that Hebrew was the original language.

So why did past writers connect Nimrod with Babel? They figured there had to be a king somewhere, huh? And people were trying to make sense of what appears to be the sudden, jarring appearance of Nimrod in the middle of the Table of Nations. They figured, "There must be something really significant about this guy." And the logical conclusion was, maybe he was part of the Tower of Babel. There are reasons for this. One is that it says he began to be a mighty one in the earth. First of all the whole earth was of one speech when God wanted them to be scattered abroad; this can lead to a picture of the whole earth being under one dictator. Secondly the Bible says he began to be a mighty one in the earth. Maybe "mighty hunter before the LORD" doesn't just mean someone who gets venison, but someone who hunted people, hunted for power. Finally we read, "the beginning of his kingdom was Babel." That seems to make a clear connection.

But this misses some basic logical points. We have to realize that saying, "the beginning of his kingdom was Babel" is not at all the same thing as saying that the beginning of Babel was his kingdom. That's the syllogistic error that people have made in interpreting this scripture. No, the beginning of Babel was not his kingdom. And the Bible does not say only, "the beginning of his kingdom was Babel." It says, "And the beginning of his kingdom was Babel, and Erech, and Accad, and Calneh, in the land of Shinar." (Genesis 10:10) How did he build all those other cities when all the world was scattered away from him? And I have a hard time believing that at the time the city of Babel was built there were so many people alive that they would have built four cities.

In fact what we know about Sumer is that there were individual cities which were all independent and self-governing city states. Later the cities started to clump around strong men. That is to say, one city would dominate over others, and there would be one king ruling over two or three or four cities. Nimrod was one such king. This is what is significant about him: that he was one of the first people in Sumer to rule as a king over other cities, rather than cities governing themselves. That's why his moniker, "a mighty hunter before the Lord" came to be the moniker for other people.

So when we read, "wherefore it is said, Even as Nimrod the mighty hunter before the LORD." (Genesis 10:9b), it might be a proverb, but it might also be a kind of title that was tacked onto a name—just as, for example, the king of Kish at one point in Sumerian history gathered enough prominence that other mighty kings, even when they didn't rule over Kish, were referred to as "King of Kish". That was just one way of saying this was one big powerful king. This may be what this passage is explaining: the institution of kingship in Sumer—and by extension the beginning of kingship in the postdiluvian world.

The fact that "the beginning of his kingdom was Babel and Erech and Accad, and Calneh in the land of Shinar," also makes very plain the fact that Nimrod was a Sumerian and led a Sumerian dynasty. Erech we know was a Sumerian city; Accad is where the word Accadian comes from, it was a Sumerian city; Babel definitely was originally a Sumerian city; Shinar in fact is the same as Sumer. Nimrod was one of the first Sumerian kings. Nimrod only came on the scene long after the Tower of Babel had been attempted to be built, long after the tongues were confused and the nations were scattered.

"Out of that land went forth Assher"—of course that's exactly what happened: Assher is the nation of Assyria. The Assyrians did in fact invade Sumer "and builded Nineveh, and the city Rehoboth, and Calah." (10:11b) So this is an important summary of the beginning of all these violent militaristic dictatorships that we call kingdoms and dynasties in the ancient Near East. That's the purpose of this little interruption. It has nothing to do with the building of the Tower of Babel.

The genealogy of Ham continues with Mizraim, which as we've already seen is not a single individual human being, or even originally a single, homogenous ethnic group, but different ethnicities amalgamated into two kingdoms. And it does go on to say, not surprisingly, therefore, that the descendants of the Mizraim are not listed as individual human beings either, but as more tribes (indicated by the suffix -*im*).

> And Mizraim begat Ludim, and Anamim, and Lehabim, and Naphtuhim,
>
> And Pathrusim, and Casluhim, (out of whom came Philistim,) and Caphtorim. (Genesis 10:13,14)

Interestingly most of these are peoples who lived *outside* of the land of Egypt. For example, Ludim refers to the Lydians who lived in Anatolia, or Asia Minor, what we now call western Turkey.[10] Lehabim, otherwise known as the ancient Lybians, lived west of the land of Egypt in what is now Lybia. We don't know much about the Casluhim, except that the Bible does say that out of that tribe came the Philistim—that's the Philistines. These of course were the so-called Sea People, the people who traveled along like vikings of the ancient eastern

---

[10]This also explains where some of the Afroasiatic influences on the Anatolian languages came from.

Mediterranean coast, raping, pillaging, conquering and so forth. And of course the Philistines gave the Israelites a whole lot of trouble because Israel was on the eastern coast of the Mediterranean. The Caphtorim are the Minoans, Caphtor being the ancient name of Crete,[11] and Crete was the cradle of Minoan civilization that spread also to Thera and other places in the Mediterranean. They were descended from Egypt, which coincides very nicely with the fact that Minoan civilization has been linked with the legendary civilization of Atlantis. Plato, writing about Atlantis, says that they were allied with Egypt. This passage in Genesis gives the underlying fact behind Plato's "alliance": more than allies, the Egyptians and Minoans were relatives. So this amalgam of peoples that made up the two kingdoms of Egypt went on to spawn lots of colonies that became kingdoms and ethnic groups of their own.

There are some groups of Mizraim here that are mentioned that lived within the borders of Egypt as well: the Anamim, the Naphtuhim, and the Pathrusim (who inhabited Pathros). All the others, though, are peoples that we don't think of as Egyptian, but who developed their identities outside of Egypt.

The name *Phut* is probably the same as the Ancient Egyptian name *Pitu*, which referred to the ancient people to the west of Egypt whose descendants today are called Berbers.

Canaan begot Sidon, his first born, and Heth. Sidon was ancestor to the Phoenicians in what is now Lebanon. Heth was ancestral to the Hittites, who lived in Turkey, but also in Syria.

> And the Jebusite, and the Amorite, and the Girgasite,
>
> And the Hivite, and the Arkite, and the Sinite,
>
> And the Arvadite, and the Zemarite, and the Hamathite: and afterward were the families of the Canaanites spread abroad. (Genesis 10:16-18)

The tribal names above derive from names of places, not patriarchs. The Sinites weren't descended from someone named Sin, but from their living in/around Sinai or the wilderness of Sin. So of all the descendants of Canaan the only two we know who appear to have been actual men were Sidon and Heth. Whatever other sons Canaan may or may not have had, did not beget specific

---

[11]This is a clear demonstration of the fact that these peoples—Caphtorim, Pathrusim, and so on—were named not from common ancestors, but from the names of the places that they inhabited.

tribal/ethnic groups. Rather their descendants all blended together into a single cultural continuum, which separated and identified themselves only by the geographic place where they settled. If you settled in Jebus you were a Jebusite, if you settled near Sin you were a Sinite, and so forth. They probably adopted an Afroasiatic language, namely Proto-Canaanitic, simply because of the influence of Egypt over the whole Mediterranean world.

> And the border of the Canaanites was from Sidon, as thou comest to Gerar, unto Gaza; as thou goest, unto Sodom, and Gomorrah, and Admah, and Zeboim, even unto Lasha.

> These are the sons of Ham, after their families, after their tongues, in their countries, and in their nations. (Genesis 10:19,20)

Curiously enough it is Shem's genealogy that reveals something significant about Japheth. It is significant in what it tells us about biblical genealogies in general.

> Unto Shem also, the father of all the children of Eber, the brother of Japheth the elder, even to him were children born. (Genesis 10:21)

The sons of Noah are always listed in the same order: Shem, Ham, and Japheth (Gen 5:32; 6:10; 10:1; also 1 Chr 1:1). If they were listed in order of birth, that would mean Japheth was the youngest son. Yet in Gen 10:21 it refers to Shem as the brother of "Japheth the elder". Japheth is listed last, not in age, but in importance for sacred history. Shem is listed first in the genealogy of Noah because he's the most important. Abraham and all of his sons, including the Israelites and the Ishmaelites, all come from Shem. Ham is the next most important in a somewhat negative way because the Philistines, the Egyptians (and partly therefore the Ishmaelites), and the Canaanites, including the Hittites, all come from Ham. And then there's the other guy: Japheth the elder. Elder or not, he's mostly nowhere when it comes to sacred history, at least during the time when the Bible was written, so he's listed last.

Some think Lud was the ancestor of the Lydians, but we've already seen that the Lydians were descended from the Ludim from Egypt. On the other hand, the various groups descended from Mizraim are mostly or entirely named after places:

Pathrusim from Pathros, for example. So Lud may have been ancestral to the Lydians and the Ludim from Egypt were later immigrants to the land of Lud. At the same time, it may well be also that Lud was the ancestor of the Lurs, one of the original ethnic groups in Iran, who to this day consider themselves an ethnic "nationality" unto themselves.

Elam was very straightforwardly the ancestor of the Elamites, an ancient empire in what is now Iran. As such Elam was an ancestor of modern Iranians (as was Madai). Based on linguistic evidence to be discussed further in Chapter 12, the descendants of Elam also migrated into what is modern India and are ancestral to the Tamils and other Dravidian ethnic groups of southern India. Additionally, Elam may be partly ancestral to the indigenous population of Australia and to peoples of southeast Asia.

It seems likely that the four sons of Aram are all end points, but the name Aram itself is reflected in the names *Aramean* and *Aramaic.* Of the four sons, only Hul has a fairly clear extra-biblical homologue: the Hurrians, which in turn are associated with the later civilization at Urartu. Gether seems to be the ancestor to the Guterites, Mash with the area of Mount Mashu in Sumerian writings (the Mons Masius in Strabo), Uz perhaps with the land of Uz which was near Edom, east of Israel.

For Arphaxad (Arpachshad) the closest geographic homologue is *Arphachiya,* an ancient settlement about four miles from Niniveh. After that the nearest resembling name we have is *Abkhaz,* an ethnic group in the Caucasus mountains near northern Syria. They live in a region near a handful of ancient towns with names like Haran, Terah, and Nahor. Since Abraham's ancestry came from Arphaxad, this seems to be a good fit.

Another descendent of Arphaxad was Peleg. Peleg's brother's name is Joktan—in the original language *Yoqtan*—and from that name we get the name of the Qahtani Arabs who live on the Gulf Coast of the Arabian Sea and the Gulf States. So the Kuwaitis, the Yemenis, all the peoples of the Gulf states are descendants of Joktan. And if we look at his name, not only does it mean something in an Afroasiatic language[12], but it says

> And Joktan begat Almodad, and Sheleph, and Hazar-maveth, and Jerah,
> And Hadoram, and Uzal, and Diklah,

---

[12]The name *Joktan* is the active form of the verb *qaton* meaning 'be small,' 'insignificant'. The name means 'he will be (made) small, insignificant'. (Strong, (1996:394)).

And Obal, and Abimael, and Sheba,
And Ophir, and Havilah, and Jobab: all these were the sons of
Joktan. (Genesis 10:26-29)

The table of nations has not been directly connected to every single ethnic group in the world, but the descendants listed in the table of nations do account for those populations by mixing together.

Elam and Raamah ⇒Dravidians, Native Australians

Raamah and Magog ⇒East Asians, Yupik, Inupiat

East Asians and South Asians ⇒Southeast Asians

Australians and Southeast Asians ⇒Pacific Islanders

Southeast Asians and Pacific Islanders ⇒Native Americans

This would be a good place to discuss the language of people of the earth from the time of Adam to the time of Noah and the languages after the flood.

12
The Confusion of Tongues

"Because without our language, we have lost ourselves. Who are
we without our words?"
— Melina Marchetta, *Finnikin of the Rock*

What was the original human language? That is a question which has enticed
people for centuries and for a very understandable reason: it's another origins
question. Looking for the original human language gives a sense of story and a
sense of foundation, a sense of grounding: we know where we came from; we
know what we spoke. And language is so integral to what it means to be human,
that to understand the original human language is a lot like understanding the
original human state.

So people have always wanted to know what the original human language was.
People who have believed the Bible have advanced the idea that Hebrew was the
original language. This is for the simple reason that as near as anyone can tell,
Hebrew was the original language of the Bible. Theories have been advanced
about the Hebrew Bible having been borrowed from Sumerian legend via Hebrew
contact with Babylonian culture—but that theory, though still popular, is actually
quite old and obsolete[1]. The fact remains that the Bible as we have it was originally
composed in Hebrew. And if you believe that that Bible is the inspired word of
God, and its original language was Hebrew, then, so the argument goes, the
language of God must be Hebrew and the original language that God gave
humanity must have been Hebrew.

It turns out that there are problems with that idea. These problems stem from
both what we see and what we believe. First what we see (and hear). The fact of
the matter is that those who have advanced such theories know nothing or next to
nothing about historical linguistics. And they don't know about linguistics itself as
a discipline. One of the basic facts about language is that language changes.
Language is always changing. It could well be argued that the very mechanism that
generates language just as certainly and inevitably generates language change. The

---

[1] P. J. Wiseman, *New Discoveries in Babylonia about Genesis* (1936); republished as *Ancient Records
and the Structure of Genesis* (1985). Also R.K. Harrison, *Introduction to the Old Testament* (1969).

very act of using a language generates change in the system of that language. If language is constantly changing, then it doesn't make sense to say that one language which is spoken today has always been there and was in fact the Original Human Language.

Most people don't recognize that language naturally changes. They see language change as a corruption; that if people were really pure in heart and in mind, and intelligent and diligent and strong in character they would never change their language from generation to generation. That's just not true. If language changes then it doesn't make sense that Hebrew would have been an unchanged language forever and ever. And there are strong reasons for concluding that that was not the case.

Those reasons have to do with the fact that all the names of the postdiluvian patriarchs—all those people that are mentioned in the table of nations—are names which don't mean anything in Hebrew. Ashkenaz, Ripat, Togarmah, Meshech, Lamech—none of these is a Hebrew name. They mean nothing in Hebrew. Why would people speaking Hebrew just make up arbitrary names? If you look these names up in an etymological dictionary, it'll tell you, "probably of foreign origin." It makes sense therefore that the survivors of the flood did not speak Hebrew because they gave their children names that don't mean anything in Hebrew.

Now in a sense we do that today. Most people who speak Western European languages give names to their children that don't really mean anything in their own language because they've changed over time.

But that's an anomaly. For most people names mean something. And in fact Adam's name meant something, Eve's name meant something, Noah's name meant something. So it makes sense that they would give their children names that meant something. But if these names have any meanings at all, they're in a different language than Hebrew. Besides that, independent of any biblical considerations, historical linguistics has determined that the common ancestor of Hebrew, Arabic, Akkadian, and Amharic was Proto-Semitic. Hebrew is not the beginning of the story as far as languages are concerned.

Now it's true that biblical names from Adam to Noah (for the most part[2]) are Hebrew names. So if Hebrew is not the original language then how did all those people have Hebrew names? We might well also ask if they all had Hebrew names and spoke Hebrew, how did they stop speaking Hebrew and stop giving Hebrew names to their children right after the flood? Both those questions actually have

---

[2]Tubal-cain and Lamech being notable exceptions.

the same answer.

A name is more about what the name means than about how the name sounds. This is not true for every culture—it's not true about our culture—but it's true for most cultures. My wife's Yoruba name is Yétúndé. What's significant about that name is not how it sounds, but what it means: "Mother-came-back". She wasn't given that name because it sounded pretty, or because it blended well aesthetically with her last name. She was given that name because it means, "Mother came back." She was born shortly after the death of her father's mother. In Yoruba culture if a girl is born shortly after the death of her father's mother, she's named Mother-came-back because of the traditional belief in reincarnation. The meaning of the name is what's significant, not the sound. In some cultures the meaning is so much more significant than the sound, that when one speaks a different language one translates the name into the language being spoken.

This is, I believe, exactly what has happened in the biblical narrative in the first six chapters of Genesis with the individuals up to and including Noah. Who knows what their names sounded like? That's not important. It's the meaning that's important. God named the first man, Man. And the man named the first woman, Woman. The first man also named the first woman, as the first mother, Giver of Life or Having Life. When Eve had her first son she named him I Have Received, I Have a Possession; that's what the name Cain means. Clearly in each case the pronunciation itself is of no significance whatsoever. As these origin stories were recounted they were recounted with the names translated, until they were written down in Hebrew.

That's why Cain's name is in Hebrew or pre-Hebrew. To us the pronunciation is what's important so we don't translate *Qayin*, even though it has a definite meaning. That's unusual.

The implication of this is that Noah's name, for all we know, could have been *Shubachak'le*. That could have been the actual pronunciation of his name. Or *Hembererr*. We don't know how it was pronounced. But translated into ancient or pre-Hebrew it was *Noah* meaning, 'Rest', or perhaps from a longer name meaning, 'He Has Given Us Rest'.

When we come to the table of nations on the other hand, it's a different matter. We don't care about what those names mean because there's no story behind the grandchildren and later descendants of Noah. Ashkenaz, for example, presumably means something in some language, but who cares? It doesn't matter because we don't know anything about him or his life and the Bible says virtually nothing about his descendants. If we did know what his name meant, it still wouldn't be relevant to us.

But if we know how it is pronounced, we can actually trace where that name shows up in history and in geography and the names of peoples. We can say, "Sure enough, there are the descendants of Ashkenaz today." The same with all the descendants of Noah. From that point on, the sound of the names is just as important as, if not more important than, the meaning of the name. Once we move on to Abram, we're dealing with Semitic names anyway, so the Hebrew text gives both the accurate pronunciation and the meaning of the name.

The names of Noah's sons, Shem, Ham, and Japheth, actually appear to be like those of their descendants (like the Ashkenaz example above). Many have thought that these names were Hebrew (making an unbroken chain of Hebrew names from Adam to David, strengthening the idea that Hebrew was the original human language). But it appears that Shem, Ham, and Japheth are not Hebrew names. Why do I say that? After all, Shem is a word in Hebrew: it means 'name'. And *Ham* (Kham) means something in Hebrew: 'hot'. *Japheth* (Yapet) has at least been linked to a couple of different Hebrew roots: more commonly with the root meaning 'to expand', and Japheth's lineage certainly expanded; but also with a root meaning 'fair' (the etymology preferred by the race-obsessed).

But we can tell that these are not Hebrew names for a couple of reasons. For one thing, if these are Hebrew names, they're severely truncated. They don't make any sense on their own: would you name *your* kid Hot? Would you name your kid *Name*? That one's really wack-o. "What do we name our son?" "Let's name him Name." He may have been the youngest one so one could claim that they ran out of names and said, "Let's just call him Name. I can't think of a name so let's just name him Name." No, I don't think so.

"Oh, Name! Name! Dinner's ready, come home, Name!" "How many times do I have to call you, Name? Didn't you hear your name, Name?" Sound absurd? Oh, yes. It does.

It's likely then that this is a coincidence. After all, if we're dealing with names that are monosyllables, that start with a consonant, end with a consonant, and have a vowel in the middle, what are the chances that it's going to sound like a Hebrew word? *Ham* is a word in English, too, but it's not an English name. *Shem* is nearly identical to English *shame*. And it would fit, right? We could say Ham was named Ham because he was such a ham (or such a pig) about the way he reacted to his father's nakedness, while Shem was different because he showed shame about it.

Obviously that's not where these names came from, so the fact that *Ham* and

Shem happen to sound like a couple of Hebrew words that don't work as names doesn't mean they are Hebrew names. *Yapet* kind of looks Hebrew, but it hasn't convincingly been connected with any Hebrew root. Two have been advanced: one meaning 'to expand', the other 'fair'. It's not obviously one root or the other, and it may just be coincidence that it sounds a little bit like either one.[3]

Another clue to this is that for reasons we have already examined, the language of Noah and his sons couldn't have been Hebrew. Therefore their names couldn't have been Hebrew. Yet those names do show up in other parts of the globe. The Egyptian word for themselves was *Kemet*, straightforwardly related to *Ham (Kham)*. The Greeks, who were descended from Japheth, believed the father of all mankind was a man (or giant or titan) named *Iapetos*, clearly from Japheth (Yapet). And, sure enough, Japheth was the father of all mankind from the Greek point of view. This clearly goes back to the story of Noah and his sons.

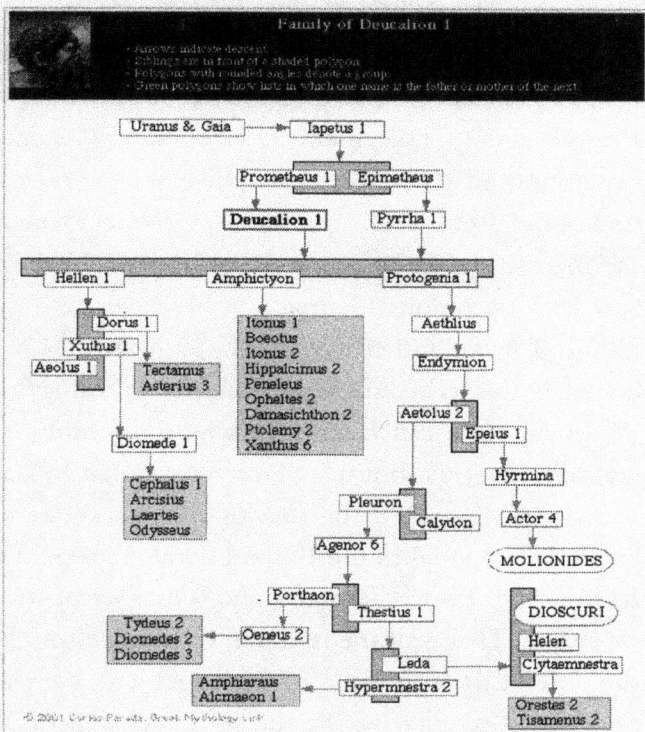

Figure 14: Greek mythological view of Iapetos. Note that the Greek Noah, *Deucalion*, is actually descended from Iapetos.

Family of Deucalion 1

- Arrows indicate descent
- Siblings are in front of a shaded polygon
- Polygons with rounded corners denote a group
- Green polygons show lists in which one name is the father or mother of the next

Uranus & Gaia ----- Iapetus 1
Prometheus 1 — Epimetheus
Deucalion 1 — Pyrrha 1
Hellen 1 — Amphictyon — Protogenia 1
Dorus 1 | Itonus 1, Boeotus, Itonus 2, Hippalcimus 2, Peneleus, Ophaltes 2, Damasichthon 2, Ptolemy 2, Xanthus 6 | Aethlius
Xuthus 1
Aeolus 1 | Tectamus Asterius 3 | Endymion
Diomede 1 | Aetolus 2 — Epeius 1
Cephalus 1, Arcisius, Laertes, Odysseus | Pleuron — Calydon | Hyrmina — Actor 4
Agenor 6 | MOLIONIDES
Porthaon — Thestius 1 | DIOSCURI
Tydeus 2, Diomedes 2, Diomedes 3 — Oeneus 2 | Leda | Helen, Clytaemnestra
Amphiaraus Alcmaeon 1 — Hypermnestra 2 | Orestes 2, Tisamenus 2
© 2001 Carlos Parada. Greek Mythology Link

---

[3] "Japheth is the one name among those found in the narratives of Genesis 6-9 which has neither a West Semitic etymology nor an onomastic environment. Unlike Ham's son Canaan, it has no comparison with place names, either. Thus we must look elsewhere for a source for this name. Neiman (1973) observes the origin of the descendants of Japheth in the Table of Nations as located in the region of Hellas and the islands of the Aegean Sea (p.122). Whether every group mentioned can be so located is beside the point. We have sufficient evidence in the preponderance of place names and gentilics to seek Japheth among the Greeks and their ancestors. It is there that Neiman finds a comparable name in Iapetos, the Titan father of Prometheus and the progenitor of Humanity. The figure already appears in Homer's Iliad (VIII, 479) and in Hesiod's Theogony." (Hess,1993:31).

A most remarkable occurrence of Japheth's name was revealed in a very back-handed way by Bill Cooper, author of an online book entitled *After the Flood*. In it he attempts to trace the table of nations to our own time. His method is to examine ancient genealogies written shortly after the Christianization of Western Europe and to take them at face value. Generally these were genealogies that superimposed Biblical genealogies from the new religion (Christianity) onto oral traditions. One such genealogy Cooper extracts from the *Historia Brittonum* ascribed to the ninth century Welsh monk Nennius. The names in this genealogy that lead to various Germanic tribes begin as follows: Noah father of Iapheth, father of Iavan, father of Iobaath, father of Baath. Cooper takes this at face value, believing this to be an authentic partial genealogy of Japheth.

In fact one can clearly see where the biblical names end and the traditional genealogy begins. But what he misses is that Iobaath, regarded in the *Historia* (and in Cooper's book) to be one of the descendants of Japheth, is in fact Japheth himself. If one takes the Biblical name *Yapet* and applied the sound change rules from PIE to Proto-Germanic and West Germanic, *Yobāth* is exactly what the result would be. That is, if the tradition of an ancestor named *Yapet* were preserved from the time of the confusion of languages and afterward by the Germanic tribes then one would predict exactly the pronunciation of *Yobāth* by the time of writing in Germanic languages. Sound change rules that have been independently discovered and which consistently applied throughout Germanic vocabulary apply here.
The change would be something like this: Yapēt > Yafēth > Yōvāth >Yōbāth (spelled *Iobaath* in the *Historia*).

And this is not a translation, either. These are not translations of ancient names into Hebrew. Clearly long before Moses' time, right from the flood, these names had passed on from generation to generation down to the ancients of India and of Greece and Northern Europe. So these were the original names of Shem, Ham, and Japheth and they have to be in the same language as Ashkenaz and Gomer and so forth, coincidentally sounding *something* like Hebrew, but not meaning the same thing.[4]

So the original language of Noah is probably lost forever. God might have kept the original language for one of the groups of people that were scattered

---

[4]Interestingly, in stories of a universal flood that appear in Eurasia, the names of Noah's sons appear in the same pronunciation as in Genesis; but the name of Noah himself is not in the Hebrew pronunciation, but a phrasal name in the language of the area. So for example, the Sanskrit Noah is *Satyavarman*, 'Keeper of Truth'; in Greek, *Deucalion* 'Sweet Fisher'; in Babylonian, *Utnapishtim* 'He Found Life' or 'He Who Saw Life'; in Sumerian, *Ziusudra* 'Length of Life'.

abroad, or He might not have, so that all of the languages were new and the original language was lost completely. So far the latter seems to be the case. Nobody can translate these names and if we knew the original language(s) that the names are from, we would be able to translate them. But in spite of our

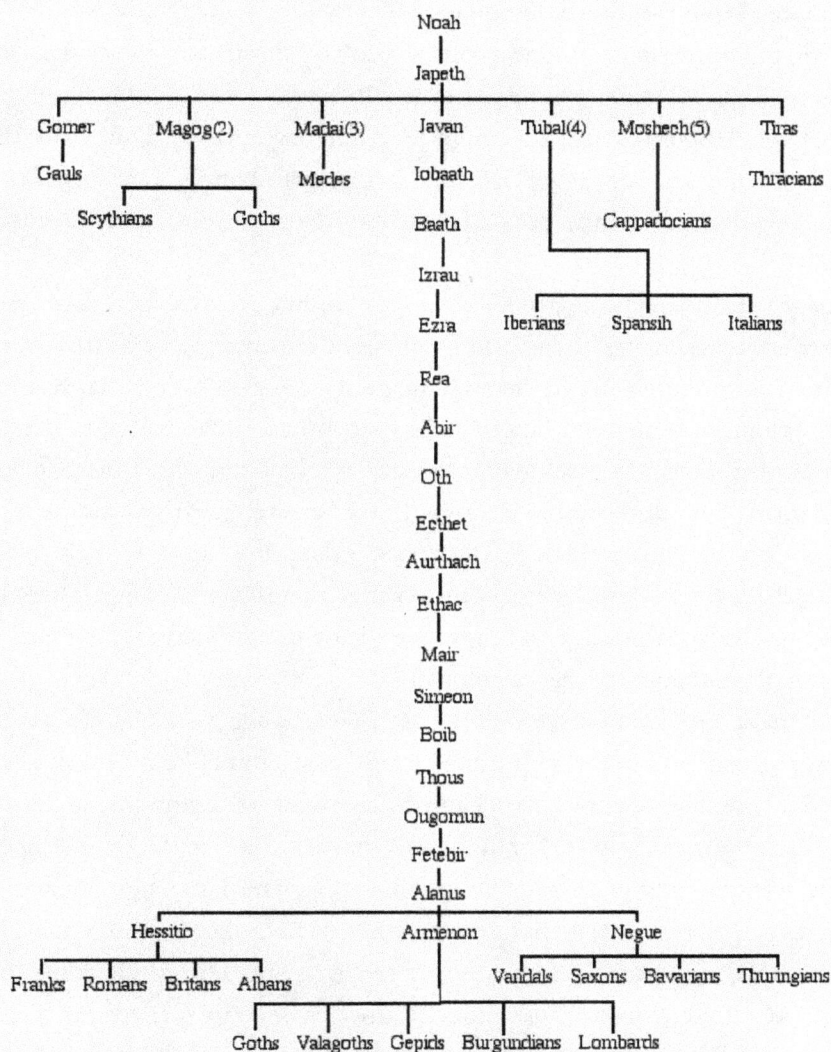

Figure 15: the Biblically influenced mythical Germanic genealogy, showing both Biblical Japheth and traditional Iobaath, himself from Biblical Japheth

knowledge of all the original languages (admittedly very limited knowledge in some cases), these names remain untranslated. So it appears that the language of Noah was lost forever, ever since the confusion of tongues.

That leads to our next subject of inquiry. How were these languages confused? How many languages were there when the languages were confused? What were they? And what have they become today?

Since this chapter necessarily involves a lot of discussion about languages, a few points made in advance will be extremely helpful.

First of all, languages must change. All languages. It is built into the very nature of language and language use that languages change. The popular notion that language change is some sort of corruption or degeneration, is completely incorrect.

Languages do not evolve from "lower to "higher" forms. Likewise languages don't degenerate from "civilized" to "primitive" forms. It is human nature to imagine this is happening in our own language. Every generation that has paid any attention to changes in its own language has attributed such change to degeneracy. This is because language change presents a challenge to the efficiency of communication, an undesirable thing. Furthermore, change happens across generations and an older, more experienced generation is not likely to ascribe superior wisdom to the younger generation that manifests language change. Thus it is human nature combined with ignorance of the inevitability of language change to regard language change as degeneration.

But all these are misperceptions. Languages change the way clouds change. There aren't advanced clouds, primitive clouds, just clouds of different shape and type. When a language changes it isn't improving or degenerating. Just changing.

Secondly language change, for the most part, is very regular. This holds true particularly for changes in pronunciation. In any given language, sounds change with such regularity that these changes are referred to by linguists as sound laws.

For example, English, German, Scandanavian, and Dutch all come from an earlier language called Proto-Germanic (PGmc), which in turn came from a still earlier language which today we call Proto-Indo-European (PIE). As PIE changed to PGmc, all voiceless stops (that is *p*, *t*, and *k*) changed to the consonants called fricatives (*f*, *th* as in *thin*, and *kh*; the *kh* eventually changed to *h*) unless they occurred right after *s* or before *t*. This change didn't just happen in some words and not others, but with every such occurrence of voiceless stops.

Such laws often apply to an entire category or class of sounds in a language (like voiceless stops in the example above) rather than to a single sound. But the same sound laws don't apply to all languages, or all languages would sound the same. Rather, countless sound laws are possible and each language experiences different sound changes at different times.

For example, in the case of the name *Yapet* above, the sound law changing voiceless stops into voiceless fricatives would have changed Yapet to Yafeth. Then a later change turning voiceless fricatives to voiced fricatives at the beginning of a stressed syllable would have changed Yafeth to Yaveth. Furthermore, long *e* (meaning here the vowel sound in the word *name*) would change to a long a (that is the sound "ah" for a slightly long time; something like "ahh") while original *a* would change to *o*. In some dialects a voiced fricative between vowels at the beginning of a stressed syllable would further change to a voiced stop. So Yapēt > Yafēth > Yōvāth >Yōbāth.

Also necessary to a discussion of the confusion of languages is the concept of *language primes*. In the last chapter we defined end points in the Table of Nations.

For example, "And the sons of Ham [were]; Cush, and Mizraim, and Phut, and Canaan." (Genesis 10:6). Phut is an end point. There are no descendants listed after Phut. There were the Phutites with their own, single language. Cush, on the other hand is listed as having five sons: Seba, Havilah, Sabtah, Raamah, and Sabtechah. Every one of those, except for Raamah, is an end point. So I don't believe that all the Cushites lived together and had one language. We know that some of Ham's descendants settled Africa and that Cush is the only "available" descendant of Ham to be the ancestor of sub-Saharan Africans. We also know that the one to two thousand languages of sub-Saharan Africa do not come from one single language. Rather each of those end points was its own nation with its own language, its own identity; Sabtah, Sabtechah, Seba, for example, each was a separate nation with its own language, its own identity; and so with all the other end points.

So, given the fact that each of these end points in this genealogy can be seen as a separate nation or tribe, with it's own language, its own identity, its own history, we can then try to determine what language that group spoke. There is a one-to-one correspondence between endpoint and language. That is, not only did a single tribe or clan get only one language, but each language spoken at the confusion of tongues was "assigned" to only one end point.

If we look at all those end points they turn out to number just under two dozen. That means the mother tongue spoken after the flood was confused into about two dozen languages. That means not only is it the case that Seba, Sabtah, and Sabtechah did not all share the same language; it's also true, in a sense even more clearly true, that Sabtechah did not share a language with Phut. Sabtah did not share a language with Elam, the son of Shem. Sabtechah did not share a language with Tubal, the son of Japheth. So we have to assume that each of these end points had a unique language. We'll call these original languages *language primes*.

This is very significant. Here's just one example of why this is so. There is a language family known as the Afroasiatic language family. That family includes Ancient Egyptian, Coptic, Arabic, Hebrew, also the Cushitic languages, languages like Galla, Somali, and so on. Languages like Galla and Somali are spoken by descendents of Cush (which ones is an issue we can explore further on). Ancient Egyptian was spoken by the Ancient Egyptians who were also descendants of Ham. Arabic and Hebrew are spoken by descendants of Shem. A closely related language or an earlier form from which Hebrew derived was spoken by the Canaanites, who were the descendants of Ham. We could try to reconstruct Proto-Afroasiatic and say this was the language of multiple nations, but then that would mean that all these nations that were scattered away from each other shared the same language at the time that they were scattered. There's no reason why they would be scattered away from each other if they shared the same language. So clearly the ancestors of those people who now speak Afroasiatic languages (Cush, Mizraim, Canaan, Arphaxad, and so forth), didn't all originally speak the same language at the time that they were scattered from the Tower of Babel. They must have spoken different languages.

How God actually confused the languages is an interesting question. When we look at the languages that we can reconstruct that we can propose as being the two dozen or so languages spoken when the languages were confused they have a few things in common even from what little we can reconstruct in the vocabulary lists, and it makes one wonder if there isn't a parallel between the way those languages were formed and the IBO theory of biology (see Chapter 5). That is, we have a common pool of language features and these can be combined and recombined in different ways to form the various languages that God essentially created at the confusion of tongues.

There are occasional similarities in vocabulary in the language primes, and similar parallels may exist in morphology as well as in syntax, but we don't know enough about these language primes to really reconstruct what the original language could have been like. We can, however, tell a fair amount about the language primes and how those languages developed into the languages that we have today.

We will now go through the list of end points and identify the language primes of each.

Of the seven sons of Japheth (Gomer, Magog, Madai, Javan, Tubal, Meshech, and Tiras) four (Gomer, Madai, Javan, and Meshech) are ancestors of people who today all speak Indo-European languages. IE languages can be traced back to a single language, Proto-Indo-European. Of these four, Gomer is not an end point; Gomer has three end points: Ashkenaz, Riphath, and Togarmah, so we're really talking about Madai, Javan, Meshech, Ashkenaz, Riphath, and Togarmah.

In fact, if we review how these groups were traced to their descendants in the previous chapter, they actually match up to groups of people who correspond to branches of the Indo-European language family:

Madai = speakers of Indo-Iranian

Javan = speakers of Greek

Meshech = speakers of Slavic

Ashkenaz = speakers of Germanic

Riphath = speakers of Celtic

Togarmah = speakers of Tokharian

This is born out by how the names have changed through the centuries. Again following regular sound change laws that we know on independent grounds, in most Classical Greek dialects, *w* disappeared. So the *w* in *Yawan* disappeared completely, perhaps influencing the rounding of the *a* on either side of it beforehand, resulting in the name *Iōn* exactly the Greek name for an ancestor of their people and the name of one of their islands.

If we take the name *Ashkenaz* and Indo-Europeanize it, take a native speaker of PIE and have them pronounce *Ashkenaz*, they'd pronounce it something like *Askenas*.[5] Then if we take *Askenas* and change it according to the sound changes that took place from PIE to PGmc we get something like *Askanaz*, or just *Skanaz*. Looking at *Skanaz*, the *-az* ending happens to be identical to the masculine nominative singular suffix in Proto-Germanic and could have been reanalyzed as such, *Skanaz* being reanalyzed as *Skan-az*. Later, in northern dialects of Proto-Germanic, the last *a* would drop out, leaving *Skanz*, which would be pronounced [skandz]. Newly reanalyzed *Skand-z* would have the genitive plural form *Skand-ōn*. The Proto-Germanic word for wetlands was **aujā*.[6] The northern European

---

[5]Because there were no phonemes /š/ or /z/ in PIE as near as we can tell.

[6]Asterisks here indicate a word that is not attested in written records, but can be reconstructed by the methods of historical linguistics.

homeland that the descendants of Ashkenaz settled in was indeed a group of wetlands, the wetlands of the *Skandz* people. And so the Skandz people called it the wetlands of Skandz, or in their tongue, *Skandōnawja*. The Latin spelling for this was Scandinavia.

Likewise, the name of Riphath. As mentioned in Chapter 11, the closest name in antiquity to Riphath is the name of the Raeti, as they were known by the Romans. In Latin, *-i* is the plural suffix as *-oi* was in Classical Greek, so the root of the name is *Raet,* which looks suspiciously like it could be from *Ripat* (the actual pronunciation of Riphath), except for the conspicuous absence of the *p*. It turns out that in Celtic the regular sound changes included the change that PIE *p* disappeared in Celtic (PIE **pH₂tér* 'father' > Old Irish *ath(a)ir* [aθəρ']; **prH₂éy* 'before' > Old Irish *ar;* PIE **epirom* 'back, again' > Old Irish *iar*).

So if a Proto-Celtic speaker had a name like *Ripat* for their tribe, that would quickly become *Riat*, and through lenition and palatalization or metathesis that would easily change from *Riat* to *Rait,* which is the name of this ancient tribe which the Romans recorded, who lived right there in Switzerland, which is where Celts lived.

But we also saw that all these groups could not have spoken the same language at the confusion of tongues. In fact each one of those six end points spoke a language prime: a unique, completely unrelated language and just one of the end points spoke a language like PIE. Then somehow PIE spread to all the other tribes and displaced their original languages. How did that happen? How did that all fit together? Who spoke PIE as their original language? How did it spread? What were the five other original languages that were all displaced? That's part of what we have to figure out.

The original language of Ashkenaz was not PIE; the Germanic people originally spoke a completely unrelated language which has been called Folkish. Because the descendants of Ashkenaz were completely illiterate, and rather primitive, they did not leave any written records in their language. We only know this language existed because of the multitude of words borrowed into PIE when the descendants of Ashkenaz began speaking that language. They did retain nearly one third of basic vocabulary from Folkish which, of course, is not found in any other branch of IE because it comes from a language unique to those people. Words that are borrowed from Folkish that we have are words like *hus, dogga,* and *folk*. This was a definitely thriving language for a while before being completely replaced by a PIE dialect which became PGmc, and evolved into the various Germanic languages.

Until recently people used to think that the language of the Raeti, which is slightly recorded by the Romans, was in fact Celtic. Now there is apparently some evidence that it was not Celtic.[7] This fits with the idea that they had to have had a distinct language. The best fit, based on where the Celts were, and other evidence, suggests that distinct language was Basque. There are three reasons for this. First, Basque stubbornly resists classification with any language; it's clearly a distinct language, a language prime (or descended from a language prime). The Basque live right in the midst of what was once totally Celtic country in the Iberian Peninsula. Before they were backed up into the Pyrenees mountains, Basque speakers lived throughout what is now France and Spain.

Furthermore, as isolated as Basque speakers are, there's virtually no genetic difference between Basque speakers and surrounding populations in France and Spain, who are at least partly descended from Celts. There is of course the famous predominance of Rh⁻factor in the blood of Basque populations, but apart from that there's no genetic difference between the two.[8] These aren't a unique, isolated pocket of people, with a completely different ancestry; these have the same ancestry as people of the surrounding region whose ancestry we know was Celtic.

As for the descendants of Togarmah, their unique language could very well have been Proto-Turkic. So we have the Uzbeks, the Kazakhs, the Turkmens, and the Turks themselves descended from Togarmah. In fact the very name Turk can be derived from Togarmah through the application of sound change laws.[9] There was an Indo-European language that did develop among them from the PIE they borrowed This language is today still called Tokharian, which was spoken for a time in northwestern China, exclusively. It's extinct today.

In the previous chapter, we saw that the descendants of Javan were not all individuals, but groups of people: the Kittim and Dodanim, that is, the inhabitants of Kitt (Cyprus) and Dodan or Rodan (Rhodes). This raises the possibility that the generation after Javan in the Table of Nations were not end points.

So it seems as though Elishah and Tarshish, much less the Kittim and Dodanim, were not speaking distinct language primes.[10] The language prime

---

[7]"Raetian language," Encyclopedia Brittanica, 9:898 (1989).

[8]"In Rosser's work, the closest population to the Basques is in Cornwall, followed closely by Wales, Ireland, Scotland, England, Spain, Belgium, Portugal and then northern France." Stephen Oppenheimer (2006:367).

[9]On Tokar from Togarmah see footnote above (number). The process for this could be *Tokar > Toker > Töker > Tökre > Törke > Türke*.

[10]But again, this is not certain. It is possible that they *did* speak different languages, if the Kittim and Dodanim appeared *after* the Indo-Europeanization of the Greeks.

belonged strictly to Javan.

　　　This wasn't PIE, though. Rather, Javan's language was something else. It might have been Etruscan, it might have been something else altogether that we don't know. My hunch is that whatever the language was, it was the language which was written in the script known as Linear A.

Linear A and Linear B are ancient scripts written on tablets found on the island of Crete. Both were undeciphered until 1952 when Michael Ventris discovered that Linear B recorded a dialect of Greek. Linear A remains undeciphered. Scholars speculate that it could be Minoan or Eteocretan. Linear A is found on tablets dating from about 1700 BC to 1600 BC, while Linear B dates from about 1400 BC to about 1150 BC. Some believe Linear B script to be a later development of Linear A script. My supposition is that, since Linear B appears just after the time of the most recent Linear A tablets, Linear A was the original language of the Greeks.

Some of the Javanites adopted IE from the descendants of Meshech, as the Celts did, but some of the descendants of Riphath clearly maintained Basque right up till today. There may have been a series of migrations where one wave had everyone speaking Basque and another wave in which there were Basque speakers who were bilingual in Proto-Celtic and subsequent migrations were more monolingual in Proto-Celtic. The same thing happened in Greece. Greece was subject to several waves of IE (Greek) migration, but in this view, the Greeks would have been more Indo-Europeanized with each new wave, the earlier waves of migration might have been speaking this earlier language so that these two languages may have existed side by side for a while.

If the descendants of Ashkenaz, Riphath, Togarmah, and Javan were not originally IE speakers, the question arises: who were originally IE speakers? PIE no doubt was one of the language primes. Which nation(s) spoke it originally? By process of elimination, it had to be either Madai or Meshech for sure, and probably Meshech.

Madai, being ancestral to the Medes (and probably the Persians as well) and to the ancient invaders of northern India who drove the Dravidians to southern India, were at one time speakers of Proto-Indo-Iranian. But it is not likely that PIE was their language. There are communities of people in the mountains of the Punjab who speak a language isolate called Burushaski. These people are parallel to the speakers of Basque in Western Europe: though isolated from the surrounding area for generations and speaking a language unrelated to any other language spoken in the world, they are nonetheless genetically identical to the surrounding population. The logical conclusion is that their story is parallel to the Basques': As the Basques are the last descendants of Riphath to speak their non-IE language, so the Burushaski are the last of the descendants of Madai to speak their original, non-IE language.

This means that by process of elimination, Meshech must have been the one whose descendants were the original speakers of PIE. This confirms with paleolinguistic and archeological evidence that the original speakers of PIE lived in East Central Europe, right in the heart of the territory inhabited by the descendants of Meshech. Further it has been suggested that the Baltic languages, another branch of IE, originated from language mixing between pre-Slavic and pre-Germanic IE dialects. That means the speakers of these languages were at least partly descended from Meshech; and Baltic languages are particularly conservative syntactically. Finally, there is the interesting fact that Meshech's name occurs in very ancient literature as Mosoch. This is the only patriarchal name which exhibits an e/o variation very reminiscent of the e/o ablaut in PIE.

We have seen a connection between Magog and Magyar, the Hungarian name for themselves. The Hungarian language is a Finno-Ugric language which in turn is part of the larger Uralic language family. Linguistic observation and genetic evidence identify speakers of Uralic as constituting a distinct population both linguistically and biologically and this population seems to correspond to the patriarch Magog. Magog's descendants, then, spoke Proto-Uralic.

Tubal has already been identified with people living in the Republic of Georgia. These are speakers, not only of Georgian, but of several other languages which constitute a language family as distinct as IE or Uralic. This language family is known as Kartvelian, and it's mother tongue, Proto-Kartvelian, was apparently the language of the descendants of Tubal after the confusion of tongues.

Tiras, was traced in Chapter 11 to many ancient and modern peoples: Thracians, Etruscans, Armenians, Romanians. Only one of these groups spoke a language prime: the Etruscans. Etruscan, then, was evidently the language prime spoken by Tiras' descendants.

In Chapter 11 we saw that Egypt was the first kingdom to preserve or recapture the vision of an intertribal state. They identified themselves more by place and loyalty to a king than by lineage. Their origin was after the nations were scattered. So they don't seem to have been descended from a single common ancestor (after Ham) and that means they didn't speak a language prime. They must have borrowed a language from some tribe.

And that raises the question: whose language did the Egyptians speak? Did they borrow from the Canaanites? No, it seems to be the other way around because the Canaanites had their own language prime and that was Hattic. Did they borrow from Cush? Maybe, but there are already so many other language groups from Cush, anyway. By contrast, there is no hint anywhere that the Berbers ever spoke any other language than Berber languages. So Proto-Berber seems to have been Phut's original language. If that is the case, then the direction of influence would have been from Proto-Berber to Egyptian rather than vice versa. After all, the Berbers are referred to by the Egyptians as Lybians. The original Lybians were really an offshoot of the Egyptians (*Lehabim* in the Table of Nations). So there seems to have been a close identity between the Egyptians and the Berbers, maybe at the point of contact with the Lybians or Lehabim---as there was also throughout their history a close connection between the Egyptians and the Cushites. So the Egyptians seem to have been literally a mixture of Cushites, Phutites, and maybe even Canaanites, and they end up with this sort of language derived from Phut, but perhaps containing elements from the original language of Cush[11].

So the conclusion of the matter is that there are at least three actual sons of Ham, and only three that we know of by name: Cush, Phut, and Canaan. Phut is ancestral to the Berbers, who probably spoke Proto-Berber, the original Afroasiatic language, and that lent itself to the Egyptian language, a language spoken by descendants of a mixture of Phutites, Cushites, and Canaanites. This language that arose from that mixture ended up, in turn, being foisted upon the Cushites (Nubians) and the Canaanites through Egyptian domination.

Canaan is recorded as having had two sons that are really individually mentioned: Sidon and Heth. The remaining descendants of Canaan are all described as just tribes: Jebusites, Amorites, Girgasites, Hivites, Arkites, Sinites, Arvadites, Zemarites, and Hamathites. This is just like the Kittim and the Dodanim (and the Mizraim, for that matter).The Canaanites apparently kept no distinct lineages, they just all blended in together. Which, again, suggests that the Canaanites maintained their ethnic and therefore linguistic unity after the confusion of tongues.

As mentioned above, the earliest recorded language of the descendants of Heth was Hattic, which again is a language prime, unrelated to any other language. If Heth's descendants spoke Hattic, then probably all the descendants of Canaan spoke Hattic. Proto-Canaanitic, the language ancestral to the Canaanitic languages,

[11] Again, not to be confused with the Cushitic languages, which are Afroasiatic and related directly to Egyptian, among others.

was apparently a creolized language derived from Egyptian.

As for Cush, they were not a single unified group. In the table of nations he is listed with five sons, and they really are sons. They are Seba, Havilah, Sabtah, Raamah, and Sabtechah. And furthermore, the sons of Raamah are given as Sheba and Dedan. That gives every reason for thinking that these are all end points. Each one of these tribes spoke a different language prime.

In the conventional wisdom of comparative and historical linguistics, all the languages of sub-Saharan Africa are clumped into three large superfamilies, but that classification has come under close scrutiny in recent years; enough so that it can be seen that three language groups do not really take care of all the languages in sub-Saharan Africa; there were probably more than that. But let's go with the three that we know about. There are Niger-Congo or Niger-Kordofanian, Nilo-Saharan, and Khoisan. According to Sands (1998), you can't really relate Khoisan to all languages attributed to it. When we examine Central Khoisan versus the other Khoisan languages, it looks very much like a creole type relationship.[12] My suspicion is that the Central Khoisan languages are the original and the other Khoisan languages are a creolized version of Central Khoisan.

We saw in the previous chapter that the descendants of Seba lived roughly in the Sahara or in what is now northern Chad. That is exactly where Nilo-Saharan (or Chari-Nile) languages are spoken today.

Nilo-Saharan is a large language family one branch of which is the Chari-Nile family of languages. It is not clear whether Nilo-Saharan languages are directly descended from a single language (Proto-Nilo-Saharan), or whether the language prime was Proto-Chari-Nile and the other Nilo-Saharan languages are derived from Chari-Nile by creolization.

Sabtah is probably ancestral to the speakers of Khoisan languages (or Central Khoisan languages) and those seem pretty exotic. It would seem that they would be even farther away from classical writers because they're spoken in southern Africa. However, as we know from Hidatsa, which is a Khoisan language and which is spoken in Tanzania in east central Africa, we can connect the dots, so to speak, and see that originally Khoisan languages were spoken all along eastern Africa. As the Bantu speakers moved in, they spread their languages across central and eastern Africa, right through the middle of that "bar" of Khoisan languages, replacing them. But originally Khoisan was all along the east coast which is why we see it in Greek sources. They were briefly on the east coast, and the Greeks had at

---

[12]Bonny Sands, *Eastern and Southern African Khoisan : evaluating claims of distant linguistic relationships* (Köln : R. Köppe, 1998).

least indirect contact with their descendants.

The only name that's conspicuous by its absence in ancient literature is Sabtechah. And precisely because it is so absent from the records it probably is connected to the Niger-Congo languages which are spoken in western and central Africa far, far, away from any classical writer.

And that's where arose this so-called diversity belt of languages where most of the one thousand-plus African languages are spoken. This diversity belt results from compounded creolization, a continual mixing and remixing of languages along that area with all these migrations from eastern Africa to western Africa. And one group of languages that came out of that mix was the Bantoid languages. Proto-Bantoid speakers migrated from West Africa across central Africa all the way to East Africa, replacing the Khoisan languages, and finally moving down to southern Africa. Those are the descendants of Sabtechah.

What was the language of Sabtechah? This is also difficult to determine. Because of all this compounded creolization and language blending it's impossible to tease out the original ancient language of Sub-Saharan West Africans and the Africans in that diversity belt.

Which language primes were spoken by whom however, is another matter. For reasons given in Chapter 11, Sabtah seems to be the ancestor of Southern African tribes which migrated from West Africa. This means they would be speakers of Niger-Congo languages. But the names *Sabtah* and *Sabtechah* are so similar that Sabtechah might just as well be the ancestor of southern tribes. Havilah we surmised to have descendants in modern Sudan and Ethiopia—linguistically this would correspond to the Chari-Nile language family if those languages are not related to Nilo-Saharan, or possibly to some other language family that has since been completely absorbed in the meta-creolization of the diversity belt. Meanwhile, Sheba and Dedan of Raamah seemed to belong near the Persian Gulf. This would correspond to Sumerian and the languages east of the Persian Gulf not otherwise accounted for. We can represent this as follows:

Seba		Nilo-Saharan
Sabtah		Niger-Congo
Sabtechah		Khoisan
Havilah		? Chari-Nile, Other
Sheba		Sumerian
Dedan		languages east (e.g. Proto-Sino-Tibetan)

This is a possible arrangement, but there is a lot of ambiguity here and even this vague hypothesis rests on speculation almost as much as on linguistic and historical evidence.

Sheba and Dedan were likely end points and each one had its own distinct language. It makes sense that they should, interpreting this genealogy in a consistent way. This would mean that one of them spoke Sumerian and the other spoke another language that contributed to, say, Proto-Sino-Tibetan or the languages of Southest Asia.

The original language of Havilah might have been the Chari-Nile languages in the southern Sudan and southern Ethiopia, or possibly Kordofanian.

Elam's descendants, the Elamites, spoke Elamite, which is also related to Proto-Dravidian. Currently the best understanding of the relationship between these languages is that they are both daughter languages of a common ancestor, Proto-Elamo-Dravidian; this split into Elamite and Proto-Dravidian, which eventually spread through southern India and became the modern languages of the Dravidian family.

Asshur of course was the ancestor of the Assyrians. What was Asshur's original language? What did Asshur speak before Akkadian?[13] Sumerian perhaps? Probably not because the Sumerians were descended from Cush; they couldn't have been descended from Asshur also. It might have been one of the Caucasian language families.

And the language of Arphachshad? Almost certainly it turns out to be the Northwest Caucasian family of languages, where to this day there are nations and languages with names like Abkhaz, which strongly resembles the name Arphachshad. And of course the descendants of Arphachshad include Abraham.

Traditionally, "Ur of the Chaldees" Abraham's home town has been identified with Ur in Sumer, but there are strong reasons for concluding otherwise. Genesis 15:2 states that Abraham's chief servant would be his heir in the absence of children. This was not the way of southern Mesopotamia. Servants did not inherit property; servants were property. But in the law of the Hurrians, recorded on tablets from Nuzi, the chief servant did become the master of the household. Further, the Nuzi tablets also record the law of using a maidservant as a surrogate mother in the event that the wife of the head of the household was unable to conceive children. Finally, the route from Ur in Sumer to Haran is hundreds of miles north, whereas the region of Urartu in the Caucasus is some distance, but

---

[13.]The Akkadian language was a Semitic language and as discussed above, the Semitic languages may have been formed from Egyptian by creolization.

not too far from Haran, where Terah and his family (including Abraham) first stayed before moving on to Canaan.

Even practices, such as the use of concubines and the sale of birthright, which occur later in the history of Abraham's descendants (specifically with Isaac's and Jacob's families) find exact counterparts in the laws inscribed from Abraham's time at Nuzi. This seems to make it clear that Abraham's culture and point of origin was not Sumer, but the Caucasus region. An internet author who identifies himself as "Bob x" states, "Can we really view Abraham as a city boy who just decided one day to buy a bunch of sheep and goats and start roaming all over? On the contrary, it makes more sense to assume that he was natively of the nomadic north, not the urban southeast." Arphachshad's descendents, then, settled in the NW Caucasus region.

So the Ishmaelite Arabs, the Jews, the Moabites, the Midianites, they're all descended from Arphachshad. None of them seem to have survived to the present; the Ishmaelite or Bedouin Arabs, and the Jews are the only ethnic groups in the Middle East that have any identity at all from Arphachshad. Of course they don't speak a NW Caucasian language, but that was apparently the first language of Abram. He learned Canaanitic because Canaanitic was indeed a lingua franca of the Middle East in the third millennium BC, alongside Sumerian and, to a lesser extent, Elamite. He picked up Canaanitic and his sons grew up speaking Canaanitic.

As for the descendants of Lud: the Lydians of Anatolia spoke an Afroasiatic language, and later an Anatolian language of the IE language family. In Iran the Lurs today speak an Iranian language, but originally they must have spoken something else. What that was, we don't know.

> And the children of Aram; Uz, and Hul, and Gether, and Mash.
> (Genesis 10:23)

The linguistic situation with Aram is similar to that of Cush: Aram's sons were end points, but which language primes apply to them is difficult or impossible to determine. Of the four sons of Aram—Uz, Hul, Gether, and Mash—the descendants of Hul may have spoken the language ancestral to Hurrian and Urartu. There seem to have been several language isolates, two of which may have been spoken by two of the three remaining groups. One of the tribes descended from Aram may have spoken Eastern Caucasian languages.

> And Arphaxad begat Salah; and Salah begat Eber. (Genesis 10:24)

At this point we're at least four generations past the flood, right up to the time of the confusion of tongues.

> And unto Eber were born two sons: the name of one was Peleg; for in his days was the earth divided; and his brother's name was Joktan. (Genesis 10:25)

Here the phrase "was the earth divided" is most logically referring to the confusion of tongues. And notice that Peleg actually has a meaning in Afroasiatic because Afroasiatic started to exist.

The descendants of Joktan probably did speak the same language because this is after the confusion of tongues, and at any rate all those names can be found in the area of the gulf states. So the Bible is clearly very accurate there.

> And their dwelling was from Mesha, as thou goest unto Sephar a mount of the east.

> These are the sons of Shem, after their families, after their tongues, in their lands, after their nations.

> These are the families of the sons of Noah, after their generations, in their nations: and by these were the nations divided in the earth after the flood. (Genesis 10:30-32)

At this point I suppose this is a good segue into talking about how the Tower of Babel was built, why it was built, and how the nations were scattered.

It's really as much by tradition as by anything else that we talk about the Tower of Babel because Babel was actually the name of a city, not just of a tower.

> And they said, Go to, let us build us a city and a tower, whose top may reach unto heaven; and let us make us a name, lest we be scattered abroad upon the face of the whole earth.

> And the LORD came down to see the city and the tower, which the children of men builded.

The point was to have a city. Those verses show whose idea it was. It was the idea of the people. They wanted to make themselves a name, make a single identity for everyone on the earth. As it says,

> let us make us a name, lest we be scattered abroad upon the face
> of the whole earth.

"Making a name" for themselves meant establishing a unified identity to prevent themselves from being scattered abroad into different ethnic identities. That city was to be the city that would unify them. Later as they grew, got too big for one city, and spread out over the land, that city would have remained the central focal point of the people's identity. Perhaps the tower would also have been a symbol of their identity.

And this leads to arguments for or against the tower being a ziggurat. The word used for tower is מגדל (*migdal*). Since this word is often used in the OT for a watchtower or a defensive tower (e.g., Judg 9:45, 51; 2 Kgs 9:17; 17:9; Isa 5:2) and nowhere else refers to a ziggurat, what reason is there to believe that in Gen 11:4 it refers to a ziggurat?

There is a parallel between the phrase used for this "tower" and the phrase regularly used to describe ziggurats in Babylonian literature.

"Whose top [head][14] may reach unto heaven" – Genesis 11:4
"its head in the heavens" – Nabopolassar
"the head of his ziggurat...as high as the heavens" – King Samsuiluna
"lofty in the heavens" – Hammurabi
"to the heavens I raised its head" – Esarhaddon

Then there's the argument of loan translation. *Ziggurat* comes from the Accadian word *ziqqaru*, 'to be high'; Hebrew *migdal* is from the root *gedal* 'to be large'. Furthermore, while *migdal* usually means a military tower, the Greek word used by Herodotus for ziggurat was *purgos*, which also is usually used to designate a military tower.

It was a vision to keep all the people of the world united as they spread over the whole world. Because when people are alienated from each other they have conflicts, strife, wars. The idea is that if everybody stays together there won't be any wars because there will be no one to fight against them, and no one for them to fight against. They could have peace, security, they could maximize their human resources because all people with all different talents and gifts would all be in one place.

---

[14]The word translated 'top' (*rosh*) literally means 'head'.

Ultimately this was the first attempt to build what Augustine called the City of Man, which is to say, the City of God without God. There's no mention of God in this plan, no mention of the name of God, only the name of the people: Let us make us a name. Why is that a bad idea? Because anything without God tends to corruption. The Kingdom of God is the best kind of community. And the worst of anything is a corruption of the best. The ideal community is corrupted by leaving God out of it and it becomes the worst nightmarish hell of a kingdom anybody could have. This is the truth expressed in God's statement:

> And the LORD said, Behold, the people is one, and they have all one language; and this they begin to do: and now nothing will be restrained from them, which they have imagined to do. (Gen 11:6)

"Nothing would be restrained from them" because nobody would be able to stop them. Even God would not be able to send an army as a scourge against them because there wouldn't be any other people. Now, of course, God could always send some great natural disaster: He could make the city blow up, He could strike them with lightening. But because God is merciful, God understood that the better path would be not to let them get there in the first place. Instead of waiting until they committed unspeakable evil and then destroying them violently, the peaceful course of action was to just stop it from happening in the first place. So rather than violently smite them He just confused their languages and thus compelled people to separate from each other, compelling them to have separate identities according to their tongues and families and nations.

A postscript to this chapter in scripture relates to the origins of paganism. Interestingly Nimrod's name has been connected with the town or city of Marad in Sumer, which is near the city of Kish, which became one of the first major Sumerian dynasties. Kish has what some would regard as evidence of the origins of paganism. Paganism undoubtedly originated independently in many places, but the tablets from Kish indicate a possible development from the monotheism of Noah to the paganism that was found ubiquitous in Gentile nations.

I'm quoting here from G. Frederick Owen, D.D., Ed.D., in his archeological supplement to Charles Thompson's Chain Reference Bible:

> The excavators found a bone stylus which for the first time showed how cuneiform characters were produced, along with hoards of cuneiform tablets and other objects of interest. One of

the tablets seems to bear on its face the earliest forms of pictographic script yet discovered in Babylonia. 300 tablets of a slightly later date disclosed the fact that the occupants' pantheon of gods included only a sky god, an earth god, and a sun god. The sky god was represented as being the original god from whom all other gods had descended—eventually about 5,000 gods in all. after reading these tablets and considering other evidence found at Kish, Erech, and Shuruppak, Langdon wrote, "In my opinion, the history of the oldest religion of man is a rapid decline from monotheism to extreme polytheism and widespread belief in evil spirits. It is, in a very true sense, the history of the fall of man."

The tragedy of this postscript to the confusion of tongues is that humanity was on the path to repeating the state of the world that led to the flood. Yet God had promised not to send a second global flood. He did, however, call a second Noah. As Noah was called from all the corrupt world to come out of it and be protected while God destroyed the rest, so God called Abram from all the corrupt pagan world, but this time it was not so that God could destroy the world, but so that God could redeem it. Likewise Abram, like Noah, was chosen to repopulate the earth—not so much with his biological children as with his spiritual children.

And the rest, as they say, is history.

Conclusion

"I have gathered a posie of other men's flowers, and nothing but
the thread that binds them is mine own."
– John Bartlett, *Familiar Quotations*

There are two themes in this book. One has to do with epistemology. The
other has to do with creation and origins. These two themes address each other.

The epistemological theme is that what we hold true is not just based on what
we observe through our senses. It is based on what we believe—and everyone
believes, from the most profoundly dedicated religious devotee to the staunchest
atheist. Everyone has, by logical necessity, a foundation that is inviolable, by which
all other beliefs, ideas, and conclusions must be measured to be considered
thinkable and true. For westerners this foundation has come to be science, even
evolution in particular. Even westerners who believe in divine revelation hold
science as their solid rock. But I have argued here that it is not only possible, but
necessary to regard as our solid rock that the Bible is the infallible record of divine
revelation.

This leads to the theme about origins, including the origin of creation itself.
Given that the Bible is the solid rock, our truth tester, I have rejected all thoughts
that are founded on rejecting it. I have attempted to show which ideas about
science were based, not primarily on empirical observation, but on the rejection of
the Bible and of Genesis in particular. Such ideas have been woven into a new
mythos that was intended from its conception to replace Genesis and to give an
account of origins in the absence of divine revelation. This mythos guides the
scientific community to reject many conclusions made by brilliant, and often non-
religious scientists. In this book, we have revisited those scientific ideas and seen
how they are in line with a literal account of Genesis.

All of that said, it's worth pointing out here that beyond what we read directly
from the Bible and observe empirically, everything else we hold to is just what we
think. And that means much of what I have written here can be mistaken and
superceded by more knowledge.

Understanding the Bible to be our way of knowing, we can confidently say:
what the Bible states we know. What we observe directly with our senses we
know. Once we propose hypotheses based on deductive and inductive reasoning,
we have moved from what we know to what we think. What we think *may* be right,

but it may not and that's why it changes as we gain more observation through experiment and other forms of learning. So there's room in this account for change, but it gives us a very strong basis to start with to have a clear understanding.

We can understand how an evolutionary account of early man compares with the biblical account. If we start with the Bible as our way of knowing, we can tease apart what the evolutionary account is and what the biblical account is; what we believe and what we don't believe, what we can trust and what we cannot trust. We can start with the biblical account and not have to be influenced by any account that is founded on rejecting the Bible.

We have also seen that choosing one way of knowing over another is not motivated by the inherent superiority of that way of knowing, but by spiritual factors. In particular, the choice of the scientific method as the way of knowing was motivated by a spiritual disillusionment resulting from religious wars in Europe. In general, though, can one make a broad principled statement about what spirituality motivates choosing one or the other way of knowing? Being consistent with the method of this book, we can look to the Bible as our starting point to answer this question.

Based on Rom 1:20-32 it does seem, in fact, that there are, broadly, two spiritualities that human beings orient themselves toward: pantheistic, self-centered vs. monotheistic, other-centered. Since by definition pantheism is identifying the physical universe with God, it further seems logical to reason that the scientific method as a way of knowing is motivated primarily by having chosen pantheistic, self-centered spirituality, while having the Bible as one's way of knowing stems from a monotheistic, other-centered spirituality. Here, of course, spirituality is different from and more basic than religion, although clearly spirituality and religion have a great deal to do with each other.

It is possible to have a pantheistic, self-centered spirituality and a monotheistic religion at the same time and vice versa. Monotheistic other-centered spirituality results in love and valuing love, while pantheistic, self-centered spirituality results in an endless cycle of self-worship and self-loathing.

When one has either pantheistic spirituality with monotheistic religion, or monotheistic spirituality with pantheistic religion, this leads to a confused religion and a confused life. Gradually the spirituality conforms the religion to itself. In the case of self-centered spirituality with monotheistic religion, one gradually abandons faith in the Bible and embraces New Age/pagan beliefs and values. In the case of other-centered spirituality with pantheistic religion, one gradually develops more interest in the Bible and the person of Jesus Christ until one is met by the Holy Spirit with conviction for sin leading to repentance and newness of life.

As spirituality shapes religion, so it shapes intellectual life and perception as well. We see how the loss of true Christian spirituality in Europe (and thus the adoption of pantheistic self-centered spirituality) led away from a Bible-centered epistemology and toward science as a way of knowing; away from Genesis and toward evolution. Likewise Christian spirituality leads away from evolution and toward Genesis. But when a society presents only one way of knowing as acceptable and that is contrary to one's own spirituality, the result is very debilitating.

On the other hand, when one's spirituality, religion, and intellect are in harmony then one can be strong. For generations now, westerners have had their pantheistic self-centered spirituality, religion, and intellect in harmony, and have been strong emotionally and psychologically, secure and comfortable in their worldview. This book is a demonstration of how monotheistic other-centered spirituality, monotheistic (specifically Christian) religion, and the intellect can be in harmony with one another and connected to each other. When this happens in individuals, Christians will be emotionally secure, strong, and stable in a way they have not been for a long time. And when Christians are emotionally secure, strong, and stable, we will be better able to live in real fellowship and value relationships the way our Master has ordained. This will also result in the fellowship of holy ones to be more distinct culturally than ever from the world. And individuals in the world will be more compelled than ever to make a decision about the Gospel. In other words, the church will be effective.

Here's to the advent of that community. Here's to reclaiming the source.

Appendices

Appendix 1
The Four Ages in Asia, Europe, and North America

Hindu

Indo-Aryan culture has four ages of the earth. These have been incorporated into Hinduism as the Maha Yuga (the great cycle). That these four ages originally stood alone is reflected in the fact that when they were seen as part of a cycle they were labeled the Great Cycle, and are still called that today, even though other cycles have been built around it to the point that the Maha Yuga is actually the smallest cycle in Hindu chronology.

The first age is called the Satya Yuga (also called Krita Yuga) or "Age of Truth" and lasts 1,728,000 human years. The qualities of this age are: virtue reigns supreme; human stature is 21 cubits; lifespan is a lakh of years, and death occurs only when willed.

This second age is called the Treta Yuga and lasts 1,296,000 human years. The qualities of this age are: the climate is three quarters virtue and one quarter sin; human stature is 14 cubits; lifespan is 10,000 years.

The third age is the Dvapara Yuga and lasts 864,000 human years. The qualities of this age are: the climate is one half virtue and one half sin; lifespan is 1,000 years.

The fourth and last age is the Kali Yuga ("Evil Age") and lasts 432,000 human years. This is the age in which we are presently living. The qualities of this age are: the climate is one quarter virtue and three quarters sin; human stature is 3.5 cubits; lifespan is 100 or 120 years.

Math is behind much of this and centers on the number 4. The simple but elegant arithmetic principle 1+2+3+4=10 (that is, the first four counting numbers add up to the base of the number system) is applied to the length of the ages. So the age before the present one (Dvapara) was twice as long as this one, the age before that (Treta) was three times as long as the present one, the age before that was four times as long as the present one and all four ages add up to one great age (Maha Yuga) that is ten times as long as the present age.

Human stature is increased from the present by the 4:3:2:1 ratio. Human life span is increased by one order of magnitude in each age from the present.

Since there are four ages, the progressive moral deterioration of the ages is reflected mathematically in fourths: four quarters virtue, ¾ virtue, ¼ sin; 2/4 virtue, 2/4 sin; ¼ virtue, ¾ sin.

Greek

The Ancient Greeks recorded four ages of the earth as well.

In the Age of Gold, the time when Cronus (Saturn) was king in heaven, the Olympian gods made a golden race of mortals who lived as though in a paradise, without toil, trouble, or cares. All good things were theirs in abundance and the fertile earth brought forth fruit of its own accord. Although they were mortal, they never aged and when they did die it was like falling asleep. Their spirits still lived on earth after their bodies died.

In the Age of Silver, childhood ended after only one hundred years, and adult life was short. People were arrogant and would not worship the gods. Zeus punished them by hiding them all under the earth and making a new race of mortals. This seems to reflect the godlessness of the antediluvian period.

In the Bronze Age weapons and tools were made of bronze. People engaged in endless war. They killed on another off "without leaving a name."

This tale of constant warfare may have been inspired by the violence of the antediluvian world or by the warfare of the postdiluvian Bronze Age. The idea that this age ended with all the people wiped out "without leaving a name," is reminiscent of the Tower of Babel and the people's failure to "make us a name." (Gen 11:4)

The Age of Iron is the current age, marked with misery and toil, when childhood is at its shortest. It is characterized by increasing wickedness, strife, and impiety. It is interesting that, while lifespan does shorten through each successive age, the emphasis is on the shortening of childhood.

In addition to these four, one writer, Hesiod, added the age of Heroes, which he placed after the Bronze Age.

The Age of Heroes. Zeus made still another race, also valiant in war but more just and more civilized. This was the race of the heroes, also called demigods, who were involved in the legendary events of Greek saga. They fought, for example, at Thebes and in the Trojan war. When they died, Zeus sent some of these heroes to inhabit the Islands of the Blessed, a paradise at the far ends of the earth, ruled over by Cronus (Saturn), who had been deposed and freed by Zeus.

This was placed after the Bronze Age because of certain historical events (such as the Trojan War) which took place after the actual Bronze Age (and after the confusion of tongues). But the ultimate origin of the stories of semi-divine heroes like Acchiles and Herakles is to be found in the time immediately preceding the flood, i.e. at the end of the Second Age.

Dine

The Dine in North America also speak of four ages, manifested as four worlds.

The version recounted here is based on the version told in Joseph Bruchac, Native American Stories (Golden, Colorado: Fulcrum Publishing, 1991), pp. 10-18.

"Before this world existed, and far below it, the First World lay in darkness. Here lived six beings: First Man, First Woman, Salt Woman, Fire God, Coyote, and Begochiddy, the golden-haired child of the Sun. Begochiddy made four mountains in this first world - white to the east; blue to the south; yellow to the west; and black to the north. Then Begochiddy made insects and plants. But conflicts arose and the first beings, tired of the First World and its darkness, decided to leave.

"At the center of the First World, Begochiddy made a red mountain and planted a giant reed. The first beings gathered all of Begochiddy's creations and crawled inside of the hollow reed. The reed grew and grew and carried them into the Second World. In the Second World, which was blue, Begochiddy created still more new things. When the Cat People, who lived in the Second World, fought the newcomers, First Man used magic to overcome them. Conflicts again disrupted the harmony of this world and the first beings collected their possessions and traveled in the giant reed up to the Third World.

"The Third World was beautiful, yellow and filled with light. There, Begochiddy created rivers and springs, animals and birds, trees and lightning, and many kinds of human beings. When the men and women began to quarrel, Begochiddy separated them. But they were so unhappy that Begochiddy reunited them, warning that the Third World would be flooded if there was any more trouble.

"And then Coyote caused trouble. Walking by the river, he spied in the water a baby with long black hair. He lifted the baby from the river and hid it under his blanket, telling no one. Colorful storms and torrential rains approached from all directions. Everyone fled to the protective hollow of the giant reed, which carried them upward. But the reed stopped growing before it reached the next world. So Locust helped Begochiddy make a hole that led to the Fourth World, an island surrounded by water.

"Seeing the waters still rising in the Third World, Begochiddy asked who had angered the Water Monster. Coyote tightened his blanket about his body and Begochiddy ordered him to open it. There was the water baby. Coyote returned the baby to the Third World and the waters receded. In the Fourth World, Begochiddy set out the mountains and placed the moon, sun, and stars in the sky. Begochiddy taught everyone the right way to live, including how to care for plants such as corn, squash, and beans, and how to give thanks."

Aztec

The Codex Vaticanus offers the following history of mankind[1]:

"First Sun, 'Matlactli At': duration 4,008 years. Those who lived then ate water maize called 'atzitzintli'. In this age lived the giants... The First Sun was destroyed by water in the sign 'Matlactli Atl' (Ten Water). It was called 'Apachiohualiztli' (flood, deluge), the art of sorcery of the permanent rain. Men were turned into fish. Some say that only one couple escaped, protected by an old tree living near the water. Others say that there were seven couples who hid in a cave until the flood was over and the waters had gone down. They repopulated the Earth and were worshiped as gods in their nations...

"Second Sun, 'Ehecoatl': duration 4,010 years. Those who lived then ate wild fruit known as 'acotzintli'. This Sun was destroyed by Ehecoatl (Winged Serpent) and men were turned into monkeys... One man and one woman, standing on a rock, were saved from destruction...

"Third Sun, 'Tleyquiyahuillo': duration 4,081 years. Men, the descendants of the couple who were saved from the Second Sun, ate a fruit called 'tzincoacoc'. This Third Sun was destroyed by fire...

"Fourth Sun, 'Tzontlilic: duration 5,026 years. Men died of starvation after a deluge of blood and fire....."

---

[1] From the Vaticano-Latin Codex 3738, cited in Adela Fernandez, *Pre-Hispanic Gods of Mexico*. (Mexico City: Panorama Editorial, 1992), 21-2.

Appendix 2
"Transitional Forms" of the Evolutionary Story

I have already stated that this book is not a forum for debate between creationism and evolutionism. A strictly biblical worldview is presented. But one inevitably has to ask where the record of transitional forms comes into play in such a worldview. The position taken here is that transitional forms are an illusion. That is, they are not transitional, but are interpreted as such by the evolutionary worldview.

Almost all distinctive traits of animal classes, certainly the most reliable distinguishing traits, are not accessible in the fossil record, but consist of internal organs and other perishable tissues:

fish/amphibians:	gills vs. lungs
amphibians/reptiles:	smooth skin vs. scales
	soft-shelled vs. hard-shelled eggs
reptiles/ mammals:	scales vs. fur
	eggs vs. live birth
	absence vs. presence of mammary glands

None of the above, or transitions between any of the above features can be found in a fossilized skeleton. And the second trait of reptiles/mammals is not even reliable: there are egg-laying mammals (monotremes). There are skeletal distinctions between these classes, but these are far from reliable. For example, reptiles have undifferentiated dentition, while mammals have different kinds of teeth: canines, incisors, premolars, molars—unless they're cetaceans like orcas or dolphins which have completely undifferentiated dentition, as reptiles do. Then there are other cetaceans along with monotremes and anteaters that have no teeth at all. This has led to incorrect conclusions about prehistoric creatures.

For example, *Pteranodon* is assumed to have been a flying reptile, but traces of hair have been found on a mummified pelt along with its skeleton. Moreover, on independent grounds flying reptiles are thought to have been warm-blooded. So we have a fur-covered, warm-blooded reptile. Another word for a fur-covered, warm-blooded reptile is 'mammal'. Whether it laid eggs or gave birth to live young is immaterial because some mammals lay eggs. The only other trait, mammary glands, is irretrievable. The only reason for calling *Pteranodon* a flying reptile instead of a flying mammal is that it's too big and too specialized a mammal for the evolutionary myth. If its skeleton is not typically mammalian that is to be expected in a highly specialized animal (cf. cetaceans again).

Another case of such misinterpretation is the case of *Archaeopteryx*, seen as a transition between reptiles and birds. It cannot be ancestral to birds: the bones in birds' wings are homologous to the second, third, and fourth digits in the forefeet or hands of vertebrates, but the digits on the forelimbs of *Archaeopteryx* are homologous to the first, second and third digits. That *Archaeopteryx* is not an ancestor of birds is well attested in general science literature. It is essentially a feathered thecodont; it's skeleton is identical to that of *Compsognathus*. In fact Hoyle and Wickramasinghe claim that it *is* in fact *Compsognathus* with a furcula artificially inserted from another skeleton and feather prints made on wet cement spread over certain areas of the fossil's stone. A strong case has been made by Hoyle and Wickramasinghe that the only *Archaeopteryx* fossil with feathers is a fraud.[1] This case has been strengthened by the subsequent action of the British Museum in locking up the fossil and prohibiting its showing to the public.

More emotionally loaded is the issue of transitional forms from apes to humans in the evolutionary scheme. Once again, the difference between the evolutionary story and the biblical view is not a matter of observation or data, but of interpretation—what we think.

There is a great deal of detail and complexity when it comes to the evolutionary story of human ancestry, but there is one main group of hominids one deals with in telling the story:

Australopithecus (africanus, robustus, etc.). The skeletons that actually exist clearly show *Australopithecus* to be an arboreal ape. Always in popular literature, *Australopithecus'* skeleton is completely human (with the exception of the pelvis which is just slightly simian) and a skull that is very chimp-like. A website that purported to show the skeleton of Lucy, that of a chimp, and that of a human showed a hand different from Lucy's, but alleging it to be "hers"; evidently because Lucy's was not as human looking as the drawings of *Australopithecus* skeletons make out. When one visitor to the website pointed this out, tremendous abuse was heaped upon him. *Australopithecus* appears to be merely an ape.

Homo erectus, the next major step in the evolutionary story of humans, was definitely not an ape, but with a smaller brain case, *H. erectus* might seem to be a daunting challenge to a biblical perspective. But here also there is no real problem. The apparent difficulty arrives from the fact that comparisons between "*H. erectus*"

[1]Fred Hoyle and N. Chandra Wickramasinghe, *Archaeopteryx, the Primordial Bird: A Case of Fossil Forgery* (Swansea, England: Christopher Davies, Ltd., 1986)

and "modern man" are based on *drawings* of skulls that never reveal the variations that occur in real life. When variations, modern and ancient, are taken into account, fossils of *H. erectus* are just seen as part of that variation. Several paleoanthropologists have written on this conclusion. Milford Wolpoff summarized the position succinctly in an interview: "There was no such thing as *Homo erectus*. The species that appeared two million years ago, the species that fundamentally became us, is us: *Homo sapiens*."[2] In his book, *Race and Evolution: a Fatal Attraction*, Wolpoff quotes John Robinson as saying that, "most of the obvious physical change had already occurred" by the time *H. erectus* appeared. The presentation is that there is a smooth transition in the fossil record between apes, australopithecine, *H. erectus*, Neanderthal man and modern man. This is achieved by completely misrepresenting *Australopithecus'* skeleton to be almost completely human, thus making *Australopithecus* more human than it was, and suppressing information about modern and ancient variation in humans, thus making *H. erectus* less human than he was. These two efforts combined serve to close the gap between ancient apes and men, if only in people's minds. But in propagating and maintaining a worldview, people's minds are all that matter.

Neanderthal man (*Homo (sapiens) neanderthalensis*) Considering Neanderthal man to be *H. sapiens* or a separate species goes in and out of fashion; evidence enough that the evidence is inconclusive even within an evolutionary perspective. Biblically, Neanderthal man was of course fully human. Brain capacity is the same as or greater than "modern" man's. It's just a different physical type.

In truth apes have always been apes and humans have always been humans. "*H. erectus*," Neanderthal, and Cro-Magnon types were all present before the flood, while *Australopithecus* was one of many types of apes living before the flood.

---

[2]Milford Wolpoff, To the Best of Our Knowledge, interview with Judith Strasser , Program 97-01-19-B.

Appendix 3
Post-diluvial catastrophic floods

Around the world there is evidence for various floods which were not global, but were on a scale unimaginable today. In the evolutionary paradigm these are mostly connected with the end of ice ages and the subsequent melting of massive glaciers. Whether the floods were caused directly by glaciers or not, they seem to at least indirectly result from the global flood as kind of aftershocks from the one global catastrophe. Chapter 10 lists some of these catastrophic, but regional, floods; here they are described in more detail.

When the sea levels had been lowered (see Chapter 11) the Tigris and Euphrates rivers, and the Shatt-al-Arab (the river resulting from their confluence) flowed through broad wetlands. Moreover the bed of the Persian Gulf which today has an average depth of only thirty-five meters, would have been well above sea level. The exploration ship "Meteor" has confirmed this. One can trace the Shatt-al-Arab into the gulf where the former river bed can be seen on the floor near the Iranian side.

Leonard Wooley famously discovered a layer of wet silt eight feet thick near Ur in southern Mesopotamia. This layer of wet silt covers an area of about 40,000 square miles, clearly a large part of which had been inundated. Whether or not this coincided with the flooding of the Persian Gulf is unknown.

Another wetland joining what are today disconnected land masses during the ice age connected the greater Sunda islands, Sumatra, West Malaysia and SW Borneo. It is thought that an extreme version of the monsoon weather of that area served as the catalyst for the flooding of that entire region, cutting off the Sunda islands from the Asian mainland.

What is now the Gulf of Carpentaria was during this time a large plain, connecting Indonesia and New Guinea with Australia. Together with the Sunda wetlands this plain made it possible for people and animals to literally walk into Australia.

One of the local catastrophic floods that received a great deal of attention recently is the filling of the Black Sea. What is now the Black Sea was once a freshwater lake until the Aegean Sea flooded and poured into the Black Sea basin.

The Aegean itself may have been a marshland which was flooded after the

Mediterranean Sea rose to its present level. Archeologists have actually looked for sunken remains of a neolithic village at the bottom of the sea, remains of a society that lived in what were the marshy plains of the Aegean. Such a society is thought to have been the source of pottery and ornamental artefacts found in Franchthi Cave, on the coast of Greece, the oldest Neolithic artefacts found in Europe.

It was after the flooding of this plain, creating the Aegean Sea, that the sea eventually poured through the Marmara Lake into what is now the Black Sea. Ryan and Pittman regard this as *the* flood, but we can see it as only one of many outbreak floods—floods which nevertheless may have inspired local alterations in the received story of the global deluge.

Since 1998 it has been understood that the shallow waters off the coast of the North Sea formed a plain now designated as "Doggerland" (named by archeologist B.J. Coes after the Dogger Bank in the North Sea). This area was populated by hunter-gatherers until the rise of the ocean levels inundated the entire region.

In North America a number of post-glacial lakes formed. Ice melted from the glaciers, but rather than draining into rivers and oceans, it pooled up, held back by a wall of ice. Eventually the wall of ice, acting as a dam, itself began to melt until pressure from the water behind it forced it to burst, suddenly sending all the water from the lake surging an raking over the land beyond it. Such catastrophes have occurred in modern times, called a glacial lake outburst flood (GLOF), or *jökulhaup*. This is an Icelandic term because Iceland is especially vulnerable to this kind of event. In 1996 a jökulhaup occurred in the wake of a volcanic eruption under a sub-glacial lake. The flood reached a flow rate of 50,000 cubic meters per second and moved 185 million tons of silt.[1]

Astonishing and destructive as these events are, GLOFs on an incomparably greater scale occurred in North America in the wake of the global flood. On such GLOF was in Montana. A sub-glacial lake now referred to as Glacial Lake Missoula burst through its ice dam and permanently drained across the Columbia Plateau, forming the Washington scablands.

Lake Agassiz and Lake Ojibway, two post-glacial lakes which ultimately joined,

---

[1] Sefán Benediktsson and Sigrún Helgadóttir, "The Skeiðarðá River in Full Flood 1996," Skaftafell National Park: Environment and Food Agency, UST March 2007.

forming a freshwater body larger than all of today's Great Lakes combined. The retreat and advance of post-diluvial glaciers resulted in several GLOFs which impacted sea level and even climate. When the glacial dam holding this lake back from Hudson Bay catastrophically failed, it drained permanently into the bay.

Another outburst flood, one which did not involve a glacial lake, involved two mega-lakes in what is now Arizona, called Hopi Lake and Grand Lake. Underground drainage from Grand Lake through the Vermillion Cliffs eventually resulted in a sudden breach of the southwestern wall of Grand Lake, rapidly eroding through the sedimentary rock and eroding a channel eighteen miles long, twelve miles wide, and two thousand feed deep. This breached the northwestern boundary of Hopi Lake which also drained. The massive erosion which resulted led to the rise and splitting of the funnel-shaped channel, forming Marble Canyon and leading to the catastrophic formation of the Grand Canyon.

Whenever humans inhabited the area near one of these catastrophic local floods, they led to new flood stories which added unique local details to the original flood legend. Some of them (The Carpentaria Flood, The Black Sea flood, the Lake Agassiz flood, the Tigris/Euphrates flood) have each been proposed in recent times as *the* flood that inspired the flood myths found all over the world. But these local events were by products of the global flood. No one of them was the original event that inspired the flood stories told all over the world.

Modern descendants of peoples listed in the Table of Nations

Gomer	W. Europeans
Ashkenaz	Germanic peoples (Germans, Scandinavians, English, Icelanders, Dutch, etc.)
Riphath	Irish, Scottish, Welsh, Basques
Togarmah	Turkic peoples
Magog	Finnish, Hungarians, Estonians, Sami
Madai	Iranians, Indians (esp. northern Indians)
Javan	Greeks
Tubal	Georgians
Meshech	Russians, Polish, Serbians, Croats, Bosnians, Czechs, etc.
Tiras	Northeastern Caucasian peoples
Elam	Elamites (Iranians), Tamils, and other southern Indians
Asshur	Iraqis
Arphaxad	Ishmaelite Arabs, Jews, northwestern Caucasus (Abkhaz and others)
Lud	Lurs (Iran)
Aram	peoples of the NE Caucasus
Uz	
Hul	Kurds
Gether	
Mash	
Joktan	Most other southern, or Qahtani Arabs (Arabs of the Gulf States)
Cush	Sub-Saharan Africans
Seba	Songhai, Kanuri, people of eastern Sahara Africans
Havilah	Sudanese, Ethiopians
Sabta	San, Khoikhoi, etc.
Sabtechah	see below
Raamah	Sumerians and people who migrated further east into Asia; not possible to tell which branch (Sheba or Dedan) was ancestral to the Sumerians
Sheba	
Dedan	
Mizraim	Egyptians
Put	Tuaregs and other Berbers
Canaan	Syrians

Names on the Table that are tribes, not individuals:
Kittim
Dodanim
Mizraim
Ludim
Anamim
Lehabim
Naphtuhim
Pathrusim
Casluhim
Philistim
Caphtorim
Jebusites
Amorites
Girgashites
Hivites
Arvadites
Sinites
Zemarites
Hamathite

Some examples of mixing between lineages:

Gomer and Heth ⇒ Indo-European Hittites, Albanians

Hittites and Riphath ⇒Latins (Romans)

Romans, Ashkenaz, and Riphath ⇒French

Elam and Raamah ⇒Dravidians, Native Australians

Raamah and Magog ⇒East Asians, Aleuts, Yupik, Inupiat

East Asians and South Asians ⇒Southeast Asians

Australians and Southeast Asians ⇒Pacific Islanders

Southeast Asians and Pacific Islanders ⇒Native (South) Americans

Appendix 5
Names of peoples and Place Names derived from the names in the Table of Nations

Gomer	Gamir (Arm.); Cymru (Wales); Cimbershawen (Den.)
Ashkenaz	Lake Ascanius; Scandinavia
Riphath	Rhaetia (Switz.)
Togarmah	Turkey
Magog	Magyar (Hung.); ? Mongolia
Madai	Medes
Javan	Ionia
Elishah	Elis
Tarshish	Tartessos
Kittim	
Dodanim	Rhodes
Tubal	Tblisi (Georg.)
Meshech	Moscovia; Moscow
Tiras	
Elam	Elam
Asshur	Assyria
Arphaxad	Arpachiya (anc. settlement 4 mi. from Niniveh)
Lud	
Aram	
Uz	
Hul	Hurria, Kurdistan
Gether	
Mash	
Joktan	Yectan (town near Mecca)
Almodad	
Sheleph	Sula (60 mi. N of San'a)
Hazermaveth	Hadramaut valley
Jerah	Jerakon Kome (near Hadramaut)

Hadoram	
Uzal	Azal (= mod. San'a)
Diklah	Hi-Dikel (Tigris R.)
Obal	Abil/Ubil (between Hadeida & San'a); ?Ebla
Havilah	Hawlan, Huwailah (Iraqi shore of Persian Gulf)
Jobab	Juhaibab (close to Mecca)
Cush	Kush; Hindu Kush; ?Kish
Seba	
Havilah	Aualis (near Djibouti)
Sabta	??Shabwat
Sabtechah	
Raamah	
Sheba	
Dedan	
Mizraim	
Ludim	Lydia
Anamim	
Lehabim	Libya
Naphtuhim	
Pathrusim	Pathros
Casluhim	
Philistim	Philistia, Palestine
Caphtorim	Caphtor (Crete), ?Egypt
Put	Punt
Canaan	Canaan
Sidon	Zidon (Sidon)
Heth	
Jebus	
Amorites	
Girgashites	
Hivites	
Arvadites	
Sinites	Nahr as-Sinn, Sinn Addarb (close to Arqa)
Zemar	?Sumra? (N of Tripoli)
Hamathite	Hamath (Orontes R.)

Appendix 6
Proto-Euphratean Vocabulary

These are words found in Sumerian which do not match the lexical structure of Sumerian words and therefore are recognized as borrowed from the language spoken in Sumer before Sumerian, a language dubbed "Proto-Euphratean". From what has been said about Sumerian in Chapter 12, "Proto-Euphratean" would be none other than the language of Noah and his family. Hence, apart from antediluvian names, these are the only recoverable words from that language.

Common Nouns

engar	*farmer*
udul	*herdsman*
shuhadak	*fisherman*
apin	*plow*
apsin	*furrow*
nimbar	*palm*
sulumb	*date*
tibira	*metalworker* (note similarity to *Tubal*)
simug	*smith*
nangar	*carpenter*
addub	*basketmaker*
ishbar	*weaver*
ashgab	*leatherworker*
pahar	*potter*
shidim	*mason*
(damgar	*merchant*)*

Place Names

Eridu	Lagash	
Ur	Nippur	
Larsa	Kish	(note similarity to *Cush*)
Isin	idiglat	*Tigris*
Adab	buranun	*Euphrates*
Kullab		

*This word may or may not be Sumerian

Appendix 7
Proposed Etymologies of Nimrod's Name

W. F. Albright

interest,[14] since its perfected form, found in the myth of Lugal-banda and Zû, is written in Sumerian, while our Gilgames-epic is a Semitic composition, however much it may have drawn on Sumerian sources. Besides the Assyrian translation of over a hundred lines (*KB* 6. 1. 46 ff.) we now possess goodly fragments of the original Sumerian: *CT* 15. 41-43; *HGT*, Nos. 14-19, and probably also 8-11 (see above); in Nos. 20-21 we have part of a chronicle dealing with events during the reigns of Lugalbanda and his successor Tammuz (cf. *HT* 117). Most of the latter text apparently refers to Lugalbanda, since Tammuz is not mentioned until the close. Along with victorious invasions of Elam, Ḥalma (= Guti), and Tidnu[m] (= Amûru), a disastrous flood which overwhelmed Eridu is described (obv. 11-12): *a-urú-gul-la-gè* [ ] *NUN-KI a-gal-la si-a* [ ] = 'the waters of the destructive deluge......Eridu, flooded by the inundation [ ].' In connection with this the *deus ex machina*, Ninlil, comes on the scene; despite the pseudo-historical setting we are dealing with myth.

The story of Lugalbanda and Zû, personification of the hurricane, is primarily, as has often been observed, the contest between

---

[14] It is possible that the saga of Nimrod may be an offshoot of the Lugalbanda cycle rather than of the Gilgames cycle, especially since the former seems to have been much more important than the latter in early times, and from a home in Marad more likely to influence the west than the latter, whose hearth was Erech. As lord of Marad Lugalbanda is the *Lugal-Maráda* or the *Nin-Maráda, just as Nergal-Lugalgira is the *Nin-Girsu*, the lord of Girsu, and as Marduk is the *Nin-Tintir* (IIR 59, obv. 47), Ellil the *Nin-Nibru*, or Lord of Nippur (*ibid.* 9); cf. also Sin the *Bêl-Ḥarrân*, etc. The heroic shepherd and conqueror of wild-beasts, *Nimarád, may thus have become the mighty hunter, *Nimród*, just as *Dagán* becomes *Dagón*, and *Hadád* 'Αδωδος. Similarly the shepherd Damu (Tammuz) became in Byblos the hunter Adonis. The figure of Nimrod was probably influenced by the impressive monumental representations of the Assyrian Heracles; he may easily reflect a western 'Orion,' but Eduard Meyer's view that he was primarily a Libyan 'Jagdriese' is gratuitous. The recent historical theories are still less felicitous: Sethe (Hastings' *Encyclopaedia of Religion and Ethics*, Vol. 6, p. 650) holds that Nimrod is a corruption of the official name Nebmu'ʻerēʻ of the indolent Amenophis III, appearing in cuneiform as Nimmurija; Van Gelderen (*Expositor*, 1914, pp. 274 ff.) explains Nimrod as a corruption of Narâmsin, historically possible, but phonetically incredible. Jensen's explanation, deriving *Nimród* from *Namurta, his reading of *NIN-IB*, is antiquated by the discovery of the correct reading *Ninurta*, which became *Inušta* (*JAOS* 38. 197), a form quite unlike Nimrod.

From "Gilgames and Engidu, Mesopotamian Genii of Fecundity," by W. F. Albright
Journal of the American Oriental Society, Vol. 40. (1920), pp. 307-335.
Stable URL: http://links.jstor.org/sici?sici=0003-0279%281920%2940%3C307%3AGAEMGO%3E2.0.CO%3B2-F

prefix *patiy*. The *prius* of the Mod. Pers. compound is more probably to be found in the Anc. Pers. *pā* 'protect.' The *nomen agentis pātar* 'protector' would appear in the Mod. Pers. as *pād*, cf. Bartholomae, *Altiranisches Wörterbuch*, 887, Hübschmann, *Persische Studien*, 35. The Mod. Pers. *pādišāh* < Anc. Pers. *pātar* + *xšāyaθiya*, 'protector-king' would illustrate Iranian *r* changed into *i* as in New Pers. *giriftah*, Bal. *gipta*, cf. Av. *gərəpta* 'seized'; New Pers. *xirs* cf. Av. *arəša* 'bear'; New Pers. *dil*, Bal. *zirdē*, cf. Av. *zərədaya* 'heart'; New Pers. *tiš*, cf. Av. *taršna* 'thirst.' Cf. change of Skt. *r* to *i* in the Indian dialects, Skt. *kṛta*, Prak. *kita;* Skt. *ghṛta*, Bang. *ghi*, Sindhī *gihu*, Anglo-Indian *ghee*, cf. Gray, *Indo-Iranian Phonology*, 71.

Herodotus (3. 61) states that Cambyses had left Patizeithes τῶν οἰκίων μελεδωνόν. If this is not a title but his real name as Hdt. implies, we find his Magian designation in *Oropastes* (Justin. 1. 9.). This reverses the now generally accepted theory which would find in the latter the proper name and in the former the title. The derivation of *Oropastes* is clear—*prius* Anc. Pers. *aura* 'lord,' *posterius upastā* 'aid.' Just as his brother Gaumāta (*nomen proprium* as given in the Behistan Inscription) bore the Magian appellation Σφενδαδάτης according to Ctesias, *Pers*. 10, which is the YAv. *spəntōdāta*, 'created by the Holy,' so we can believe that in **auraupasta* 'possessing the help of the Lord' we restore the Magian title of Patizeithes.

H. C. TOLMAN

Vanderbilt University

A possible Sumerian original of the name Nimrod

According to the tradition recorded in the genealogical tablet, Gen. 10. 8 ff., Nimrod, son of Cush, founded the empire of Babylonia. This Nimrod is mentioned in v. 8, as having been 'the first great warrior in the land' (this seems to be the meaning of the words: (החל להיות נבר בארץ), and in v. 9 it is stated that Nimrod was a 'great warrior hunter before Jahve,' i. e., so great as to attract the attention of Jahve (הוא היה נבר ציד לפני יהוה), a tradition which does not appear to have any connection with the rest of the text. For this reason some scholars have concluded that verse 9 is a gloss (Procksch, *Die Genesis*, 1912, p. 74).

been an epithet of the first great Semitic Babylonian king Hammurapi, who, however, was not distinguished in the chase, but, like the Biblical Nimrod, was an empire builder, which would correspond with the expansion attributed to Nimrod, Gen. 10. 10 ff., and, so far as the historicity of Nimrod is concerned, it is highly probable that we have in this obscure character a reminiscence of early Semitic territorial extensions in the Euphrates valley. But it is doubtful whether Hammurapi is intended.

How can the description of Nimrod as a great hunter in the presumably glossated text of Gen. 10. 9, be accounted for? In the absence of any known tradition confirming this statement, the next step would be to examine the form *Nimrod* itself, to discover whether the name does not offer some suggestion of the chase. Assuming *Nimrod* to be a Sumerian name or epithet, it is highly probable that the first syllable *nim* contains the Sum. *nin*, with gloss *ni-ni* (Del. *Glossar*, p. 204) $= câidu$, occurring in *lu edin ni-ni* ($= kili$), 'field huntsman.' That this stem *nin* (*ni-ni*) is identical with *nigin* $= saxâru$, 'turn, seek,' which itself contains *gin*, *gi* $= târu$, 'turn around, seek,' is highly likely. In *nin-nini*, the final *n* was probably nasal *ng*, as in the equation *gi* $= ni$ = 'man' (also $= lu = nu$, 'man'; Prince, *JAOS* 39, pp. 270, 275). This *nin-nini* also has the meaning *napxaru*, 'entirety,' a variant of *saxâru*, 'surround,' in which sense the sign has the val. $kili =$ nasal $k + l = n = ningi\text{-}ningin$.

The element *-rod* in *Nimrod* is more difficult. It may stand for Sum. $ \acute{g}ud^2 = ellum $ 'bright, distinguished' (*Glossar*, p. 215), a very common epithet. In this case, *ning-ḫʿud* = 'distinguished hunter.' It is, however, possible that a later tradition may have confounded this guttural $\acute{g}ud$ with $gud = qarradu$ (*Glossar*, 108), the exact equivalent of the Biblical גבֹּר. If this supposition is correct, *Nimrod* is merely the original of the rendering גבֹּר צִיד. This suggestion has never been made before, so far as I know, and would serve to explain the introduction of the supposed gloss, Gen. 10. 9, implying that the glossator connected the idea of a huntsman with the name *Nimrod*.

J. DYNELEY PRINCE

Columbia University.

---

[2] Variant *ḫad* $= ellum$, *ebbum*, 'shining, distinguished' (*Glossar*, p. 209).

From "A Possible Sumerian Original of the Name Nimrod," by J. Dyneley Prince, Journal of the American Oriental Society, Vol. 40. (1920), pp. 201 and 203. Stable URL:

http://links.jstor.org/sici?sici=0003-0279%281920%2940%3C201%3AAPSOOT%3E2.0.CO%3B2-E

pose that the Israelites have borrowed even the number of seven ancestors; for the number seven is so common to Israelite traditions of old days and to their religious and mythological conceptions, that they may very well have created the conception of seven ancestors without any knowledge of Babylonian tales about the antediluvian kings. Mr. Albright thinks the derivation of *Nimrod* from *Ninurta* is wrong. Well, I have only to take that *ad notam*. But the conclusion to be drawn from these facts, as regards *my* problem, is at all events the following: J has no other Babylonian material than the name and the figure of Nimrod. His opinions about creation and the first human things are based on genuine Israelite or Hebrew, at all events non-Babylonian, conceptions and traditions, only with a little touch of Babylonian mythology, in a rather altered form (the cult-god Ninmarada (?) has become a human king and founder of Assyrian cities). *This* Babylonian influence may really go back to early pre-Israelite times, but the fact that no other Babylonian matters are found in the oldest source (J) seems to prove, as Mr. Albright also seems to mean, that the Babylonian influence on the "origin of *early* (the italics are mine) Hebrew cosmogony and ethnogony" has been a rather small one.

As regards the primeval history of E, as above mentioned, I have got to drop the *amêlū —'enōš*. But that does not overthrow my main thesis with regard to E, namely that we find here several Babylonian matters, which are new as compared with J and apparently not known by him. In the Sethite list of ancestors we have to admit some more Babylonian influence than that of the number only (ten); in the figure of Henoch there certainly are other features than those of an old Hebrew clan forefather. Mr. Albright himself intends to prove in a later investigation that the '*ēd* of Gen 2 6, which I ascribe to E, is originally the name of a Sumero-Accadian water-god (*op. cit.* 231). And above all we have the Flood story, which J does not know. The Babylonian origin is beyond doubt. From these facts I have concluded, that *these* Babylonian matters in all probability have come to the Israelites in the interval between J and E. Maybe I am wrong in regarding some of these

From "The Babylonian Matter in the Predeuteronomic Primeval History (JE) in Gen 1-11," by .

Sigmund Mowinckel, WF Albright,

Journal of Biblical Literature, Vol. 58, No. 2, 87-103. Jun., 1939 (p.89)

Bibliography

Albright, William F. "Abram the Hebrew: A New Archaeological Interpretation." *Bulletin of the American Schools of Oriental Research* 163 (1961):36-54.

_____. "Gilgames and Engidu, Mesopotamian Genii of Fecundity." *Journal of the American Oriental Society* 40 (1920):307-335.

_____. *History, Archaeology and Christian Humanism.* New York: McGraw-Hill, 1964.

_____. "Historical and Mythical Elements in the Story of Joseph." *Journal of Biblical Literature* 37.3 (1981):112-43.

Astruc, Jean. *Conjectures Sur Les Memoires Originaux Dont Il Paroit Que Moyse S' Est Servi Pour Composer Le Livre De La Genese.* (1753) Whitefish, MT: Kessinger Publishing, LLC, 2009.

Augustine of Hippo. *Genesi ad Litteram.* Transl. by John Hammond Taylor. 2 vols. New York: Newman Press, 1982.

Barnett, Michael and Andria Erzberger. *The Particle Adventure.* 1999-2012. http://www.particleadventure.org/standard_model.html

Bauvais, Vincent de. *Speculum Naturale.* Beauvais at Internet Archive Speculum naturale (Google Books), Hermannus Liechtenstein, 1494.

Beckwith, Carol, and Angela Fisher, "The African Roots of Voodoo", *National Geographic,* 188.8 (1995):102-13.

Berlinerblau, Jacques. *Heresy In The University: The Black Athena Controversy and the Responsibilities of American Intellectuals.* New Brunswick, NJ: Rutgers University Press, 1999.

Bernal, Martin. *Black Athena: The Afroasiatic Roots of Classical Civilization (The Fabrication of Ancient Greece 1785-1985, Volume 1)* New Brunswick, NJ: Rutgers University Press, 1991.

Bourke, John G. *Scatalogical Rites of All Nations*, Washington, DC: W. H. Lowdermilk 1891.

Brown, Walt. *In the Beginning: Compelling Evidence for Creation and the Flood.* Phoenix, AZ: Center for Scientific Creation, 2008.

Bruchac, Joseph. *Native American Stories.* Golden, CO: Fulcrum Publishing, 1991.

Buffon, Georges Louis Leclerc, comte de. *Histoire Naturelle.* 36 v. Paris: Imprimerie Royale, 1749-89.

Chalmers, David. "Facing up to the Problem of Consciousness," in *Journal of Consciousness Studies* 2.3 (1995):200-19.

Clark, Kenneth. *Civilisation: A Personal View.* New York: Harper and Row, 1969.

Constable, George. *The Neanderthals.* New York: Time Life Books, 1973.

Cooper, Bill. *After the Flood: The Early Post-flood History of Europe Traced Back to Noah.* Chichestor: New Wine Ministries, 1995.

Cremo, Michael A., and Richard L. Thompson. *Forbidden Archeology: The Hidden History of the Human Race.* Los Angeles: Bhaktivedanta Book Publishing, 1998.

Cremo, Michael A. *Human Devolution: A Vedic Alternative to Darwin's Theory.* Los Angeles: Bhaktivedanta Book Publishing, 2003.

Darwin, Charles. *On the Origin of Species: A Facsimile of the First Edition.* Rockville, MD: Wildside Press 2003 [originally pub. 1859].

De la Preyrere, Isaac. *Prae-Adamitae: Sive Exercitatio Super Versibus Duodecimo (1655) (Latin Edition)* Whitefish, MT: Kessinger Publishing, LLC, 2009.

"DNA Shows Neandertals Were Not Our Ancestors." *The MCC Hominid Journey.* Richard Effland and Ken Costello with assistance from Kathryn Wullstein. 11 July 1997.

http://www.mesacc.edu/dept/d10/asb/origins/hominid_journe
y/neandertal_dna.html.

Dobzhansky, Theodosius. "Nothing Makes Sense Except in the Light of
    Evolution." *American Biology Teacher* 35.3 (1971):125-29.

Dolphin, Lambert. "The Bountiful Fullness of Empty Space." *Lambert Dolphin's
    Library*. Lambert Dolphin. April 27, 1999, February 6, 2000.
    www.ldolphin.org/emptyspace.html

_____. "The Uniqueness of Creation Week." *Lambert Dolphin's Library*.
    Lambert Dolphin. revised March 6, 2003.
    http://www.ldolphin.org/Unique.html

Dwyer, James D. *Is There a Case for Created Time?* online book at *A Quest for Creation
    Answers* James D. Dwyer. March 20, 2011.
    http://www.creation-answers.com/time.htm

Eichhorn, Johann Gottfried. *Einleitung in das Alte Testament (5 vols)*. Leipzig:
    Weidmann, 1780–1783.

Eichhorn, Johann Gottfried, and George Tilly Tollop (translator) [1888]
    Introduction To The Study Of The Old Testament. Whitefish, MT: Kessinger
    Publishing, LLC, 2009.

Farrar, Steve "Speed of light 'slowing down'", *The London Sunday Times*, November
    15, 1998.

Fernandez, Adela. *Pre-Hispanic Gods of Mexico*. Mexico City: Panorama Editorial,
    1992.

Ham, Kenneth, and Paul Taylor. *The Genesis Solution*. Grand Rapids: Baker Book
    House, 1988.

Hamblin, Dora Jane, "Has the Garden of Eden Been Located at Last?" *Smithsonian*
    18.2 (1987):127-35.

Harrison, Roland K. *Introduction to the Old Testament.* Grand Rapids: Eerdmans, 1969.

Hawkes, Nigel "Is Einstein about to be dethroned?" *The London Sunday Times*, April 5, 2000.

Hess, Richard S. "The Origins of the Personal Names in Genesis 1-11." *Studies in the Personal Names of Genesis 1-11.* [*Alter Orient und Altes Testament*, band 234]. Kevelaer: Verlag Butzon & Bercker Kevelaer. 1993.

Hobbes, Thomas. *Leviathan: With Selected Variants from the Latin Edition of 1668.* Indianapolis: Hackett Publishing Company, 1994.

The Holy Bible. New York: The Reader's Digest Association, Inc., 1971.

Irenaeus of Lyons. *Adversus Haereses.* Alexander Roberts, James Donaldson, A. Cleveland Coxe (Eds.). CreateSpace Independent Publishing Platform, 2012.

Irenaeus of Lyons. *St. Irenaeus, Bishop of Lyons', Five Books Against Heresies (Volumes 1 & 2): Greek and Latin Edition.* Rev. William Wigan Harvey S.T.B. (Editor). CreateSpace Independent Publishing Platform, 2013.

Josephus, The Complete Works. William Whiston (translator). Nashville: Thomas Nelson, 1998.

Kaiser, Walter C., Jr. "How Many Generations in Egypt?" in *Hard Sayings of the Bible*, pp.140-2. Downers Grove, IL: InterVarsity Press, 1996.

LaFreniere, Gabriel. *Matter is Made of Waves.* 2002. Revised April 19, 2011. http://matterwaves.info/index.html

Lee, Scarlett. "Faster than light", *Varsity Publications*, 1999.

Lefkowitz, Mary R. *Black Athena Revisited* The University of North Carolina Press, 1996.

Lewis, C.S. *They Asked for a Paper*. London:G. Bles, 1962.

Mattox, Jeffrey. "A layman's summary of the new theory:" *Independent Birth of Organisms*. Jeffrey Mattox. http://www.mattox.com/genome/

Milton, Richard. *Shattering the Myths of Darwinism*. Rochester, VT: Park Street Press, 1997.

Mishlove, Jeffrey. *Thinking Allowed* (Tulsa: Council Oak Books, 1992) 65-74.

Morton, Glenn. Old Earth Ministries. 2014. http://www.oldearth.org/

Mowinckel, Sigmund and W.F. Albright. "The Babylonian Matter in the Predeuteronomic Primeval History (JE) in Gen 1-11." *Journal of Biblical Literature* 58.2(1939):87-103.

Nennius. *The History of the Britons: Historia Brittonum*. Charleston, SC:Forgotten Books, 2008.

Nugent, Christopher. *Masks of Satan: The Demonic in History*. London: Sheed and Ward, 1983.

Parrot, A. Review of *La Pénétration des Arabes en Syrie avant l'Islam* by René Dussaud. *Syria* 32.1955.

Pollard, William G. *Physicist and Christian: A dialogue between the communities*. Greenwich, CT: Seabury Press, 1964.

Prince, J. Dyneley. "A Possible Sumerian Original of the Name Nimrod." *Journal of the American Oriental Society* 40 (1920):201-203.

Oppenheimer, Stephen. *The Origins of the British*. London: Constable & Robinson, 2006.

"Raetian language," *Encyclopedia Brittanica*, 1989.

Robertson, Steve. 2/14/98 email to Glenn Morton, published in "Steve Robertson's Story: a Case History of What Happens to a Young-earth Advocate who works in Geology" (http://home.entouch.net/dmd/robertso.htm)

Rolston, Bruce "Speed Of Light May Not Be Constant, Physicist Suggests." University Of Toronto *Science Daily* October 6, 1999.

Sands, Bonny. *Eastern and Southern African Khoisan : evaluating claims of distant linguistic relationships.* Köln: R. Köppe, 1998.

Senapathy, Periannan. *Independent Birth of Organisms. A New Theory that Distinct Organisms Arose Independently from the Primordial Pond, Showing that Evolutionary Theories are Fundamentally Incorrect.* Madison: Genome Press, 1994.

Setterfield, Barry. "Creation and Catastrophe Chronology." *Lambert Dolphin's Library.* Lambert Dolphin. September 9 1999. www.ldolphin.org/emptyspace.html

Sewell, Curt. "The Tablet Theory of Genesis Authorship." *Bible and Spade*, 7.1. (1994) http://www.trueorigin.org/tablet.asp

Sheldrake, Rupert. *A New Science of Life: The Hypothesis of Morphic Resonance.* Rochester, VT: Park Street Press, 1995.

Simon, Richard. *Histoire critique du Vieux Testament.* Paris, 1678. *A critical history of the Old Testament* (1682), available at archive.org.

Strong, James. *Strong's Concordance.* Nashville: Thomas Nelson, 1996.

"The Creation of the World." *A Series of Bible Studies.* 1:1-3. Portland, OR: The Apostolic Faith Church. Undated.

Taylor, Charles V. *The Oldest (Science) Book in the World.* Slacks Creek, Queensland: Assembly Press, 1984.

Taylor, Charles V., "Who Wrote Genesis? Are the Toledoth Colophons?" *Journal of Creation*, 8.2 (1994) pp.204-211.

Troitskii, V.S. "Physical Constants and the Evolution of the Universe." *Astrophysics and Space Science*. 139.2 (1987):384-411. also online at http://www.ldolphin.org/troitskii/

Ventris, Michael; Chadwick, John. Documents in Mycenaean Greek. Cambridge: Second edition (1974). Cambridge UP, 1956.

Wasson, R. Gordon, "The Soma of the Rig Veda: What was It?" *Journal of the American Oriental Society* 91.2 (1971):169-86.

Watson, DMS. "Adaptation." *Nature* 124.3119 (1929):231-4.

Wellhausen, Julius. *Prolegomena zur Geschichte Israels*. Berlin, 1882. 3rd ed., 1886. Eng. trans., Edinburgh, 1883, 1891; 5th German edition, 1899; first published in 1878 as *Geschichte Israels*; English translation *Prolegomena to the History of Ancient Israel*. Charleston, SC:Forgotten Books, 2008. Also available on Project Gutenberg (http://www.gutenberg.org/dirs/etext03/prole11.txt)

White, Andrew Dickson. *A History of the Warfare of Science with Theology in Christendom, vol. 1* London:Macmillan, 1896; reprint ed, New York:Dover, 1960.

Wiseman, P. J. *New Discoveries in Babylonia about Genesis* (1936); republished as *Ancient Records and the Structure of Genesis*. Nashville:Thomas Nelson, 1985.

Wolpoff, Milford, and Rachel Caspari. *Race and Human Evolution: A Fatal Attraction*. New York: Simon & Schuster, 2007.

Wong, Kate "Neandertal Genome Study Reveals That We Have a Little Caveman in Us." *Scientific American*, May 6, 2010.

Woodmorappe, John. *Noah's Ark: A Feasibility Study*. Dallas: Inst for Creation Research, 1996

Yamauchi, Edwin *The Stones and the Scriptures*, Grand Rapids: Baker Book House, 1972.

Index

www.ingramcontent.com/pod-product-compliance
Lightning Source LLC
Chambersburg PA
CBHW080500110426
42742CB00017B/2950